1992

READING AUDEN

READING AUDEN

THE RETURNS OF CALIBAN

JOHN R. BOLY

CORNELL UNIVERSITY PRESS

ITHACA AND LONDON

First published 1991 by Cornell University Press.

Excerpts from *W. H. Auden: Collected Poems*, edited by Edward Mendelson, copyright © 1976 by Edward Mendelson, William Meredith, and Monroe K. Spears; *The Dyer's Hand and Other Essays*, copyright © 1962 by W. H. Auden; and *The English Auden*, edited by Edward Mendelson, copyright © 1977 by Edward Mendelson, William Meredith, and Monroe K. Spears reprinted by permission of Faber and Faber Ltd, and Random House, Inc.
Excerpt from *Selected Poems* by W. H. Auden reprinted by permission of Random House, Inc.
Excerpts from *The Enchafèd Flood* by W. H. Auden reprinted by permission of the University Press of Virginia.

International Standard Book Number 0-8014-2565-4
Library of Congress Catalog Card Number 91-6948
Printed in the United States of America
*Librarians: Library of Congress cataloging information
appears on the last page of the book.*

♾ The paper in this book meets the minimum requirements
of the American National Standard for Information Sciences—
Permanence of Paper for Printed Library Materials, ANSI Z39.48-1984.

FOR LINDA AND CARI—
MORE ACUTE AUDITORS

Contents

Preface

This book argues that W. H. Auden wrote his poetry to help people become more aware of what happens when they read. In itself that is an innocent enough, maybe even banal claim. But if patiently pursued, it leads into perilous territory, the uncharted marches, badlands, deserts waiting calmly beyond the horizon of Auden's verse.

It is natural to assume that reading is a practical affair, a matter of figuring out what must have been an author's original intention. And it follows from this assumption that reading is a most intimate encounter, the irresistible possession of a rapt subject by a mastering voice. But for Auden that is not it at all. He saw reading as an activity that takes place in a cultural arena, where murderously opposed interests compete for status and power. Contrary to widespread belief, reading is not the referee of this mayhem but its chief goal and prize. The rivals of the arena try to seize control of reading, to claim its activity of meaning-making as their own. Auden knew that to hold power over someone is not to impose a specific (and easily forgotten) truth, but to induce that person to construct reality in a predictable way. Insofar as reading designates the entire shaping process through which a too fluent world is forged into solid truth, the stakes are quite high.

Poetry fascinated Auden because it offered a chance to arrest and anatomize the subtle disciplines of the cultural arena. As social beings, we are ordinarily, and quite rightly, preoccupied with the accurate transmission of sense. But poetry offers a respite from this concern. It stages an imaginative saturnalia and pokes fun at a violence that would otherwise be imperceptible. *Violence* may seem too strong a term, but it is not, at least for a poet. To Auden, words are inscribed, which means they retain the varied accents and nuances they have accumulated during the course of their wanderings through history. Each cultural moment naturally has its enforced designations for a word. Yet its inscriptions remain. To the thoughtful writer and patient reader, this neglected memory, language's recollection of itself, offers continuous resistance to that most subtle violence, a tyrannically contrived normality or truth.

The motive for being interested in this resistance is a firm conviction about the fate of civilized humankind. For Auden, modern society is composed of technologies and bureaucracies that, though invented by human beings, are no longer controlled by them. Anywhere one turns, including (especially) the depths of the inmost self, a presiding voice, vestige of the romantic *genius loci,* stands guard as the agent of these social forces. Language offers a particularly effective means of repression, because it gives these interests the capacity to enter an individual and, in effect, to become that person's own voice. As an anatomy of this seductive coercion, the voice of an Auden poem is typically a negative force. Its task is to intimidate the reader into compliance with its limits and to manage the text so that its inscriptions remain unobtrusive, marginal, as *insignificant* as possible. Reading Auden, then, is partly a matter of outwitting a dominant voice (in effect, outwitting oneself as the conjurer of that voice) by patiently tracing its repressive stratagems.

Were that all, though, reading would be a forlorn project, a fatalistic obsession with an efficient restraint. But there is more. In the course of imposing its disciplinary measures, the spiritualized voice necessarily consorts with a material text. In this sense, the voice retains a tangible body, the historical medium of the language it must occupy. And as a body, the text performs an intricate array of gestures, mute yet enacted movements. Auden's early inquiries into psychosomatic medicine explore the possibility that this accompanying body offers a continuous resistance to the presiding voice. So reading Auden involves not only an attentiveness to repressive disciplines but an inventory of the gestures enacting those disciplines, gestures that by means of their tacit dissent furnish a point of return for the silenced inscriptions. In this sense, Auden redefines reading so that it becomes a continuous challenging of its always too restrictive permissions.

Such concerns may seem quite distant from our traditional image of Auden. He is rightly known as one of the first poets to break with the dismayed isolationism of the high modernists and willingly to concern himself with contemporary events: the fall of the Weimar Republic, the rise of German fascism, the civil war in Spain, the outbreak of the Second World War, the terror of the nuclear era, the cynical travesties of the cold war. But his concern with reading is perhaps less irrelevant to these affairs than at first appears. What can a poem hope to accomplish? If it simply equips a reader with a countertruth, little has been achieved. The ordinary person is inundated with authoritative messages, from newscasts, papers, well-meaning colleagues, persuasive strangers. To put the comparatively frail powers of poetry in direct competition with these more strident forces is to play a losing game. But if poetry has a different cultural role, if its task is to promote an awareness of how truths are formed, and how in the process of that formation they provoke the resistance of a historical medium, then the poet might fulfill a cultural duty after all. By offering an opportune site for the anatomy and disruption of repressive disciplines, poetry might contribute to the open society Auden never stopped hoping would one day be built.

Every approach has its limits, and this one is no exception. To trace the intricate patterns of discipline and disruption that Auden saw as essential to the process of reading, it is necessary to spend much longer with a text than would otherwise be the case. But is that so objectionable? For some reason, it is rarely noted that a poem might take weeks, months, or even longer to compose, and yet not fit into a tidy summary. The discussion here unapologetically lingers with its texts. Although the poems considered have been drawn from the entire range of Auden's half-century-long career, many splendid works have had to be omitted because of insufficient space. Still, if reading is an activity rather than a result, a continuing dialogue rather than the attainment of some final truth, then a more reflective approach is justified.

Anyone who writes about W. H. Auden is the fortunate heir of some excellent scholarship. The studies of M. K. Spears, John Fuller, Justin Replogle, Frederick Buell, Herbert Greenberg, and Samuel Hynes have played an important role in clarifying my own ideas. Special mention must be made of two works that have been particularly helpful. Edward Mendelson's *Early Auden* gives a thorough account of Auden's recurrent critical preoccupations. Richard Johnson's *Man's Place* offers a crucial insight into how Auden understood the social responsibilities of the modern poet.

Preface

My colleagues at Marquette University have been both good-natured and generous in their willingness to read portions of the manuscript. I remain grateful to Cate McClenahan, Paula Gillespie, Christine Krueger, Claudia Johnson, Camilla Nilles, Michael McCanles, and Albert Rivero for their sound advice. Michael Gillespie took friendship to the point of heroism by reviewing and commenting on each draft of the entire book. My many conversations with him about the fate of reading within modernism and its various sequels have certainly been the most enjoyable part of the project. As is only fair, I accept responsibility for whatever faults the argument may have, but admit that its strengths are mainly the result of an extended dialogue with such friends. To Linda Krause, for her unflagging patience and support, I owe a debt beyond measure.

JOHN R. BOLY

Milwaukee, Wisconsin

Abbreviations
of Works Cited

CP   W. H. Auden, *Collected Poems*, ed. Edward Mendelson. New York:
     Random House, 1976.
DH   W. H. Auden, *The Dyer's Hand*. London: Faber and Faber, 1963.
EA   W. H. Auden, *The English Auden*, ed. Edward Mendelson. New York:
     Random House, 1977.
EF   W. H. Auden, *The Enchafèd Flood*. Charlottesville: University Press of
     Virginia, 1979.
SP   W. H. Auden, *Selected Poems*, ed. Edward Mendelson. New York: Random House, 1979.

READING AUDEN

Reading Auden

Looking back, however, I now realize that I had read the technological prose of my favorite books in a peculiar way. A word like *pyrites*, for example, was for me, not simply an indicative sign; it was the Proper Name of a Sacred Being, so that, when I heard an aunt pronounce it *pirrits*, I was shocked.
—"Making, Knowing and Judging"

Every encounter with a work of art is a personal encounter; what it *says* is not information but a revelation of itself which is simultaneously a revelation of ourselves.
—"Cav & Pag"

Commentaries on Auden have explored a range of essential topics: his varied poetic sources, historical events that provide a backdrop for many of his works, themes distilled from a life of unusually eclectic interests—in social and political theory, psychology (both Freudian and Jungian), theology, economics, modern science, classics, anthropology. To illustrate Edward Mendelson's claim that "Auden was the first poet writing in English who felt at home in the twentieth century" (SP, ix), a writer who welcomed rather than dreaded the new era's divergent discourses, one need only glance at the notes the poet originally appended to *New Year Letter*. But what is still lacking in the repertoire of Auden commentary is a consideration of reading itself. Obviously something happens when a poem is read, and clearly it is different from what is ordinarily meant by reading. If we are to be more precise than this, however, certain questions must be elaborated. What does Auden ask from the reader? How does the poetic text articulate that demand?

What liberties or devious subterfuges, features imperceptible and even inadmissible from the standpoint of a successful communication, does the poem enlist: not to impart information, but to embark on a revelation that might never be completed, which is always just begun?

The initial problem is that reading bears such a variety of meanings. In an ordinary sense, it indicates a basic competence: a virtually rote procedure in which signs are deciphered, translated, and ultimately discarded so as to reveal an underlying, intended content. However useful for everyday purposes, this familiar sense of reading is not only unhelpful but obstructive when applied to poetry, or for that matter any form of imaginative literature. To read for content is also to accept, even if unconsciously, a specific contract. One agrees to honor certain associations, exclude or repress others, credit proper authorities, observe required practices. One agrees, in other words, to accept a role, a prescribed identity, which like any imposition entails a restriction of rights. The reader who adheres to a regimen of basic competence thus becomes an effigy: a fixed image, motionless, docile, at best a commemoration (though perhaps an intricately wrought one) of a formerly vital and surprising life. To be sure, this dire entombment provides the basis not just for ordinary communication but for the entire elaborate apparatus of a culture's understanding and truth. So there must be no thought of abolishing the effigy, no anarchic dream of pure liberation. In Auden, such never-never lands remain faithfully out of reach.

> Cold, impossible, ahead
> Lifts the mountain's lovely head
> Whose white waterfall could bless
> Travelers in their last distress.
> (EA, 159)

Nonetheless, Auden resisted any surrender of freedom, especially one grown so familiar as to become unnoticeable. In addition to the docile effigy, his poetry offers the reader another role, that of the auditor. This term also bears a plenary sense: as a meticulous and not terribly reassuring reviewer, a contentious respondent, the difficult person, someone who hears a bit too well. To put the matter in brief, the main task for poetry is to maintain the possibility of an auditor's alternative reading, as a noncompliant, dissenting respondent.

2

But is this distinction anything more than a theoretical refinement, entertaining in its impractical way but otherwise quite worthless? Perhaps, though, as some remarks he made in "Balaam and His Ass" suggest, Auden saw the difference between a routine competence and an imaginative response as leading to the heart of what distinguishes us as human beings.

> There are other social animals who have signal codes, e.g., bees have signals for informing each other about the whereabouts and distance of flowers, but only man has a language by means of which he can disclose himself to his neighbor, which he could not do and could not want to do if he did not first possess the capacity and the need to disclose himself to himself. The communication of mere objective fact only requires monologue and for monologue a language is not necessary, only a code. But subjective communication demands dialogue and dialogue demands a real language. (DH, 109)

Like so much of Auden's notoriously lucid prose, the passage is deceptively complex because of its peculiar mode of logic. Auden wrote with categories, but the distinctions are imbricated, overlapping rather than opposed. The difference between a "signal code," as a system of fixed equivalences, and a language, as an arena of disclosure, seems to suggest a binary pair. But since language can also operate (in fact usually does) as a signal code, the distinction is not simply between different systems but between different ways of using them. When language is taken simply to impart information, it functions monologically. That is, an initiating subject sends a message through a means of conveyance so as to reach a receiver, preferably with as little interference as possible. In operating such a system, humans, mosquitoes, and crows have much in common, though the creatures are in many respects better at it. As noted in "Natural Linguistics," they often transmit and receive their data with fewer mistakes.

> Since in their circles it's not good form to say anything novel,
>   none ever stutter on *er*, guddling in vain for a word,
> none are at loss for an answer.
>   (CP, 636)

But when language is used as a means of disclosure, this linear design no longer works. It is important that the dialogue Auden mentions begins within subjectivity. For this dialogue is not simply a reversal of monologue, in which the structure remains the same but the direction changes when the receiver becomes the sender. Rather, the dialogue Auden has in mind commences in an encounter with a more elusive other, a source of responsiveness that does not require another person because it stems from within the linguistic medium itself. "But subjective communication demands dialogue and dialogue demands a real language" (DH, 109). To engage in a dialogic exchange in Auden's sense, then, has little in common with the conversations that occur in fiction and drama, or for that matter in everyday speech. Rather, the dialogic process that frees language from the restrictions of the informational circuit involves a relentless deliberation that occurs within the medium of language itself.

If tracing such a conversation seems a strange thing for reading to do, that is mainly because so little effort is required to forget the violence on which its arrest of meaning depends. The canons of rhetoric, ancient as they are venerable, strive to imbue language with a combination of certainty and authority so that words might offer scant resistance to the will of a presiding voice. This confident assurance is of course a complete hoax. If words were indeed untainted in their meaning, purified of any intrusive or distracting accents, they would not be certain, only incomprehensible. The ciphers of a language, having in most cases outlasted several epochs and traversed numerous historical situations, arrive at the threshold of an utterance in a quite contaminated state. They are radically impure, unfaithful, even promiscuous, or, to put this in a nonmoralistic way, they are inscribed. The words marshaled by a voice are always preoccupied, densely filigreed with a fine tracery of differing nuances and accents. It is this play of inscriptions that a presiding voice must suppress in order to preserve an origin that is also a violence, however modest, the repressive authority of a ruling intention or underlying sense.

Yet Auden did not endorse that violence. Poets enjoy an unusual right. They can in part excuse themselves from the violence prerequisite to a successfully communicated truth. That is why Auden was not being flippant when he wrote in *The Prolific and Devourer*, "Artists, even when

4

they appear to hold religious or political dogmas, do not mean the same thing by them as the organizers of their church or party. There is more in common between my view of life and that of Claudel than there is between Claudel's and that of the Bishop of Boston" (EA, 404). The bond between imaginative writers involves not a political, religious, or otherwise thematic congruence but a shared interest in a specific function. Poets have little, perhaps ultimately nothing, to say. They are sovereignly absent; their departure as intending subjects suspends any thought of ordinary communication. Rather, their absence releases a dialogue that occurs across a preoccupied medium, an exchange between a presiding violence and its patiently waiting inscriptions.

But the departure of an author does not necessarily entail the departure of a dominant voice. Auden's poetry offers what seems an unlikely site for a dialogic exchange, if only because its various speakers are so adept at self-authorization. Indeed, perhaps the most evident feature of an Auden poem is its singularly monologic quality. In what becomes a recurrent drama, an unchallenged voice holds sway over an abandoned (emptied, silenced, repressed) landscape. This voice's oppressive enforcement of a meaning closes off the reaches of the past and thus excludes the possibility of any dissident overture emerging from lapsed or bygone discourses. It carefully intimidates and silences any contemporary rivals. And insofar as this is possible, it vigilantly guards against future intrusions, from later discourses that have yet to emerge. But though authoritative, Auden's voices are not authorial. They are no more than a collection of functions, actually disciplines. For Auden, a poetic voice is merely what it does, an aggregate of certain restrictions. It has no special or privileged status in the text, whose dissonant impulses exceed the range of any regulatory voice.

That dissonance is real enough, though tacit. If an auditor looks harder or listens more attentively to one of Auden's landscapes, it proves to be neither as abandoned nor as unresponsive as at first appears. The scenes are preoccupied, littered rather than haunted, strewn with a variety of material remnants. Even complete emptiness and unrelieved silence are not empty or silent but figures of inscription, preludes to an incalculable response as in this eerie passage from "Hammerfest":

> Was it as worldly as it looked? I might have thought so
> But for my ears: something odd was happening

> Soundwise. A word, a laugh, a footstep, a truck's outcry,
>   Each utterance rang singular, staccato,
> To be cut off before it could be contradicted
>   Or confused by others: a listening terrain
> Seized on them all and never gave one back in echo,
>   As if to land as desolate, as far up,
> Whatever noise our species cared to make still mattered.
>   Here was a place we had yet to disappoint.
>
> (CP, 545–46)

Auden's forsaken landscapes, with their dilapidated ruins and derelict machinery, furnish images for the disruptive potential of the text. For that disruption emerges not only from the detritus of contemporary usage but from the wreckage of industries once in demand and now abandoned, remnants of war, shards of forgotten civilizations, bones and artifacts of feral ancestors. The voice is never the first element to occupy a scene, only the most obvious. It in fact presides over a comic prospect, an unmanageable because preoccupied stage.

But how can the unvoiced ever hope to obtain a hearing? The habits of ordinary reading are so easy and natural: simply embrace a normality that is reassuring and not a little smug (the heartiness of common sense), revert to a docile acceptance of the voice, and brightly forget all about the troublesome inscriptions. Even so, such reading persistently stumbles on a troubling remnant, something left over that refuses to fit.

> But somewhere always, nowhere particularly unusual,
> Almost anywhere in the landscape of water and houses,
> His crying competing unsuccessfully with the cry
> Of the traffic or the birds, is always standing
> The one who needs you.
>
> (CP, 204)

Literary works are written in response to assumed questions, and as a common critical practice considerable effort is expended in finding answers to these queries. But the far more important issue is to decide what the apt questions are.[1] With Auden's poetry, a primary concern

---

1. See Auden's comment in "Reading": "A critic shows superior insight if the questions he raises are fresh and important, however much one may disagree with his answers to them. Few readers, probably, find themselves able to accept Tolstoy's conclusions in *What Is Art?*, but, once one has read the book, one can never again ignore the questions Tolstoy raises" (DH, 9).

is, How can an auditor trace a dialogic process within so eminently monologic a violence? The comedy of inscriptions, if inescapable, is also inaudible. How is it possible to conjure a responsive voice from the tumult of the everlastingly unvoiced? Auden's carefully evolved response to this leads into some of the most fascinating aspects of his poetic practice.

As if to make up for the certain disruption that stems from the text, the voices of the poetry adopt an aggressive stance toward their prospective recipients. Inscriptions are ultimately unmanageable. Their dissidence may be forestalled but not averted. But a real audience, the historical beings caught within the fine web of cultural determination and restraint, offers a good chance for intimidation and control. That is why Auden's voices have such a demonically manipulative quality. Obliged to inhabit a text that will eventually betray them, they almost overcome that predicament by more or less skillfully managing the audience. Their task is to confine reading within the protocols of an intended truth. The speaking voice in an Auden poem, the mystifying force of a dominant persona, must see to it that the audience cannot break the trance of intended meaning long enough to begin tracing its responsive inscriptions.

The tactics for this mystification vary according to the nature of speaker and audience. Auden's voices carefully observe rhetorical contracts, the unwritten and often unconscious agreements through which a delimited meaning may be safely conveyed. Yet they honor these bonds not to communicate a truth but to help illustrate a variable apparatus of repression. In his earliest poetry, Auden was fascinated with the techniques used by interior voices: the remnants of early threats and prohibitions which, as a result of being so deeply embedded in memory, eventually attain the status of a privileged inwardness, the *authentic* voice of conscience, reason, wisdom, and the like. In subsequent poetry, he turned his attention to more public voices. Thus the arena shifts from the surrealist dramas of the self to the sites of a more banal repression, where a culturally empowered persona holds others in its grip. During the middle and later parts of his career, Auden contended with perhaps the most insidious contract, the peculiar coercions that an author, by way of the habituated and thus easily forgotten technology of the book, might bring to bear upon a dispersed, disembodied, and all but silenced public.

As the result of the tyranny it so variously and at times brilliantly exercises on its recipients, Auden's poetry has the capacity to inspire not just passion but animosity. At this late date it can be admitted that there exists a vociferous group, in some ways a school, of Auden despisers.[2] Many are frankly incensed at the demonic bullying of his voices. No doubt they have good cause. It would be an exercise in masochism to defend Auden's personae, somewhat akin to inventing clever excuses for the gnostic and life-hating sermon on Hell in Joyce's *Portrait.* Yet if the dictates of common sense and obviousness can be set aside, it becomes apparent that the readers who despise Auden indict only themselves. In effect their animosity is an admission: that the demonic voices have succeeded and, for them at least, drawn attention away from the inscriptions so that the routine, abject transmission from sender to receiver remains safely intact. Despising "Auden," of course, initiates a rich confusion, between biographical myth (a residue of anecdotes, memoirs, and in some cases outright fabrications), scriptor (a hypothetical point of orchestration for conflicting discursive elements), and poetic persona (a voice that, though entirely imputed by a reader, is customarily accorded a separate and even quasi-spiritual status). More regrettably, it shows a sluggish and impassive response to the resistances inherent in the text, thus an implied insistence that the mediocrity of ordinary reading be preserved.

But to return to the primary question, Is there a way in which the insidious belligerence of Auden's voices could contribute to, even release,

2. It is a school not because of its common ideology but because of its shared practice. Auden's detractors routinely assume that the voice of a poem is the direct and authentic expression of the poet, hence that moral categories may be freely substituted for critical ones (since the issue is character rather than discourse). Of many possible examples a particularly illustrative one is that of Marjorie Perloff in *The Poetics of Indeterminacy* (Princeton: Princeton University Press, 1981), p. 26, especially her attack on Auden's *Bucolics:* "in the end, the poet has become the victim of his own account of 'lakes'; he seems to have absorbed their impulse toward smugness and control. To settle for such charming but undemanding forms of nature is to take the coward's path." Watching a commentator take the bait with such eagerness, it is difficult not to be reminded of Auden's remark in "Genius & Apostle": "Both the dreamer and the madman are in earnest; neither is capable of play acting. . . . But the poet pretends for fun; he asserts his freedom by lying—that is to say, by creating worlds which he *knows* are imaginary" (DH, 438).

a dialogic venture? Might it be that the paired yet asymmetric aggressions of a voice, its violence to the text and its tyranny over the audience, are somehow intertwined? During his first visit to Berlin in 1929, Auden became interested in the theories of Homer Lane, as espoused by his American disciple John Layard. Prominent among Lane's ideas was the theme of psychosomatic disease, the notion that physical symptoms have their origin in intellectual dishonesty or imaginative inhibition. In general, this aspect of Auden's intellectual interests has provided commentators with little more than an explanatory gloss for some of his early poems. But a patient reading of relevant texts suggests that Auden developed Lane's psychosomatic theories into a means of discursive analysis. Just as human beings have a body, which serves as both a repository and a manifestation of divergent impulses, so does language. And just as there can be no utterance, no authoritative claim or definitive statement, without an accompanying set of dissident gestures, so there can be no meaning without a companion syntax, the movements and gestures of its predicative endeavor. Through a series of remarkable textual experiments, then, Auden explored the possibility that in the course of achieving its repression of an audience, the presiding voice of a discourse unwittingly, helplessly, enacted a series of betraying syntactic gestures. These performed cues, the unvoiced but gesticulating aspect of a discourse, provide the otherwise silent inscriptions of a text with both a provocation and a point of convergence. For it is through such neglected gestures, the forgotten body of an utterance, that the responses of a text, the impulses forbidden or denied by its usurping disciplines, are called upon to speak.

Reading Auden involves patience but is by no means an unmanageable task.[3] It begins, for all its novelty, where ordinary reading does: in subservience to a voice, committed (in the sense that mental patients are) to an accurate understanding. But rather than being confined within a speaker's intention, this beginning concerns itself with a tracework of disciplines. How is it that a potentially unruly audience is held in check? Through a diagnosis of the ensuing disciplines, another anatomy gradu-

---

3. In an early review, Auden put the relation between patience and insight even more forcefully: "the necessary preliminary, whether to scientific discovery or to artistic vision, is intensity of attention or, less pompously, love" (EA, 319).

ally becomes apparent: the syntactic body of the text, the gestures it cannot conceal in its tasks of predication. From the intimations of this anatomy, a reading listens and watches for a dialogic return, a restlessness within inscriptions through which their inherent diversity may become directed, responsive to the specific violences that safeguard the meaning of the text. Reading Auden is thus a matter of keeping varied records: of the practices of a repressive discipline, the gestures through which it is enacted, the irrepressible responses those gestures alternately provoke and direct.

Such reading has its rewards. By venturing into an arena of conflict, it brings to light some of the neglected components of the poetic text: auditor, effigy, and public as Auden developed that notion, as well as a panoply of disciplinary devices. It also illustrates the task Auden thought poetry might perform in an open society, not with its voiced themes or announced ideas, but through its more important capacity to make the origin and production of truth both apparent and questionable. Nonetheless, any reading that strays beyond the precincts of a presiding voice must also accept certain risks. As one of Auden's persistent motifs suggests, to step beyond the boundary of the passively accepted and probably approved is to accept a fate of exile.[4] Auden once wrote that books which alter one's way of thinking are often "what an expert in their field would call 'unsound' " (DH, 51). In that case, this book aspires to be unsound, though only out of deference to Auden's resolutely unsound texts. For his poems are not at all solid, secure, endowed with a unified belief or consistent design throughout. Rather, they are eerie, preoccupied, riddled with dissident overtones and obsessed with barely discernible voices. To borrow a phrase from "Missing," those who cross the margins of the monologue must accept a nomadic, suspect fate, "fighters for no one's sake, / Who died beyond the border" (EA, 28). Yet they also have the chance of listening more acutely to the confident tyrannies of a voice, so as to hear the dissidence within, the "curlew's creaking call," "the drumming of a snipe," the continuing response of "all / Whose voices in the rock / Are now perpetual . . ." (EA, 28).

---

4. But as often happens with fate, what is not accepted is imposed anyway: "the immigrant is coming more and more to stand as the symbol for Everyman, as the natural and unconscious community of tradition rapidly disappears from the earth" (DH, 334).

CHAPTER ONE

Homage to a Legend

> Language is fossil poetry. As the limestone of the continent consists of infinite masses of the shells of animalcules, so language is made up of images or tropes, which now, in their secondary use, have long ceased to remind us of their poetic origin.
>
> —Ralph Waldo Emerson, "The Poet"

To read Auden's poetry is to take up the problem of writing: why it should be so hard, almost impossible. Words are put on the page. A scene emerges. "A sentence uttered makes a world appear . . ." (CP, 473). All seems well enough, but a problem soon arises. What is the precise relation between this summoned world and its intractable textual remnant, the sentence? There can be no answer to that question, no appeal to any source or authority, other than a reading of the line itself.

The sentence in question is clearly judicial. It stages a grim Baconian drama that puts nature on the rack and thereupon ordains the fate of an external reality. It remands a low and fugitive chaos to the penal knowledge of the already evident (which it has just invented). And as befits any good creation myth, its passage from "the primordial undiffer-entiated flux" (EF, 6) into civilized order entails not only divine interven-tion, a *creatio ex nihilo*, but the familiar raptures of an epistemological rape: "make" in Auden's line should also be accorded its penetrative sense. The judicial sentence makes—impales—an obtuse and proverbially feminine matter. Its utterance masters a too fluent diversity by arresting it within a visual clarity—"appear"—and thus forcing it to stand convicted, docile, transfixed, beneath an omniscient and conquering gaze.

But there is a hitch. Auden's line does not say "*the* world," as it

11

should, only "a world." With its fatal contingency thereby exposed, the somewhat defrocked creation myth must recede into a sinister and incense-wreathed thaumaturgy. A world is not a true universe at all, only its sad parody: an entrant in a field of rivals; a calm infested with teeming life; a particle adrift within a stupendous indifference.[1] As a result of this exposed contingency, the previously judicial sentence momentarily recalls an ancient but suspect wisdom, the venerable *Sententiarum Libri Quatuor* perhaps, but also the dark sentence, an enigma the learned Fathers would try to suppress because its unguarded margins offered refuge to spectral shapes, terrifying possibilities. Taken in this sense, Auden's innocent "uttered" becomes the intonation of a spell. Through its unsuspecting voice, a long-forgotten magic springs to life. Dead signs turn into portentous charms. All too briefly, language eludes a routine limit, its habit of meaning, to deliver a ravishing diversity.[2] Yet the effect is almost too perfect. For the potent "makes" gradually acquires the character of a fabrication, a too laborious contrivance. Confronted with such illusions, the formerly arrogant "appears" begins to tremble in the presence of its illicitly engendered progeny.

There is safety, though, in dullness. A sentence is a structure whose rules, of selection, determination, and closure, must be learned. The

1. The insight here recalls Auden's title for his Eliot lectures on literary texts as cultural formations, *Secondary Worlds* (London: Faber and Faber, 1969). A world is an uneasy assemblage of not only diverse but highly self-inconsistent discursive practices.

2. Adopting an argument from R. G. Collingwood's *Principles of Art* (Oxford: Clarendon Press, 1938), pp. 57–77, Auden used magic as an image for any application of cultural signs in which their material instability recedes before the truth they represent. In this sense, magic designates both a trickery and its effect, and thus becomes another name for the familiar illusions of a passively accepted reference. Cf. Auden's essay "Squares and Oblongs," in *Poets at Work*, intro. Charles D. Abbott (New York: Harcourt, Brace, 1948), p. 173. "Two theories of poetry. Poetry as a magical means for inducing desirable emotions and repelling undesirable emotions in oneself and others, or Poetry as a game of knowledge, a bringing to consciousness by naming them, of emotions and their hidden relationships." Or the note from Auden's essay "Writing": "Poetry is not magic. In so far as poetry, or any other of the arts, can be said to have an ulterior purpose, it is, by telling the truth, to disenchant and disintoxicate" (DH, 27). Or the frequent allusions in the poetry itself, which acknowledge that its entrancing forms lend "a conjurer fine apparatus" (CP, 224), and concede along with the Stage Manager in *The Sea and the Mirror* that "the ghosts who haunt our lives / Are handy with mirrors and wire" (CP, 311).

sorcerer's warren gives way to a scene of instruction, a grammar school. A sentence assumes an elaborate process of correct formation. "Teaching is a political activity, a playing at God the political father, an attempt to create others in one's own likeness" (EA, 401). To form a proper sentence is to have been taught to shape an acceptable reality, one in which certain thoughts and actions become impossible. Only carefully selected elements may be admitted into the good sentence; their modification is closely watched; their significance must never stray beyond an enclosed thought, intended from the outset by a subject who can be held to account. But in keeping with its Narcissistic origins, the sentence eventually betrays its infatuated creator. Its logic of selection also implies a discipline of exclusion. Around each chosen element there gathers a crowd of jealous rivals, not just opposing words but differing accents within the same word.[3] Under the pressure of this silent rivalry, the syntactic linkages become strained, a deviancy rather than a necessity. If confronted with this wavering within the once stable sentence, the already badly shaken "appears" threatens to become an ellipsis: appears as . . . Susceptible to a form of auto-irritation, the sentence operates an exclusion that provokes dissidence, a finality that opens up gaps. A sentence's world thus poses a theatrical space at best, a globe like Shakespeare's stage enclosing a dramatic arena, its solemn cosmogony a slightly camp costume drama.

•

If this reading illustrates anything, it is the perils that await the unwary. Because of the pivotal quality of Auden's language, in which each word becomes a crux, it becomes impossible to find, much less impose, a limit. Any passage might be endlessly unraveled. The choice of a line from the poem "Words" is arbitrary. A thousand others might serve as well. Left with this dangerous prospect, the death (or birth) of reading, it is logical to cast about for something akin to the "Lords of Limit" (CP, 63) Auden borrowed from D. H. Lawrence: some restrictive order,

3. Auden's "Prologue" ("O Love, the interest itself in thoughtless Heaven") images these internal accents as "alive like patterns a murmuration of starlings / Rising in joy over wolds unwittingly weave" (EA, 118), that is, as an aftereffect of natural flight, or as a maze inscribed upon a permeable blankness.

13

a version of licit bounds.[4] The most readily available of these is "Auden" himself. One need only conjure a figure, benign, mature, slightly older than oneself (though this is awkward with poets like Keats or Rimbaud, who either died or stopped writing when they were young), and quite testy toward meanings that do not meet with its approval. Unfortunately, this familiar appeal to the author is one that the author specifically prohibits. Auden's calculated passive—"uttered"—abandons the line to any conceivable subject. It suspends proprietary rights. Whatever inflection, turn, or accent a historical individual might chance, it instantly becomes the fate the dubious sentence, and its dissembling world must endure, at least for a while. "Auden," like his later description of his countenance as resembling a wedding cake left out in the rain, fades into the furrows and clefts of an eroded image.

At the side of the author waits an even more powerful Lord of Limit, the good sense of plain usage. Much of Auden's poetry maintains unusually close ties with everyday speech. He took Byron's *Don Juan* as a stylistic exemplar (though he chose many others as well).[5] He preferred the epistle as a poetic form: occasional, unassuming, colloquial. This bias recalls the romantic ideal of poetic diction, a man speaking to men, and it hints at a familiar literary mission. Supposedly, the poet's job of work is to cut through distortion (the lies of government, bureaucracy, or one's ideological foes) so as to restore a natural language, authentic, pure. But appealing though it may be, the ideal of a natural language is at odds with the common experience it claims to preserve, as is illustrated in "Law Like Love." It is easy to believe in a universal language, a normative discourse that is objective and fair: "Law is the

4. Lawrence's discussion of mythic doubles or twins had a considerable influence on Auden, as is indicated by the extent to which the imagery of "The Witnesses" draws on that chapter of Lawrence's *Apocalypse* (1931; rpt. New York: Penguin, 1981), pp. 78–84. "And always they have this aspect of rivals, dividers, separators for good as well as for ill: balancers" (81).

5. The concern with originality struck Auden as a misguided value, in that it ignored or slighted the historically overdetermined quality of the artist's medium. "The absolutely banal—my sense of my own uniqueness. How strange that one should treasure this more than any of the exciting and interesting experiences, emotions, ideas that come and go, leaving it unchanged and unmoved" (DH, 95–96). "The poet is the father of his poem; its mother is a language: one could list poems as race horses are listed—*out of L by P*" (DH, 22).

one / All gardeners obey / To-morrow, yesterday, to-day" (CP, 208). But the reductivism of the garden metaphor overlooks some perennial discursive conflicts. What seems perfectly natural to one generation, "the wisdom of the old," may strike their ideological heirs as somewhat extravagant and wild, "the grandchildren put out a treble tongue." Even within the confines of a particular era, there will always be competitive versions of the one perfectly natural language, each mined with the biases and values of a peculiar interest group: for the priest, "law is my pulpit and my steeple"; for the judge, "law is The Law"; for sardonic scholars, "law is the clothes men wear"; for the powerless, "law is our Fate"; for the totalitarian, "law is our State"; for anarchists, "law is no more"; for egalitarians, "law is We"; and for the weak-minded who, despite contradictory evidence, manage to preserve their faith in instinctively grasped universals, "and always the soft idiot softly Me" (CP, 206). "Law Like Love" illustrates what might be described as Auden's discursive pragmatism. The nostalgic belief in a natural language notwithstanding, the members of a complex modern society must acquire a range of highly incongruent discourses, because what passes for natural (acceptable, appropriate, adequate) must constantly adapt to the shifting nuances of context. Besides being too rigid, the romantic ideal of a natural language is dogmatic and intolerant.

Still, it is beyond dispute that many of Auden's best-known poems are written in seemingly natural languages. But are these unreflective discourses therefore being recommended? Auden worked to reveal a choice that awaits the participants, whether as senders or receivers of any utterance: "The task of overcoming mediocrity, that is, of learning to possess instead of being possessed . . ." (DH, 321). One can accept the truth of a discourse, the residue of its constitutive assumptions and disciplines, in a passive way, grateful for the power-as-knowledge it bestows; or one can recognize that discourse as a specific entrant within a cultural arena, an always flawed configuration that is itself composed of unstable and dissonant impulses. To the extent that consciously or otherwise an individual accepts the role of gratified passivity (serious truthfulness), there is an accompanying loss of humanity. Enticed into an unreflected role, the individual shrinks to a mytheme, a definable stereotype: "Narcissus does not fall in love with his reflection because it is beautiful, but because it is *his*" (DH, 94). But to the extent that the other choice is risked (and unlike the first, this must always be done consciously), a greater degree of freedom ensues. The poet's, and by implication the contributing reader's, task is not to endorse a natural language or, for that matter, to promote any particular discourse at all. Rather, the essential task is to discover how an utterance not only entails a coercive structure but through that coercion opens a way to the clamorous interiors it bears within itself.

The task of denaturalizing language lends itself to a certain theatricality. Considered as text, a work offers neither revelation nor escape but "a rehearsal for living" (EA, 311). It provides an opportunity to take on different parts, alien words, and to explore their fields of implication. As opposed to method acting, where the performer becomes totally immersed within a dramatic identity, Auden assumes the situation of a small repertory theater, in which each member of the cast must play several roles. The challenge is to bring out something unusual in each. Of course, it is easy to ridicule such dramatic agility, as does the narrator in *The Age of Anxiety:* "Besides, only animals who are below civilization and the angels who are beyond it can be sincere. Human beings are, necessarily, actors who cannot become something before they have first pretended to be it; and they can be divided, not into the hypocritical and the sincere, but into the sane who know they are acting and the mad who do not" (CP, 395–96). Leaving aside the obvious question, whether it is possible to be sincere about being versatile, we can say the narrator's irony misstates the case. A modern culture is too complex and diverse to be encompassed within a single discourse. Further, this cultural complexity uneasily emerges from a genealogy of even more intricate and elusive beginnings. The likely images for a modern everyman are Hamlet and Falstaff, not because they play a specific part but because they play at acting itself. "Is there . . . any figure traditionally associated with the stage who could be made to stand for this imaginative faculty [a "talent for fabrication"]? Yes, there is: the actor. Keats' famous description of the poet applies even more accurately to the actor" (DH, 436). As with the persona demanded by negative capability, a figure that can have no fixed character but must instead be everything and nothing, the actor practices a quasi-religious form of asceticism. Yet this strict selflessness has a purely dramatic utility. By not identifying with any given character, the capable actor—which is to say, a composing poet as well as a participating reader—illustrates an essential cultural venture: the discovery that every discourse, every productive framework of conscious beliefs and unconscious biases, is not only contested from without because hedged around by differing rivals but challenged from within because riddled with disruptive voices.

That venture suspends (for it can never quite eliminate) the vigilant image of a controlling subject. Yet it is necessary to go further. If a text actually releases a continuous exchange within itself, if it is at once judicial order and subversive response, does the literary tradition offer any warrant for this practice? The brief answer, that the tradition shows little else apart from this textual strife, is accurate but confusing. In its haste it neglects to notice the paradox at work within the idea of "tradition" itself. Anyone who studies Auden's essays on previous writers soon discovers a contradiction. On the one hand, Auden maintains, the past must be overthrown. It is an immense inertia, a graveyard of crepuscular images. What makes this overthrow even more urgent is that the past routinely assists the reactionary forces of the present, as Auden noted in this fiat from *The Enchafèd Flood*:

> For every individual the present moment is a polemical situation, and his battle is always on two fronts: he has to fight against his own past, not only his personal past but also those elements in the previous generation with which he is personally involved—in the case of a poet, for instance, the poetic tradition and attitudes of the preceding generation—and simultaneously he has to fight against the present of others, who are a threat to him, against the beliefs and attitudes of the society in which he lives which are hostile to his conception of art. (EF, 43–44; cf. DH, 280)

But on the other hand, Auden also maintains that any attempt to sever ties with the past is arrogant folly. This position is as deeply entrenched as the first. In one of his cryptic early notebooks, Auden remarked: "The Tyranny of the Dead. One cannot react against them" (EA, 299). As he gradually defined his critical thought, he glossed this aphorism with the motif of a symbolic incest. To disown the past is to indulge an Oedipal fantasy, that is, to nurture the delusion that it is possible to be divine, self-engendered, and thus free of historical restraints and material limits. Auden noted the telling recurrence of the incest motif throughout

17

romantic literature, for example, in Wagner's *Ring.*[6] But he found perhaps its most striking manifestation in the obsession of Melville's Ahab with the unutterable polysemy of the whale. To the question of why Ahab embarks on his needless quest for revenge, Auden implicitly answers with the opening sections of *Moby Dick*, "Etymology" and "Extracts," which introduce the whale's inherent diversity and instability. Ahab, a figure of demonic domination, can neither tolerate nor resist the creature that has dismembered him, and yet on which he depends for both his livelihood and self-worth. He typifies the romantic genius's obsession to control an unmasterable medium.

> It is possible to attach too much importance to this [Ahab's self-inflicted castration wound with his artificial limb] as also to the sexual symbolism of the Whale as being at once the *vagina dentata* and the Beast with two backs or the parents-in-bed. The point is that the sexual symbolism is in its turn symbolic of the aesthetic, i.e., the Oedipus fantasy is a representation in aesthetic terms of the fantasy of being a self-originating ego, i.e., of the ego (Father) begetting itself on the self (Mother), and castration is the ultimate symbol of aesthetic weakness, of not being an aesthetic hero. (EF, 136)

To become one's own father is to transcend history, to set aside the myriad traces, influences, and disciplines through which an individual is shaped. Because romanticism resented modern society as debased and democratically degraded, while at the same time it yearned for the apocalyptic arrival of some Utopian totality, it readily became fascinated with the incest motif. The Oedipal offspring who slays a hated paternity only to become its dutiful replica is a familiar reactionary pattern.

So the contradiction in Auden's attitude to tradition is apparent. Although he advocates a necessary departure from the sepulcher of the past, he also characterizes that departure as a regressive fantasy. Nor was

6. See W. H. Auden, "Mimesis and Allegory," *The English Institute Annual, 1940* (New York: Columbia University Press, 1941), p. 9. "The whole cycle of the *Ring*, indeed, is full of incest; it is precisely this love that is never renounced. As a political allegory the birth of a hero through the incest of Siegmund and Sieglinde may be sound—only those who are not bound by the tabus of their culture can reform it—but as a psychological allegory incest is a regressive step."

he unaware of the tension. A statement such as "more than any other people, perhaps, the Americans obey the scriptural injunction: 'let the dead bury their dead' " (DH, 104) suggests more than the evident irony. Whatever its cultural misappropriation, the biblical text is itself still valid: the past can neither be escaped nor conquered.

Like many contradictions, this one stems from a vexed concept, in this case the idea of the past or tradition itself. If tradition is taken in an authoritarian way, as a set of mandated themes and strict limits, then it must be overthrown. This is the sense it bears in the lines "But their ancestral curse, jumbled perhaps and put away, / Baffled for years, at last in one repeats its potent pattern . . ." (EA, 29); and, more disarmingly:

> To you, to me,
> Stonehenge and Chartres Cathedral,
> the Acropolis, Blenheim, the Albert Memorial
> are works by the same Old Man
> under different names.
>
> (CP, 518)

But if tradition is taken in a more dialogic way, as bearing within itself a disruptive tumult, a power continuously to subvert and reassemble even its most ultimate tenets, then it is a vital resource. In this respect, there is an important distinction between Auden's critical attitude and that of a romantic apologist such as Harold Bloom. With patient thoroughness, Bloom has elaborated Freud's Oedipal complex into a general theory of literary influence. His critical narrative continuously rediscovers how a late poet, trembling in the shadow of a romantic precursor, demolishes the ancestor's incapacitating imago. But then the guilty offspring, having no further exemplar to follow, surreptitiously resuscitates the ancestor's work. The daring with which the ancestor is slain and the cunning with which his Ur-poems are replicated combine to provide an index for the strength or weakness of a poet.[7] But from Auden's perspec-

7. Harold Bloom, *A Map of Misreading* (New York: Oxford University Press, 1975). Unsurprisingly, a poet who acclaims rather than represses his literary ancestors does not fare especially well in Bloom's scheme. Auden is cast along with Swinburne and Beddoes among those "epigoni" who "drown too soon," that is, surrender to the depths of

tive this narrative, though quite faithful to its romantic mythemes, is too restrictive. Bloom's theory of influence remains entirely situated within the informing assumptions of the movement it would critique. And although this theory offers a perceptive sense of tradition as influence, it lacks a sense of the *text* as an exchange between both repressive and responsive elements. For Auden, tradition retains this nonromantic, dialogic sense. Consequently, it can play for higher stakes than the guilty son's ingenious reconcilement to an invincible paternity. In Auden's more provocative sense of tradition, it enacts the betrayal of W. Sclater's *Key,* or the damnable deliverance of sacred books into heretical hands lamented by Milman or J. H. Blunt. Utterly uninterested, the countertradition within tradition refuses the captivating fetishes of ancestor worship. Instead it fosters another task, that "literary All Souls Night in which the dead, the living, and the unborn writers of every age and in every tongue were seen as engaged upon a common, noble and civilizing task" (DH, 42).

In theory, any writing might serve as an instance of the discord Auden found ingrained within language. "The difference between different kinds of writing lies not so much in the writing itself, but in the way we look at it" (EA, 308). A word or phrase is at once a fatal finality, a death sentence, and an endless play: an entrance to a maze of historically inscribed signs from which Auden's *Anthropos apteros* (wingless man) must beguile a destiny (CP, 236). Yet some texts disclose that strife more willingly than others, which no doubt accounts for the citations of Blake in Auden's criticism. Auden found in Blake not a precursor but a creative mentor, that is, a writer whose imaginative practice made either discipleship or filiation impossible. Even more important than his citations of

---

tradition. He is admonished accordingly: "The sea of poetry, of poems already written, is no redemption for the Strong Poet. Only a poet already slain under the shadow of the Covering Cherub's wings can deceive himself this profoundly with Auden" (16). The most telling phrase in this passage is Bloom's "too soon," which quietly insinuates romanticism's Oedipal mandate: it admits that in any case, even a strong poet's recuperation of the one true maternal source, the anxiety of influence, is inevitable. Auden's attitude toward such an entropic destiny, the closed circle of a universal template that informs all worthwhile poetry, might be traced in a phrase from Blake he found cited in *A Vision* by Yeats and unhesitatingly adopted for a line in *New Year Letter,* "the bottom of the graves" (CP, 173).

Blake, especially in the early criticism, is the aphoristic technique Auden adapted from *The Marriage of Heaven and Hell*. As he explained in the foreword to *The Dyer's Hand*, "In going over my critical pieces, I have reduced them, when possible, to sets of notes because, as a reader, I prefer a critic's notebooks to his treatises" (DH, xii). This preference for notes characterizes much of Auden's criticism, from his gnomic early journals, through the terse outlines of *The Enchafèd Flood*, to the *Shorts* he appended as notes to the original *New Year Letter* and later developed into a distinct poetic form in *Academic Graffiti, Symmetries & Asymmetries, Marginalia*, and *Shorts II*. The slide from prose into poetry, though with both encompassed within the practice of criticism, is deliberate and significant. It embodies Blake's insight that, given the disruptive tensions inscribed within even the most authoritative text, criticism had to play a similarly divided part. As aphorism, a notoriously dogmatic form, criticism mock-seriously promises deliverance from imaginative excess. But as an imagery from which even the most lucid language might claim only a passing exemption (the moment of forgetfulness known as truth), this critical deliverance slips back into the textual tumult. The serious aphorism thus declines into a troping, the unruly figuration in which language both begins and ends: "In origin all language is concrete or metaphorical. In order to use language to express abstractions, we have to ignore its original concrete and metaphorical meanings" (DH, 380).

To focus this conflict more precisely, Auden turned to Blake's mythology. Shortly after arriving in New York in 1939, Auden began a critical manuscript, *The Prolific and the Devourer*. This unusual autobiographical work illuminates a historical moment that is itself an emblem of Auden's poetic concerns: an alien, the proverbial wanderer, on the shores of a strange new world (America as a collage of varied discourses), and in the background a shadow of impending doom, the deteriorating situation in Europe. Given this crisis, the manuscript defines the poet's task as one of articulating the elemental forces struggling within language, forces glossed in the Blakean giant forms Auden borrowed for his epigraph:

> To the Devourer it seems as if the producer was in his chains: but it is not so, he only takes portions of existence and fancies that the whole.
>
> But the Prolific would cease to be Prolific unless the Devourer, as a sea, received the excess of his delights.

These two classes of men are always upon earth, and they should be enemies: whoever tries to reconcile them seeks to destroy existence. (EA, 394)

Prolific and Devourer should each be accorded a generous range, as *hypostasis* and *latency*. The Devourer is not exactly truth, certainty, or even reference, but the entire complex of restrictive features that enable a discourse to achieve its thematic effect. Thus the Devourer would include most of Blake's demons: reason, consensus, morality, abstraction, authority, law. Nonetheless, it is only through the Devourer that a tumultuous medium, language as a device of pure play, can be held in check long enough not merely to perform useful service but to initiate a dialogic process in the text. Because the communicative practices of ordinary speech are so familiar, the Devourer-principal is noticed first so that it always seems to be in control. Yet here Blake's insight reveals its genius. The too obvious priority of the Devourer is entirely a result of its reception. Merely because it is noticed first does not mean it precedes its textual medium. The seeming priority of the Devourer in fact depends upon violence and repression. It achieves its illusion of order by attempting to silence any rivals. Yet the violence of the Devourer serves only to provoke and animate the Prolific, by inciting it to further creativity. Each imposed hypostasis tries to confine the text within a spell of truth, placing a certain name upon its excess. Yet this repression in turn instigates further outbursts, so that the more tyrannically a text is bound, the more exultantly responsive it becomes.

Auden never completed *The Prolific and the Devourer*; its last section trails off into a dialogue about religious conversion.[8] Nonetheless, the manuscript offers an invaluable insight into Auden's recurrent critical approach and, by implication, into his theory of how texts work. An earlier notebook proposes this variation on Blake's Prolific and Devourer: "It is the body's job to make, the mind's to destroy" (EA, 298).

8. Parts of *The Prolific and the Devourer*, however, did find their way into the notes that originally accompanied *New Year Letter* (London: Faber and Faber, 1941), pp. 79–160. As Edward Mendelson indicates in *W. H. Auden: A Bibliography, 1924–1969* (Charlottesville: University Press of Virginia, 1972), p. 49, the notes in the first English edition are more extensive than those of the American counterpart, *The Double Man* (New York: Random House, 1941).

As Auden explains, "Body and Soul (Not-Me and Me) can have no independent existence, yet they are distinct, and an attempt to make one into the other destroys. The Pagans tried to convert mind into body, and went mad or just apathetic. We attempt to turn body into mind and become diseased" (EA, 297). The textual strife can be framed in a variety of imageries, mythic as in Blake, or anthropological as here in Auden. But it would be a mistake to fashion any of these variations into a static dualism, for Auden's point has to do with a general theory of the text. Human beings live not in a neutral or objective reality but in realms of meaning composed of culturally constituted signs. In other words, human beings live in texts. "What we have not named / or beheld as a symbol / escapes our notice" (CP, 630). Yet these enveloping texts, no matter what medium they occupy, and no matter which subject they concern, inevitably display an interactive and self-destabilizing quality. In part, they serve purposeful ends. They act as obedient instruments, able to perform a master illusionist's bidding: Prospero as the emblem of the rhetor. In part, however, they also play the role of the obscured body, dense, riddled with conflicting desire, resistant. Auden never ceased to be fascinated with this textual dynamic. His return to its varied phases can be readily traced in *The Dyer's Hand*: for example, in "The Poet and the City," "Hic et Ille," "Balaam and His Ass," "The I without a Self," " Brothers and Others," "The Joker in the Pack," "Postscript: The Frivolous and the Earnest," "Genius and Apostle." In each instance, the tension between an ordering violence and its responsive subversion is considered in a new way. On one side stand the stern guarantors of a respectable truth: intending author (Poet), dominant theme (Hic), official persona (Balaam, a high priest), controlling consciousness (I), serious purpose (the Earnest), and inspired messenger (Apostle). On the other side waits a motley horde of voices and inscriptions. These can be repressed, denied, or attacked, yet neither evaded nor silenced: City (an arena of rival discourses), Ille (a corrupting marginality), Ass (the betrayals of a gesturing body), Self (a crowd of warring voices), Others (all who ever thought, lived, or loved differently), Pack (an erratic reshuffling of signifiers), Frivolous (a condition of relentless mirth), and Genius (a dispassionate function, with much to do but nothing to say).

Yet there is an important asymmetry here. The Devourer is readily defined. It is the act of definition itself, a principle of restriction. But the Prolific is elusive because it remains just over the horizons of the thinkable. The Prolific is not a theme but an event, an inherent capacity for responsiveness. The instant its textual body is named, it slips away:

> No *codex gentium* we make
> Is difficult for Truth to break;
> The *Lex Abscondita* evades
> The vigilantes in the glades.
>
> (CP, 175)[9]

Thus we have reached what would be a most convenient stopping point. Inquiry might go no farther, having stumbled on the unnameable and silent. Yet as Auden's irreverent couplets from *New Year Letter* suggest, he had little inclination to the intuitive or mystical. If the Prolific cannot be fixed or stated as such, it is still possible to inquire into the conditions that foster its emergence.

How is it that a language can be at once docile and treacherous? When in doubt about a meaning, the impulse is to secure a definition. But the lexicon's treasure trove offers only an assortment of further words. These devious equivalences extend the initially doubtful term yet still remain words themselves. The conviction of reference, their spell of an achieved reality, is pure magic. Thus the original doubt might be repeated for each of the items in the definition. It soon becomes apparent that the simple tyranny of definition releases a tumult of conflicting resonances. "That is why, for a desert island, one would choose a good dictionary rather than the greatest literary masterpieces imaginable, for, in relation to its readers, a dictionary is absolutely passive and may legitimately be read in an infinite number of ways" (DH, 4). There is nothing whimsical or poetic to this; Auden is being rigorously correct. The lexicon from which a writer's materials are drawn exceeds the work even of genius, for it stipulates the clamorous labyrinth from which a

---

9. The passage continues with an illustrative vignette that reenacts Nietzsche's parody of the Western ideal of knowledge as a characteristic violence: thought unveiled as a woman stripped. "Now here, now there, one leaps and cries / 'I've got her and I claim the prize.' / But when the rest catch up, he stands / With just a torn blouse in his hands" (CP, 175).

meaning briefly escapes, only to return. Each step of carefully refined nuance leads farther into an infinite complex. Each momentary resting point of truth conjures up ravishing ambiguities that demand a further adventure. Each branching of semantic ways opens up passages that cannot be pursued just now and yet, because they lead into a maze that has no center (save the usual reductions of the human to the bestial), must sooner or later be crossed again.[10] Behind any masterpiece, then, stands its only permanent context, the lexicon. And in the dictionary, as in the verbal universe of the poet, each member, whether scrofulous or sacred, is eventually kin to every other. Like it or not, the inscribed word must endure

> the uncritical relations of the dead,
> Where only geographical divisions
> Parted the coarse hanged soldier from the don.
> (CP, 149)

But why go to such excessive lengths? Common sense holds that for general purposes, the smaller a dictionary the better: it is cluttered with less pedantry, meandering erudition, and other such academic irrelevance. Auden conceded that in most circumstances it makes sense to restrict the range of a semantic field, the seductive allure of the Prolific, so as to obtain a clear and direct meaning. Still, clarity must not be turned into a fetish. As Auden noted in his introduction to *The Poet's Tongue*, poetry in particular demands "exactly the opposite kind of mental effort to that we make in grasping other verbal uses" (EA, 327). Instead of restricting the semantic range to a single entry, a poem calculatedly sets off "the aura of suggestion round every word through which, like the atom radiating lines of force through the whole of space and

10. Auden's imagery makes a careful distinction between the centered labyrinth, which revolves around a monster or fetish ("the Minotaur" of *New Year Letter*, CP, 166; the rustle "of famishing Arachne" in *For the Time Being*, CP, 271; or "Old Grandmother Spider" in "Circe," CP, 646–47) and the decentered maze, usually a contemporary city, whose only focal points are dispersed, transitory, and suspect, as in "Macao" ("Churches alongside brothels testify / That faith can pardon natural behavior"; CP, 145) and "Brussels in Winter" ("And fifty francs will earn a stranger right / To take the shuddering city in his arms"; CP, 146).

time, it becomes ultimately a sign for the sum of all possible meanings" (EA, 327). Although ordinary usage conceals this phenomenon, words have memories. Besides conveying a particular idea, event, or emotion, words implicate subtle networks of relation, unconscious yet nonetheless operative sets of disciplines and practices. These intricate patterns trace diverse constitutive spaces, whose topographies or scenes of production are both incongruous and competitive. Over the course of its history, a more or less lawless wandering among various discourse groups, the word gradually acquires a highly variegated assortment of these topographies. If patiently considered, then, any utterance leads in several directions at once: into an arena of contemporary competitors and, beyond that, into a realm of alien or lapsed but still responsive inscriptions. Like the epic hero in the underworld, the message-bringing word is encompassed and possessed by spirits of both the dead and the unborn: "Nights come bringing the snow, and the dead howl / Under headlands in their windy dwelling" (CP, 39). A literary text must stage the scene of this eerie, dissonant return.

An account of the word's topography might suggest a division of labor along generic lines. As noted, a word's inscriptions include both contemporary rivals and historical remnants. Dramatic and fictional genres, because of their capacity to accommodate a wide array of discourses, are well suited to explore the arena of contemporary rivals. Given a range of competitive perspectives, the playhouse and even more so the encyclopedic framework of a novel provide opportunities for juxtaposition and conflict. The artistic impulse within these dialogic arrangements is not to declare a victor but to illuminate through contrast the simulations of different discourses: to hold their incongruous structures in an imaginary conversation. In poetic genres, however, the chance for such exchanges is typically limited to the much narrower range of contrasts available to a particular persona, at a single dramatic moment. Auden was acutely aware of this limitation. At times he envied the greater discursive freedom permitted to novelists and dramatists. Whereas the poet is "encased in talent like a uniform," restricted to largely monologic forms, a novelist can easily move from discourse to discourse:

> For to achieve his lightest wish, he must
> Become the whole of boredom, subject to

Vulgar complaints like love, among the Just
Be just, among the Filthy filthy too
And in his own weak person, if he can,
Dully put up with all the wrongs of Man.
                          (CP, 147)

Yet poetic genres more readily lend themselves to an inquiry into the other aspect of a word's topography, its repository of historical inscriptions. Precisely because of their monologic and contextual bounds, poetic genres foster a compression, an almost intolerable rigor or exclusion in which the lapsed itineraries of a word may come to life. Needless to say, this generic division of labor is only a rule of thumb, with exceptions on both sides. Poetic novels such as *Finnegan's Wake* are riddled with inscriptive play; marginal poetic forms such as children's or nonsense verse can accommodate a polyglot brood of contemporary rivals. It is this latter possibility that informs Auden's interest in light verse, as well as his refusal to write only "serious" poems. As he insisted at the end of his introduction to *The Oxford Book of Light Verse*, "poetry which is at the same time light and adult can only be written in a society which is both integrated and free" (EA, 368), that is, a society able to acknowledge discursive boundaries for what they are, and yet willing to transgress them.

Nonetheless, a great deal of Auden's most distinctive poetry is written in a more formal, that is, a more narrowly monologic, mode. One voice, one dominant discourse, prevails. It would be reasonable to infer from this monologic rigor that Auden is therefore promoting some kind of dogmatic thought. But that would be a clear misstep, even though it is one sanctioned by no less eminent a theorist than Mikhail Bakhtin. Because Bakhtin assumes that a dialogic strife among contemporary rivals is the sole valid component of a word's topography, he characterizes poetry as an authoritarian form. He argues in "Discourse in the Novel" that the practical effect of poetry is to accomplish "the task of cultural, national and political centralization of the verbal-ideological world in the higher official socio-ideological levels."[11] Poetry is well-equipped for this task, Bakhtin maintains, because it assumes the existence of a higher, primordial, more complete or otherwise superior discourse: "The lan-

11. Mikhail M. Bakhtin, "Discourse in the Novel" in *The Dialogic Imagination*, ed. Michael Holquist (Austin: University of Texas Press, 1981), p. 273.

guage of the poetic genre is a unitary and singular Ptolemaic world outside of which nothing else exists and nothing else is needed. The concept of many worlds of language, all equal in their ability to conceptualize and to be expressive, is originally denied to poetic style."[12] Coincidentally, Auden took up the same metaphor, though in a comic spirit: "Any heaven we think it decent to enter / Must be Ptolemaic with ourselves at the center" (CP, 232). Certainly Auden was aware of the monologic tyranny of poetic genres. But unlike Bakhtin, Auden retained an acute sense of more elusive textual interiors, the realms of an utterance's topography that remain open to a poetic dialogism. Bakhtin makes a reasonable mistake, given his scholarly preoccupation with the novel, in overlooking the dialogic potential of poetry. But as a result, his writings show little inclination to acknowledge a text's communion with its forgotten yet still potent dead. Yet no matter how tyrannical a monologue may be, how impervious its thematic center or primordial its intentional origin, any text is simultaneously threatened, both from within and without. The arena of contemporary rivals is no doubt more familiar and accessible. But the subtler dimension of a word's inscriptions, its capacity for a poetic dialogism, must also be acknowledged if there is to be a more thoughtful approach to Auden's writing.

The different kinds of dialogism are each valid and necessary. But they have separate tasks. A dramatic or fictional dialogism offers access to the more concrete and ideological strata of a discourse. Plays and novels excel at examining opposed assumptions about current social issues.[13] A poetic dialogism, by contrast, is ill-adapted to such inquiries, for it lacks the discursive variety and contextual range. Yet there are other levels of constitutive structure, more remote and elusive, to which a poetic dialogism can offer access. As if undistracted by the bustle of the street, a poetic dialogism can patiently listen to the fainter voices

12. Ibid, p. 286.
13. As an example of indefensible yet pervasive ideologies, Auden glossed his phrase "Empiric Economic Man" in *New Year Letter* with a passage from the Lynds' *Middletown in Transition*. What Middletown just naturally believes is quite fantastic. Yet because these beliefs remain sovereignly unquestioned, their discourse constitutes an invisible or transparent mythology, a secular religion more tenacious than any of its ecclesiastical competitors (though these are for the most part shrewd enough to concur with it), because it deals not in ritual or symbol, but behavior and truth.

within the inscriptions. These distant accents, though without the urgency and passion of contemporary rivals, can speak to more elemental concerns: the often bizarre beginnings of a sober idea, the gradually eroding ground of its truth, the ultimate because untraceable destinies of its reception. Such matters may seem unimportant, but they have profound implications for the more impassioned struggles of the novel or drama. A poetic dialogism discovers, at the very site of sacred origins, an irrepressible return of responses. In a quite practical way, it tempers the fury of the contemporary arena by demanding a nerve-wracking patience and by opening a path through antagonism into play.

Perhaps that is why Auden, even when given an opportunity for ideological skirmishing, so often turned to a form of poetic dialogism. In an important essay, "Psychology and Art To-Day," Auden set about to debunk Freud's argument that the work of art originates as a compensation for personal neurosis. As is typical, however, Auden avoids polemics. He does not disagree with or even particularly resist Freud's theory. Instead he tinkers with its familiar but unquestioned convictions about the beginnings of a text.

> Just as modern physics teaches that every physical object is the center of a field of force which radiating outwards occupies all space and time, so psychology states that every word through fainter and fainter associations is ultimately a sign for the universe. The associations are always greater than those of an individual. A medium complicates and distorts the creative impulse behind it. It is, in fact, largely the medium, and thorough familiarity with the medium, with its unexpected results, that enables the artist to develop from elementary uncontrolled fantasy, to deliberate fantasy directed towards understanding. (EA, 337)

Freud describes the production of the work of art in terms of an opportunistic censorship. The artist, beset by an overpowering yet impossible desire, first purges that desire of idiosyncratic features as well as any culturally proscribed material, and then disguises it, so that the impulse may be safely consumed by others. If successful, the artist acquires, through fantasy, the wealth, fame, and love of women that had previously been attainable only in fantasy. Auden does not object to this reductive determination of the creative process. Instead he illustrates its unexamined foundations. Freud's account presupposes both a controlling intention and an obedient medium that serves to convey the intention to a historical audience. Yet these perfectly natural assumptions, so natural as to be imperceptible, provide a hopelessly inadequate framework for thinking about the work of art. As a field of force, the text resists any single, determinative impulse. A field is an array of different elements, some unknown, others volatile, all interconnected, and each capable of transforming any other. Within such a turbulent scene, the idea of a controlling intention is out of place: "The associations are always greater than those of an individual." This does not mean that the author can be ignored or discarded. A creative act is required to begin the exchange. It means only that neither an author nor anyone else can lay proprietary claim to the ensuing play.

Auden's use of the field metaphor also calls into question Freud's other tenet, namely that the artist uses the creative medium to represent something beyond itself, to arrest a referent. Yet there can be no outside beyond the textual field, no external nature or reality that somehow eludes or transcends the mediation of cultural signs. This inescapable quality of the field is an advantage, indeed the main benefit. A work of art does not try to escape or transcend the labyrinth of signs in order to achieve a lasting truth. Its task is to show how that maze operates, what its devices at once prohibit and release through an exchange of conflicting forces. For in this way the subject, whether as artist or recipient, can go beyond the obsessions of a narrow egotism, the "elementary uncontrolled fantasy." Auden concedes that this process of understanding brings with it the risk of seeming preposterous, extravagant, or worse, for the associations grow "fainter and fainter." But he adds that this pursuit might lead to an understanding not merely of what is but of what might still be gathered from the forgotten.

•

A theory of poetic dialogism, a doubled text engaged not so much with contemporary rivals as with its own inscriptions, raises certain problems. Not the least of these is its defiance of some of the most apparent features of Auden's literary image. As everyone knows, Auden is a historical poet, a writer deeply aware of the problems of late capitalist culture: unemployment, inadequate education, political charlatanism, culture: unemployment, inadequate education, political charlatanism, bigotry, and the brutalizing stupor induced by mass media. But if he is so aware of such issues, does not the idea of an internally responsive text condemn language to an ahistorical suspension, a retreat into precisely what Auden ridiculed as "la *poésie pure*" of Mallarmé and Rilke: "a celebration of the numinous-in-itself in abstraction from all cases and devoid of any profane reference whatsoever" (DH, 58). Furthermore, Auden had a well-known dislike for any kind of unruliness or disorder. This sensibility can be found in his aversion to anything that suggested chaos:

> The sea, in fact, is that state of barbaric vagueness and disorder out of which civilization has emerged and into which, unless saved by the effort of gods and men, it is always liable to relapse. It is so little of a friendly symbol that the first thing which the author of the Book of Revelations notices in his vision of the new heaven and earth at the end of time is that *"there was no more sea."* (EF, 6–7)

Later on, it can be found in his snub of a sixties radical: "Somebody shouted, I read: *We are ALL of us marvelously gifted!* / Sorry, my love, but I am: You, though, have proved that You ain't" (CP, 645). But if Auden so resisted disorder, is not this fastidious sensibility at odds with a theory that would relegate even the most simple utterance to an interminable trembling of dialogic ripples? Also, Auden often lamented the growing isolation that modern society imposed on the individual. Human beings were steadily being cut off from one another, so that they had access only to customary languages and practices, a situation well suited to both a self-righteous insularity and an encroaching state control.[14] But if Auden were worried about such isolation, does not the

14. See Auden's "Criticism in a Mass Society" in *The Intent of the Critic*, ed. Donald A. Stauffer (Princeton: Princeton University Press, 1941), p. 135. "We have heard much in the last twenty years of the separation of the modern artist from the crowd, of how modern art is unintelligible to the average man, and it is commonly but falsely supposed that this is because the artist is a special case. In my opinion, on the contrary, the lack of communication between artist and audience proves the lack of communication between all men; a work of art only unmasks the lack which is common to us all, but which we normally manage to gloss over with every trick and convention of conversation; men are now only individuals who can form collective masses but not communities."

doubled text confine experience within a prisonhouse of signs, denying any contact with others and thereby condemning us to an even more terrible aloneness? The verdict seems inevitable. On the grounds of its flagrant ahistoricism, anarchism, and solipsism, the evidence against Auden's ever accepting his own theory of poetic dialogism is overwhelming.

The strength of these objections is encouraging, for it suggests that Auden's remark about Voltaire is equally applicable to himself: "Voltaire has suffered the greatest misfortune that can befall a writer: he has become a legend, which insures that he will not be read until someone destroys the legend" (EA, 386–87). The distribution of ideas here is telling. To read an author, in the sense of faithfully grasping an intended meaning, is to confirm a minor myth, a cultural image of the origin governing a text. But as Auden suggests, these local myths are also disciplinary. They install a controlling principle, whether as author, movement, or period, and this principle serves in turn to silence the unruly responses of the text. It paradoxically follows that the act of reading is imperiled by its own result, the legends it confirms. Still, the only deliverance from the genteel tyrannies of comprehension is further reading, in the sense of a patient waiting and listening for the vestigial inscriptions of a text: "*Who are You, whose speech / Sounds so far out of reach?*" (CP, 72). To read as defined by Auden thus requires an alternation of violence with disruption, an exchange in which the evident (authorial, magisterial, coercive) and its disciplines are welcomed not as truth but as the summoning of an irrepressible return. Reading undertakes a violence to the text, whose only respite is a counterviolence on behalf of the text.

Such counterviolence, however, carries out a destruction that is curiously refined. As illustrated in his nonpolemic with Freud's theory of neurotic origins, Auden's idea of reading involves a seductive or perhaps mirthful lenience, a submission of officious legends to the play of their inscriptions, the illimitable *legenda* or forgotten events still to be read within them. What Auden repeatedly does as a reader is to show how an accompanying text surprises and overwhelms its announced themes. In this regard, it is perhaps inevitable that he began *The Enchafèd Flood*, his most thorough display of a responsive reading, with the dream sequence from Wordsworth's *Prelude*. In this parable of the text symbols of both enlightenment and romantic values (the shell and stone of the Bedouin) are set in flight, first by a twinkling on the horizon, the flood that is figuratively glossed as "an unknown Tongue," and then by the "articulate sounds" of the text's dissonance. Thus it is possible to derive from Auden's practical reading a strategy to contend with the formidable objections of the Auden Legend. Let the Legend object: that the disciplinary mytheme "Auden" would refuse the ahistorical, anarchic, and solipsistic character of his textual theory. Yet the charges must be heard repeatedly, not just once, and with an ear to their perfectly reasonable claims as well as to the unlikely responses they provoke.[15]

What does it mean to claim that Auden is a historical poet? Although different models are available for writing history (linear, cyclical, spiral, random, catastrophic), they share a consistent notion of the historical, that is, of the necessary markers for a discourse that seriously describes the past. The historical must deliver a tough-minded, compelling set of determinants. A virile enterprise, it must penetrate to the real causes of events. Implicit in the historical, then, is the assumption that explanatory causes exist and that the job of history is to find and identify them with as little distortion as possible. In effect, the historical practices a form of idolatry by claiming that "physical force is the Prince of this world against whom no love of the heart shall prevail" (DH, 83). Within this idolatrous purview, language is at best a transparent medium, at worst an intrusive nuisance, but in either case something to be used only so that it may be set aside.

But histories are also texts. Their narratives are written, that is, composed of ideologically configured and culturally inscribed signs. To the empiricist and objectivist, this wayward quality of the scriptural remnant raises spectral prospects. If there are no determinative causes within a textual field, only rival presuppositional structures, then its written status reveals the historical as a disciplinary mode. Yet from Auden's vantage, this unmanageable textual diversity is what delivers history from itself: "Culture is history which has become dormant or extinct, a second

---

15. Auden elaborates the idea of a continuous hearing, in both an anatomical and a forensic sense, by amplifying the phrase "that summary tribunal" from *New Year Letter* with an aphorism from Kafka: "Only our concept of Time makes it possible for us to speak of the Day of Judgment by that name; in reality it is a summary court in perpetual session."

nature" (DH, 97). As long as the historical prevails, inquiry is caught not so much in some iron web of determinants as in the fantastic belief that it is possible to know those determinants. Within the tumult of the textual field, however, the historical yields to a dialogic play in which consumption is superseded by production: "Man is a history-making creature who can neither repeat his past nor leave it behind; at every moment he adds to and thereby modifies everything that had previously happened to him" (DH, 278). The past cannot be made to go away, nor can it be used as a pattern of replication. For at each instant, the coercive determinants of the historical are poised at a threshold of disclosure. Because this moment of revelation is not confined to the present, but is itself part of the past, the historical *includes* the record of the continuous self-disruption through which it has become history. Thus Auden refashions history as a textual passage: from the supposedly hard causes of an event, the solidity of its legend, to the responsive inscriptions of its playful *legenda*. In this way, the historical becomes what it always was, not the "subjugated plain" of "August 1968" but a field of incessant production.

It is possible to trace some of the distinctive features of this field. Once the spell of a final determination has been broken, what is left changes from a timeless structure of signs to an arena of specific inscriptions. That arena might be thought of, to borrow Auden's adaptation of Dante's "Catholic ecology" (CP, 164), as a series of concentric rings. With the logic of the historical suspended, the word resonates outward. Closest to the center are familiar connotations, the ideological uses that echo permitted resemblances. Next met is a ring of nuances which, though acknowledged, are out of favor. These are no less ideological than the connotations, but they often bear the presuppositional structure of an alien discourse group, often one that is banished or condemned: the uninitiated, dissidents, or outcasts like the biblical Ishmael, Auden's prototype of the romantic artist. Farther out is a ring of derelict meanings, vast, abandoned, stretching well beyond the horizon. This region of a word's topography reveals structures of understanding that are contaminated with pariah beliefs and tainted with debunked practices. Such traces are of little use to the serious writer, aside from shock or comic value. But to a poet, these odd creatures of the margins offer an invaluable resource, a repertoire of inscriptions available for dialogic purposes, because their presuppositional structures are at once so apparent and so incongruous. And finally, in one of the outer rings (there is never a last one) may be found a tangle of etymological stems, fouled leads that are as cunningly interwoven as the finest lace. These solemn origins promise a lasting foundation and, just as faithfully, betray that promise through their ambiguity, contradiction, and impertinence.

Given this concentric patterning of the word's possibilities, it seems odd to portray the text's subversions of the historical as a turning away from history itself. On the contrary, the interplay of responsive inscriptions enables history, as a productive field, to at last emerge from its confinement within devious necessity and arrogant fact.

But the very interplay that brings history to life also confirms another charge of the Auden Legend: that the inscriptions of a text merely release a free-associative anarchy. If the inscriptions really are endless in their resonances, what separates them from a barbaric din? Here it is important to recall that the Prolific does not shrug off the chains of the Devourer and then proceed to take its own course. Instead its play has a specific task: it articulates and subverts the forces that would dominate it. In this sense, as Auden noted in his early essay "Writing," the text carries on an internal conversation, acute, patient, relentless. "When we read a book, it is as if we were with a person" (EA, 310). But the "as if" must be given a special emphasis, for the textual other is not the speaking voice but a voice within that voice. The person in question is a momentary hypostasis, a response that instigates a further departure. Auden made this clear when he returned to the issue several decades later in "The Virgin and the Dynamo": "A poem might be called a pseudo-person. Like a person, it is unique and addresses the reader personally. On the other hand, like a natural being and unlike a historical person, it cannot lie" (DH, 68). The textual other cannot lie because it does not belong to a system in which lying is possible. A lie presupposes a definite framework: a presiding consciousness that intends a reference it knows or believes to be false. But the pseudo-persons of the text preside over nothing. Their solid identities are porous, admitting a host of alien voices; and their apparent claims never reach the secure exterior of a reference. Yet there is nothing futile or nihilistic about their play. The inscriptive clamor of the text, though unbounded, faithfully responds to the configuring assumptions that assemble and provoke it.

35

Yet even if the inscriptions lead neither beyond history nor into anarchy, there is still the last complaint of the Legend: that the text's labyrinthine coils isolate the individual from social contact, the lively group "engaged / On the shady side of a square at midday in / Voluble discourse" (CP, 414). Many of Auden's poems seem almost deliberately to play into the hand of this charge. They frame an enclosed space, sealed, claustrophobic, where every surface is littered with fragments of different scripts. The poetry, then, does not depart from its scene of making but, as in "Nones," leads back "to a room, / Lit by one weak bulb, where our Double sits / Writing and does not look up" (CP, 482), or to the writer's burrow described in "The Cave of Making":

> For this and for all enclosures like it the archetype
>   is Weland's Stithy, an antre
> more private than a bedroom even, for neither lovers nor
>   maids are welcome, but without a
> bedroom's secrets: from the Olivetti portable,
>   the dictionaries (the very
> best money can buy), the heaps of paper, it is evident
>   what must go on. Devoid of
> flowers and family photographs, all is subordinate
>   here to a function, designed to
> discourage daydreams—hence windows averted from plausible
>   videnda but admitting a light one
> could mend a watch by—and to sharpen hearing: reached by an
>   outside staircase, domestic
> noises and odors, the vast background of natural
>   life are shut off. Here silence
> is turned into objects.

(CP, 521)

This is the only scene of origins, where the hallucinations of authority and certainty are transformed back into a field of signs. Here intricately wrought and unruly inscriptions are arranged for an ostensible purpose, which briefly quells their internecine strife, but only as a momentary stay against their eventual return.

Yet if Auden's poetry remains so attached to this scene, does it not pass judgment on itself as isolated, defeatist, in retreat? The objection rests on a familiar humanist bias: that whereas individuals are vital and independent, language is inert, subservient. Accordingly, it takes courage to interact with real people, whereas it is a sign of pathological abnormality (the stereotype of the writer as crippled, myopic, inept, deviant) to envelop oneself within language.[16] Although plausible enough, this commonplace bias confuses matters. Members of a society are held in place by powerful bonds, of rank, lineage, or obligation. As a result of this pervasive web of power, the number of people who can afford to be candid is inversely correlated to one's social status: the greater the status, the fewer the respondents, that is, those permitted to talk back. For the really powerful (unanswerable), there may be no respondents at all. In effective terms, this means that the practice of inquiry is severely restricted. Those below oneself in the social pyramid are permitted only to comply, that is, to preserve an oblivious monologue, even if it is exploiting them. As Auden explained, this fact of imposed complicity leads to a matched set of delusions. The powerful become swollen with insolence as they convince themselves that they are dealing with imbeciles; and the oppressed, refusing to acknowledge that degradation, come to believe that the masters are really extensions of their own will. "By nature we tend to endow with a face any power which we imagine to be responsible for our lives and behavior; vice versa, we tend to deprive of their faces any persons whom we believe to be at the mercy of our will. In both cases, we are trying to avoid responsibility" (DH, 62). It is against the backdrop of this disciplinary pragmatism that Auden's withdrawals into the text must be assessed.

To open a book, to read a poem, is to leave the realm of actual persons: "And the crack in the tea-cup opens / A lane to the land of the dead" (CP, 115). But what is the basis for believing that the poetic

16. Unlike the ideally well-adjusted person, for whom signs correspond to or represent a separate and preferably external reality, the artist construes signs as infinitely displaceable parables of their own production, that is, helpless simulacra of the way in which they at once orchestrate and disrupt a meaning. "The same psychologist [who examined Auden's early love of mines and mining equipment] would have also detected easily enough the complexes that were the cause of these affairs, but what was important for the future was not the neurotic cause but the fact that I should have chosen to express my conflicts in symbolic fantasy rather than in action or any other way. I cannot now look at anything without looking for its symbolic relation to something else" (EA, 398).

dead, the clamorous forces of inscription, will be even more docile than the well-disciplined living? In the aftermaths of a poem, a creative subsidence takes place. A regulatory force, the voice of approved meaning, gradually fades into the textual responses it has provoked. If attending to such responses is to be dismissed as a cowardly isolation, its rules of conduct should be compared with the codes governing an ordinary conversation. The results might be surprising. When talking to another person, there is a manageable image, hence a clear focal point. The inscriptions of the text, however, have no definite locus or center, only myriad beginnings. They might spring from a repressed present, a derelict past, an alien society, or an as yet unrealized epoch. So there is no hope of ever fixing their identity. Try as criticism might, it can find no satisfactory motive, no lasting or deep structure with which to foreclose their tumult. Of course, other persons can be unruly enough. But even with a lout and bully, some latter-day Ignatius Gallaher, there is still an ample repertoire of disciplinary devices: whether these be conciliatory (appeals to common roots, experiences), evasive (topical shifts, deliberate incomprehension), magisterial (invocations to vague authorities, hints at disapproval), or belligerent (a challenge, a summons). But none of these gestures is effective in dealing with the text. Its inscriptions are irrepressible. With all the effrontery and persistence of the dead, they have nothing to fear. Nor is there any means of appeasement, any tactic to hold them at bay. Sometimes, of course, a conversation can lead to crisis. In such cases, one simply walks away. The analogy with reading would seem to be closing the book. Yet when so denied, the inscriptions can be even more insistent than a painful memory. For not only do they wait, as do memories, at every gap and interval in the rhythm of concentration, but far worse, they patiently lurk within the devious medium of its movement, language itself. At the margins of any textually incited word, a host of dissenting voices, outcasts denied a hearing, threatens to leap into prominence, no matter where that word might be encountered. Contrary to the familiar humanist bias, then, a withdrawal from the bustle of the street to the quieter strife of the text actually involves a passage from comparative safety into a much more demanding exchange.

If the Auden Legend can be put aside, however briefly (some version of it will always reassert itself), new questions and possibilities arise.

These do not involve thematic preoccupations or intellectual debts. Rather, they are concerned with what a text might do, the performances it might commence once the shadow of its truth has been lifted. In an odd way, however, this new region of possibilities leads back to some familiar topics. The responses of the text bear a distinct social burden. They perform an important cultural task, so there must be no contradiction between the wary pragmatism of Auden's social criticism and the refined exchanges of his texts. But working out the specific terms of this exchange, between a textual play and the responsibilities of its practice, requires a further inquiry.

CHAPTER TWO

Psychosomatic Lessons

The sum total of an individual human being, physical, mental, and spiritual, the organism with all its forces, the microcosmos, the universe which is man, I conceive of as a self unknown and forever unknowable, and I call this the "It" as the most indefinite term available.

—Georg Groddeck, *The Book of the It*

in our theater
all that I cannot syllable You will pronounce
in acts whose *raison-d'être* escapes me. Why secrete
fluid when I dole, or stretch Your lips when I joy?
—"Talking to Myself"

The question of Auden's social commitment is not completely dead. In a once infamous essay, "From Freud to Paul: The Stages of Auden's Ideology," Randall Jarrell attacked Auden for a lack of high intellectual seriousness.[1] Jarrell argued that during the period of his most intense political involvement (or at least his reputation for that involvement), Auden was a spiritual magpie, stealing ideas from first a crackpot psychology, then a puerile Marxism, and finally a Kierkegaardian fideism. Jarrell's argument may be the most influential criticism ever written about Auden. Its idea of a three-step development, from personal, to social, and then back to personal (religious) concerns, has furnished a framework that both Auden's defenders and detractors have been obliged to accept. For example, even in his highly adulatory *The Poetry of*

1. Randall Jarrell, "Freud to Paul: The Stages of Auden's Ideology," *Partisan Review* 12 (1945): 437–57.

W. H. Auden, Monroe K. Spears faithfully adheres to Jarrell's three-stage model which furnishes the organizing basis for an analysis of Auden's themes.² In Herbert Greenberg's *Quest for the Necessary,* the three-stage evolution is simply the common view that has much to recommend it.³ So one of the most durable truisms about Auden is that he marched under the successive banners of psychology, politics, and at last religion. But Jarrell's study has also shaped the critical tradition in a subtler way, by fostering a tendency to separate the early secular Auden from the later religious convert (temporizer, reactionary, sellout). Two of the best recent studies of Auden, Samuel Hynes's *Auden Generation* and Edward Mendelson's *Early Auden,* both draw their inquiries to a close at 1940.⁴ While justifiable for practical considerations, because of the extensive amount of material from the thirties, such a division at least implicitly confirms Jarrell's accusation. It would seem that Auden either lost or never had the high seriousness required of a social poet.

So the debate focuses on Auden's place, if any, among the visionary company of those who had something important to say—and kept on saying it. The necessity of that thematic persistence, as if it were not self-evident, is acknowledged by Auden himself: "When a writer is dead, one ought to be able to see that his various works, taken together, make one consistent *oeuvre*" (DH, 21). As might be expected, the early commentaries on Auden are dominated by his detractors. When the disappointed hopes of thirties radicalism were still painful, and the resentment of Auden's abrupt departure for America still fresh, critics had a greater tendency to assail what Hynes calls the Auden Myth. This tendency is evident not only in the predictable skirmishes in reviews by younger poets, but also in the more considered attack of J. M. Cohen in *Poetry of This Age* and the elaborate case brought by Joseph W. Beach in *The Making of the Auden Canon.*⁵ By sifting through Auden's editorial

2. M. K. Spears, *The Poetry of W. H. Auden* (New York: Oxford University Press, 1963).

3. Herbert Greenberg, *Quest for the Necessary* (Cambridge, Mass.: Harvard University Press, 1968), p. 9.

4. Samuel Hynes, *The Auden Generation: Literature and Politics in England in the 1930s* (New York: Viking, 1977); Edward Mendelson, *Early Auden* (New York: Viking, 1981).

5. J. M. Cohen, *Poetry of This Age* (London: Hutchinson, 1960); J. W. Beach, *The Making of the Auden Canon* (Minneapolis: University of Minnesota Press, 1957).

revisions of already published work, Beach manages to catch the poet in a double bind. For such compulsive revisionism proves not only that Auden is ideologically inconsistent but that he *knew* he was inconsistent and committed a further offense by trying to destroy the evidence. Beach argues that Auden must be accorded a minor status, a sort of Aldous Huxley of poetry, because he lacks a profoundly compelling message for humankind. "We are here concerned with what is sometimes called the integrity of a work of art" (*Auden Canon*, 250), he explains.

> There can be no question about the strengthening effect for poetry of tensions set up between things which actually coexist in all our experience, such as light and dark, bitter and sweet, or the realistic and the idealistic view of human nature. What I have in mind in the poetry of Auden is opposites which cannot well coexist logically or practically, like incompatible meanings of the same word in the same context, or conflicting lines of conduct in a given situation recommended in the same breadth. (*Auden Canon*, 252)

Hence, Beach decides, Auden's greatness as a poet falters upon a question of identity. These comments conclude a painstaking bibliographical analysis and still retain considerable power. They accurately present the main charge, which is that Auden's texts are riddled with dissonant nuances and conflicting accents. But Beach has no sense of how that dissonance might contain a poetic dialogism or, more important, how that dialogism might serve a social function. Consequently, he has become the unacknowledged father of the Audenesque version of the Wordsworth Myth. That is, just as the elder Wordsworth reduced his earlier work to domesticated banality, so did the later Auden, though with this difference: whereas Wordsworth once had something prophetic to say, Auden never did.

Still, Auden does have his defenders. Yet these rescue missions are oddly unfortunate in that their arguments, however perceptive as readings, have unwittingly confirmed the framework of Jarrell's assumptions. Until that framework is challenged, the question of Auden's social commitment remains at an impasse. The defenders might be divided into two camps, the polemicists and the humanists. Taking the high road, the polemicists maintain that Auden did indeed have a prophetic message. This is certainly the most direct line of defense. But even with a deft selection of materials, the polemicists run athwart the obvious posturing of the texts. Auden's poetry retains the sense of a mask or pose, as of someone miming a part in an unnervingly overdone way. The performance has the quality of an impersonation, so that it seems less a statement than a dramatization. It is as if the poem were saying, here are the techniques for achieving an austere pathos (Rachel's lamentation from *For the Time Being,* CP 305); or for showing a resentment disguised as flippant witticism ("Friday's Child," CP 509). Consequently, when the polemicists have to make good on their claim and indicate exactly what the prophetic message might be, they must resort to vague locutions about Auden's sense of disintegrating civilization and Malrauxesque violence, as does François Duchene in *The Case of the Helmeted Airman;* or more ingeniously, they put the long-awaited prophecy out of verbal reach, as does Frederick Buell in *W. H. Auden as a Social Poet.*[6]

The other camp, the humanists, also retain the ideal of a unified message, but they shift its site from the treacherous plains of history to the more congenial sanctum of psychology. For the humanists, Auden is the upholder of individual rights and personal freedom against the insidious encroachments of mass culture and its mechanized bureaucracies: the poet of works such as "The Unknown Citizen," "The Managers," "The Chimeras," and "Progress?" Richard Hoggart's *Auden: An Introductory Essay* is an important source for the humanist tradition, since he insists that in Auden's universe the psychological is of greater importance than the political.[7] So the poetic message runs, first set your own house in order and only then worry about larger affairs. The obvious appeal of this truism, aside from familiarity, lies in its seemingly realistic accommodation to the context of reading. What more might an individual, with only a text, hope to achieve beyond a minor and momentary self-reform? Herbert Greenberg takes up this notion of self-reform in *Quest for the Necessary,* where he portrays the essential theme in Auden as a conflict between Ego and Self, conscious will and vital

6. François Duchene, *The Case of the Helmeted Airman* (London: Chatto and Windus, 1972), p. 71. Frederick Buell, *W. H. Auden as a Social Poet* (Ithaca: Cornell University Press, 1973).

7. Richard Hoggart, *Auden: An Introductory Essay* (London: Chatto and Windus, 1951), pp. 164–65.

but haphazard energy. Proceeding through Jarrell's three-stage evolution of stages, Greenberg argues that Auden's poetry is unified around the Ego's continuing quest for some necessary absolute: inward harmony, social justice, total religious commitment. Always, though, the quest upholds the exemplary humanist values of personal decision and individual freedom. A similar bias can also be found in Jan Montefiore's "Goebbels and Goblins."[8] Montefiore argues that Auden imported elements from popular and children's literature into his poetry so as to make global political issues at once comprehensible and accessible; that is, Auden used topics that need not be relegated to experts or politicians because they remain within the grasp of individual moral choice.

Like any thematic approach to Auden, the humanist defense captures certain elements of his practice, but at the cost of ignoring many others. It cherishes the notion of a free and autonomous individual, set apart from social currents and detached from ideological frays. This idea, however, runs counter to Auden's insistence that human beings are historical entities: "For we are conscripts to our age / Simply by being born" (CP, 183). Paradoxically, the humanist ideal of independence entails an insidious authoritarianism. As a former instructor at an English boys school, Auden understood quite well the lasting effects of a cultural apparatus that could mold an individual during the most impressionable period of personal development and well before its subjects were capable of understanding what was taking place. The poetry often portrays the young as caught in the mechanism of a sadistic trap: "Bones wrenched, weak whimper, lids wrinkled, first dazzle known, / World-wonder hardened as bigness, years, brought knowledge" (EA, 21). Certainly, the humanists can point to numerous passages in which Auden requires a "change of heart" or demands a new beginning. But such texts must be approached carefully. One example is a retrospective passage from "Authority in America": "Looking back, it seems to me that the interest in Marx taken by myself and my friends . . . was more psychological than political; we were interested in Marx in the same way we were interested in Freud, as a technique of unmasking middle-class ideologies,

---

8. Jan Montefiore, "Goebbels and Goblins: Politics and the Fairy-Tale in Auden's Poems," in *W. H. Auden: The Far Interior*, ed. Alan Bold (Totowa, N.J.: Barnes and Noble, 1985), pp. 73–99.

not with the intention of repudiating our class, but with the hope of becoming better bourgeois."[9] Auden says nothing here about an autonomous inwardness or a heroic decision making. Instead he emphasizes analytical procedures. Both Marx and Freud offer strategies for recognizing and reassembling discursive structures: the assumptions and practices through which meaning is fashioned. It is this "technique of unmasking," not any privileged interior or independent will, that is cited as the important contribution of psychology. To argue, as the humanists do, that a change of heart must precede any significant social reorganization is in effect a reactionary tactic. It conveniently overlooks that what is meant by "heart" (an ideologically approved value, *anthropos*, an inwardness subject to state and economic formation), or what is acceptable as "change" (a move toward carefully restricted goals), has already been fashioned by the social organization it proposes to alter.

It does not follow that Auden was either a behaviorist or a relativist. He did not believe that acculturation imposes an invincible order, nor did he maintain that any one society is as good as another. But he did insist that human freedom begins in an understanding of the discursive structures and techniques through which well-entrenched social interests attempt to supervise meaning and truth. As he noted in "I Believe," an important essay written shortly before he left England in 1939, romantic individualism and its humanist correlatives too readily neglect the complex process of social formation: "Man has always been a social animal living in communities. This falsifies any theories of Social Contract. The individual *in vacuo* is an intellectual abstraction. The individual is the product of social life; without it, he could be no more than a bundle of unconditioned reflexes. Men are born neither free nor good" (EA, 373). It is true that Auden wrote this essay during a transitional period, but then any period is transitional in one way or another. Long after his religious conversion, when he supposedly committed himself to an existential inwardness, he criticized D. H. Lawrence for having "no firsthand knowledge of all those involuntary relationships created by social, economic and political necessity" (DH, 293). Despite its rhetoric of choice and freedom, humanism unwittingly betrays those values. By invoking psychology as a means to achieve a purely personal liberation (as if

9. W. H. Auden, "Authority in America," *Griffin* 4 (1955): 5–11.

psychology's concepts of mental health were not carefully supervised), humanism achieves a freedom already subservient to the social interests it claims to reform.

One offshoot of the humanist defense, however, merits particular attention: Richard Johnson's study, *Man's Place*.[10] Johnson too seeks an integrity of concern with which to defend Auden against Jarrell's charge of intellectual charlatanism. But Johnson locates that unity in a process rather than a theme. What gives the poetry coherence is an event, an informing activity, rather than a concept or intention. One of the few critics to make thoughtful use of Auden's prose criticism, Johnson argues that Auden's recurrent concern is humanity's anxious and self-destructive flight from social worlds it has made (collectively, as cultures moving through time) yet can neither understand nor control. As Auden read contemporary events, this flight had produced alternate forms of totalitarianism: unable to contend with the complexity of the discursive arena, modern society sought refuge in either the evasive relativism of the liberals or the ironfisted absolutism of the fascists. Thus humanity's task, and by implication the social responsibility of the poetry, is to find a way out of ideological insularity and back into the frightening yet productive realm of social and historical diversity. The value of Johnson's insight is incalculable. By shifting the focus from themes to textual events, he not only reorients the debate about Auden's social commitment, which becomes a process that must be actively engaged rather than an idea to be approved or disapproved, but opens a way to reshaping the definition of what a culturally responsible literature would be. But despite his acute readings, Johnson does not fully pursue his insight. The main culprit is a tendency to reduce the arena of embattled discourses to a scene of harmonious order. Although Johnson occasionally mentions the interplay between oneness and multiplicity, it is usually the oneness that has the last word: "Poetry has for man the function of a higher calculus by which it is reasonable to see man as a totality, even though he is composed of contradictory and antagonistic elements" (*Man's Place*, 15). As Johnson admits, the omnivorous mysticism of Heidegger's *Being and Time* broods over that totality. Still, the importance of his search for integrity in an unsettling yet generative event rather than a reproduc-

10. Richard Johnson, *Man's Place* (Ithaca: Cornell University Press, 1973).

ible theme cannot be overstated. It marks an important, if neglected, turning point in Auden criticism.

It is a turning point because from Jarrell onward both Auden's defenders and detractors have assumed a common but inadequate ideal of the visionary poet. Supposedly this figure has something profound to impart, masters the treachery of words, and thereby conveys a significant message. No doubt a major reason for the unquestioned acceptance of this ideal is that it duplicates the familiar communicative model of language. In ordinary usage, a speaker passes a message through language as an instrumental medium, preferably with a minimum of distortion or noise, in order to relay an intended meaning. Yet as a poet, Auden had few such ambitions. He does not try to say or to express anything. Thus he rejects both the visionary ideal and the communicative function it assumes. This rejection serves as a means, however, the beginning not the end of his social commitment. For in refusing to play the visionary/ communicative role, Auden thereby opens a way to articulate the workings of an alternative function, one dedicated to a play of contrasts rather than a serious expression of final truth. And it is from a reader's active participation in this textual play that the social function of literary art is derived. That tenuous participation, a text's admittedly perilous dependence on the contributing imagination of a historical individual, is perhaps more valuable than a docile compliance with even the most profound truth.

Auden's rejection of the visionary ideal is readily traced. His essay on D. H. Lawrence in *The Dyer's Hand* opens with this curious endorsement:

> The artist, the man who makes, is less important to mankind, for good or evil, than the apostle, the man with a message. Without a religion, a philosophy, a code of behavior, call it what you will, men cannot live at all; what they believe may be absurd or revolting, but they have to believe something. On the other hand, however much the arts may mean to us, it is possible to imagine our lives without them. (DH, 277)

Visionaries foster the process of ideological evolution. They seize upon some powerful idea that a dominant system has not accommodated, and make it the basis of a refurbished mythology. (As Auden explains in another essay, the idea itself might be either Utopian/revolutionary or Arcadian/reactionary, depending on whether it promotes a dazzling future or a divine past.)[11] Yet having granted the importance of visionaries, Auden pointedly distinguishes them from the writer. Sometimes, as in Lawrence, the two happen to overlap. But as noted in his essay "Writing," that coincidence is unusual because visionary and writer have opposing tasks. Unlike the visionary, a writer has no message to convey.

> Writers can be guilty of every kind of human conceit but one, the conceit of the social worker. "We are all here on earth to help others; what on earth the others are here for, I don't know." (DH, 14)

> The Oracle claimed to make prophecies and give good advice about the future; it never pretended to be giving poetry readings. (DH, 16)

> As a rule, the sign that a beginner has a genuine original talent is that he is more interested in playing with words than in saying something original. (DH, 22)

By his own testimony, Auden makes an unlikely candidate for the prophetic choir of love.

It does not follow, however, that Auden abandoned all thoughts of social commitment. In addition to its communicative purpose, language has what might be called a ludic function. Instead of exercising "powers over words to persuade people to a particular course of action," as Auden explained in the introduction to *The Poet's Tongue*, this alternative function extends "our knowledge of good and evil, perhaps making the

---

11. Auden develops this contrast at some length in "Dingley Dell & the Fleet," where he suggests that it is as elemental a distinction as the one between Blake's Prolific and Devourer: "The psychological difference between the Arcadian dreamer and the Utopian dreamer is that the backward-looking Arcadian knows that his expulsion from Eden is an irrevocable fact and that his dream, therefore, is a wish-dream which cannot become real; in consequence, the actions which led to his expulsion are of no concern to his dream. The forward-looking Utopian, on the other hand, necessarily believes that his New Jerusalem is a dream which ought to be realized so that the actions by which it could be realized are a necessary element in his dream; it must include images, that is to say, not only of New Jerusalem itself but also images of the Day of Judgment" (DH, 410).

necessity for action more urgent and its nature more clear, but only leading us to the point where it is possible for us to make a rational and moral choice" (EA, 329). The distinction between the communicative and the ludic is essential to an understanding of how literary art might serve a social purpose, even though, in the well-known words of Auden's elegy on W. B Yeats, "poetry makes nothing happen" (CP, 197). In its communicative role, language must be induced to conceal its conflicting inscriptions, which are subjugated to a presiding voice so that the utterance may achieve a semantic end. But in its ludic aspect, a wholly different activity emerges. The normal concern of language, the preoccupation with a successfully achieved meaning or effect, is suspended. Instead, through a process of turning within itself, language begins to illuminate rather than apply its discursive patterns. Thus the ludic function covertly turns absolutes into contingencies and certitudes into anxious decisions.

But as Auden knew, the culture of late capitalism has little tolerance for such an impractical activity. A genteel and almost imperceptible dogmatism pervades discursive practice in the form of a belief that *only* the communicative function has any value. Auden attributed the modern writer's lack of status to a cultural ethos that had no use for play, that is, for any activity that did not serve a defined and useful end.

> In a society governed by the values appropriate to Labor (capitalist America may well be more completely governed by these than communist Russia) the gratuitous is no longer regarded—most earlier cultures thought differently—as sacred, because, to Man the Laborer, leisure is not sacred but a respite from laboring, a time for relaxation and the pleasures of consumption. Insofar as such a society thinks about the gratuitous at all, it is suspicious of it—artists do not labor, therefore, they are probably parasitic idlers—or, at best, regards it as trivial—to write poetry or paint pictures is a harmless private hobby. (DH, 74–75)

The destructive consequences of this disciplinary efficiency are extensive. Such militant seriousness of course devalues the ludic function. Moreover, it corrupts it with expectations and demands that, however necessary to the operation of the communicative function, have only an inaugural or instigative role in an imaginative art.

49

These destructive effects are readily seen by contrasting the ludic with the communicative. In ordinary use, it is the sender, the quasi-divine proprietor of a conveyed meaning, who founds the act of communication. But when the impulse is to play within diverse inscriptions, the sender becomes incidental, the site of an obscure collapse, a comically emptied threshold to a field of embattled forms. Nonetheless, literary commentary cherishes the myth of a controlling center of consciousness, a tutelary spirit that might bestow protection and guidance. (A hermeneutic daydream: to have an approving author prefer the critic's thorough, serious, mature explanations over a scriptor's disjointed, impertinent, misbegotten texts.) Nor is communication theory any less restrictive with regard to the artistic medium, the materiality of its words. Noise or distortion, the tumult of a historically accretive medium, must be rigorously purged from the act of communication. It interferes with the transmission of truth. In verbal play, however, such distracting noise attains an imaginative value. Through its myriad possibilities, the tensions, rifts, and anomalies of a discursive friction are intensified rather than quelled. The ludic task is not to consolidate a single and unified message but to release a clash of differences within a culturally and historically inscribed medium.

But the most exacting repression occurs when communication theory is used to formulate the role of a literary work's reader. If a message must be conveyed, its recipient is obligated to *get it right*, to abjure all illicit and merely subjective deviances in favor of an ascetic (strictly antihedonistic) confinement to the sender's original intention.[12] The dutiful receiver in communication theory thus becomes a tormented being, alertly imperceptive, energetically passive, ingeniously obtuse. Surely no better impediment to the dangerous pleasures of imaginative enjoyment might be found than this unspoken but tyrannical demand for a faithful reception. It is for this reason Auden proposed in "The Joker in the Pack" that the separate functions of language, to communicate and to play, be kept distinct. "Social relations," he writes,

12. Following Nietzsche in this regard, Auden characterized such rigorous objectivity as a peculiarly modern form of religious devotion: "As Nietzsche said, experimental science is the last flower of asceticism. The investigator must discard all his feelings, hopes and fears as a human person and reduce himself to a disembodied observer of events upon which he passes no value judgment" (DH, 270).

are only possible if there is a common social agreement as to which actions or words are to be regarded as serious means to a rational end and which are to be regarded as play, as ends in themselves. In our culture, for example, a policeman must be able to distinguish between a murderous street fight and a boxing match, or a listener between a radio play in which war is declared and a radio newsbroadcast announcing a declaration of war. (DH, 254)

But the inertia of habit is tremendous. The communicative functions are not only expected but planned, practiced, and rewarded daily with each instance of ordinary use. No matter how arrant the textual play, the disapproving seriousness of communication theory and its sober solidifications of dialogism into truth reimpose themselves as the perfectly natural attitude.

Like most natural attitudes, this one is neither innocent nor terribly natural. As traditionally conceptualized, rhetoric, stylistics, and semantics are unapologetically subservient to the primacy of communication. When Auden observed that the citizens of modern societies were undereducated, he meant not that they were unskillful in the ordinary use of language but that they were oblivious to the complexity of discursive systems, their presumptive disciplines as well as their inscribed subversions. On this topic there is little distance between the obscure young instructor who protested that "education in the use of the language becomes more and more necessary. At present nobody gets such an education" (EA, 307), and the internationally renowned Professor of Poetry who decades later observed:

Writers, poets especially, have an odd relation to the public because their medium, language, is not, like the paint of the painter or the notes of the composer, reserved for their use but is the common property of the linguistic group to which they belong. Lots of people are willing to admit that they don't understand painting or music, but very few indeed who have been to school and learned to read advertisements will admit that they don't understand English. As Karl Kraus said, "The public doesn't understand German, and in Journalese I can't tell them so." (DH, 15)

But Journalese, an instance of the linguistic corruption Auden insists all free societies must resist (DH, 11), is only one subcategory of the communicative function. The corruption lies not in journalism's popularity but in its transparency: its capacity to make discourse disappear by concealing as simple fact the disciplines through which its inventions of the truth are produced. Who benefits from this carefully cultivated illiteracy? There is an obvious link between an educational omission, which if not victimization itself is certainly good preparation for it, and the interests of a demand-based economy, a profit engine driven by high levels of undiscriminating and readily manipulated consumption. Bad readers make good customers.

As heretical educator, Auden needed to find an image for the ludic function—an unlikely task since that function consists of an event that cannot be summarized or repeated, only further acted out. One of his most concerted efforts to devise this impossible image occurs in a passage from "Dingley Dell & The Fleet," where he analyzes a special class of human activities, games. Like a text, a game is a social institution that demands compliance with certain rules. It must operate within bounds. Yet a game is also an intricate apparatus that can be operated with skill, even virtuosity. Because of this dual aspect, games suggested to Auden a useful analogy for the ludic function. "A game is a closed world of action which has no relation to any other actions of those who play it; the players have no motive for playing the game except the pleasure it gives them, and the outcome of the game has no consequences beyond itself" (DH, 421). Each aspect of this definition is carefully designed to suspend the privilege of a purely instrumental or practical use. Thus the players in a game have no motive beyond the play itself. "The closed world of the game is one of mock passions, not real ones" (DH, 421). If someone wants to express an emotion or convey an idea, that intention would instantly change the game into something else. But with no activity admissible beyond its own play, a game lacks an origin, any basis or center from which it proceeds. A game is simply available, a determinate structure that outlasts its specific performances, much as a text outlasts its successive readings. For not only does a game lack an origin, it also lacks a purpose or end. Framed within well-marked boundaries (the chessboard, the tennis court), the game refuses any prospect of a departure to the outside. "Within the closed world of the game the only human beings are the players; the other inhabitants are things, balls, bats, chessmen, cards, etc." (DH, 421). This is not to say that the game banishes reality, but, more precisely, that its utmost version of reality is a preoccupation with its own activities.

As noted, a game requires strict adherence to its rules. "In the game world there is only one crime, cheating, and the penalty for this is exclusion; once a man is known to be a cheat, no other player will play with him" (DH, 421). This requirement has a crucial effect when applied to language. For purposes of communication, language must be made unobtrusive, as transparent, immediate, and spontaneous as possible. The ideal is to make the very words disappear, in effect dissolving into their natural truths. But in the text as game, the object is to make the regulatory rules, the various authorities, codes, and conventions that supervise meaning, as conspicuous and as notably arbitrary as possible. Certainly each player must know the discursive rules. Yet the game becomes worthwhile to the extent that its participants can operate those rules in a way at once law-abiding and unpredictable. When this happens, "the pleasure of playing, of exercising skill, takes precedence over the pleasure of winning" (DH, 421). This attention to restrictive bounds and disciplinary practices is in marked contrast to the conduct of serious rhetoric, in which the parties are expected to comply with communicative norms in an unreflective and automatic way, so as to promote swift comprehension.

From his anatomy of games, it is possible to obtain a clearer sense of the contrasts Auden drew between ludic and communicative functions. Whereas communication requires an arc in which language somehow effaces itself to achieve a result, play remains situated within an arena of lively differences. The arrogant reticence of a truth that conceals its own production bears little resemblance to a game in which every player must be master of the rules. And perhaps most important, the rapt narcissism of communication, which seeks its own reflection in an external world, is opposed to the shuttle of an event that has no object beyond its own increasingly refined performances.

It would be logical to conclude that there must be a lively enmity between ludic and communicative functions. And indeed there is warrant for such hostility in Auden's critical views. "In earning his living, the average poet has to choose between being a translator, a teacher, a literary journalist or a writer of advertising copy and, of these, all but the first can be directly detrimental to his poetry" (DH, 77). To the extent that language is practiced to convey a point, no matter how praiseworthy, informative, or profitable its message may be, that activity has a corrupting effect upon the would-be poet. But it would be inaccurate to portray the relation between sense and play as one of mutual antagonism. Certainly, the communicative functions bear little love for their ludic accompanists. The principal mission of serious rhetoric is to keep the ludic well out of sight and sound. (Auden's Airman is obsessed with the anarchic forces poised just over the horizon.) But that keeping is an improbable task, as futile as efforts to recapture one's own echo. Its hindering involves a retention, a risk of intense scrutiny, and thus becomes a preserving, almost a celebration: as one keeps a special observance. The ludic cannot be repressed, for it constitutes a dimension of any text, whatever the period, genre, style, topic, or intent. In this sense, Auden notes, "it is a sheer waste of time to look for a definition of the difference between poetry and prose" (DH, 23). The furrow-browed treatise harbors subversive disruptions. The licentious ode practices Horace's "Persian Apparatus" (CP, 186), the machinery of a disciplinary tyranny. Furthermore, there is even a creative liaison between the two adversaries. "Though every poem involves *some* degree of collaboration between Ariel and Prospero, the role of each varies in importance from one poem to another" (DH, 338). As Auden's reference to collaboration suggests, the ludic and communicative functions not only occupy every text but have a genetic relation. Even though the communicative may strive to repress the ludic, its efforts have a contrary effect. Instead of restricting, they release; rather than intimidating, they provoke and direct. So from the instigating standpoint of a serious intention, the text stages a doomed warfare against hopeless odds, the desperate heroism of Auden's Mortmere saga.[13]

> Sharers of our own day, thought smiling of, but nothing known,
> What industries decline, what chances are of revolution,
> > What murders flash
> > Under composed flesh.
>
> > > (EA, 29)

13. The most considered treatment of Auden and Christopher Isherwood's private fantasy world of Mortmere may be found in Justin Replogle, *Auden's Poetry* (Seattle: University of Washington Press, 1973), pp. 16–20. See also Mendelson's *Early Auden*, pp. 120–21.

Yet from the standpoint of its responsive inscriptions, the text opens a space of ebullient play, a schoolboy's delight in subverting the preposterous interdicts of a moribund regime.

Fostering that play is the artist's social task. As the following passage from Auden's essay "Private Pleasure" suggests, the paradox of modern society is that as it grows more diverse and interesting it also becomes more adept at imposing restrictions on discursive exchange: "Like everything else in our civilization, the system we have made has become too much for us; we can't stop the boat and we can't get out into the cold sea. The snail is obeying its shell. All we can do is to become specialists" (EA, 312). Although surrounded with the variety of a complex culture and its differing traditions, the modern individual is increasingly driven into repressive modes of thought, the cunning refuge of the specialist. The task of literary art, then, is to discover and release the subversions that this narrowness bears within itself. Thus a poem might seem to convey an intended message or truth. But it does so only as a way of marking out, incising, the disciplines that enforce that truth's authority and, more important, of illustrating how that act of enforcement prompts dissident responses from within the textual medium. Little concerned with either conveying a message or having a determinable effect (the disruptive collusions of a reader are creative and hence incalculable events), the artist has the sole ambition *as an artist* of fostering an exchange between disciplinary and responsive forces.

> To be useful to an artist a general idea must be capable of including the most contradictory experiences, and of the most subtle variations and ironic interpretations. The politician also finds a general idea useful, but for his purpose, which is to secure unanimity in action, subtlety and irony are drawbacks. The political virtues of an idea are simplicity and infallibility.
>
> "How can one think to fill people with blind faith in the correctness of a doctrine if by continued changes in its outward construction one spreads uncertainty and doubt?" (Hitler). (EA, 404)

As Auden's citation indicates, the great communicators of every epoch firmly grasp that a discourse is merely a means to an end, the dispensable covering of an essential core. A literary artist, however, throws the verbal medium into the sharpest relief possible, to illustrate how its impassioned means are incapable of reaching their semantic ends because embarked upon obstreperous dialogues within themselves.

The cultural contribution of the poet is to deliver language from its convenient repression, even into truth. This unlikely deliverance might be figured in quasi-religious terms, as a resurrection or return from death to life, "a promise to man / Pushed on like grass-blade into undiscovered air" (EA, 42). But the redemptive figure is unduly linear, suggesting a passage from one stasis to another, since so many versions of "life" in fact offer devious cognates of death (harmony, fulfillment, peace, bliss, unity). So Auden more typically resorted to a figuration that moves from stasis to process, though with this condition: that each must be a simultaneous aspect of the other. At any instant a text might shift, because its constants as well as its variables conceal the action of a pivot: from amorphous to discrete ("That out of cloud the ancestral face may come"; CP, 47); from crystalline to fluent ("It is our sorrow. Shall it melt? Then water / Would gush, flush, green these mountains and these valleys"; CP, 105); from blank to inscribed ("An improper word / scribbled upon a fountain"; CP, 110); from inert to responsive ("Where all I touch is moved to an embrace"; CP, 203); from passive to peremptory ("Words pushed him to the piano to sing comic songs"; CP, 149). Or to gather all these turns while provoking even more, the text is both an impenetrable semantic surface, and a discrete and beckoning interior, which "by happening to be open once" let

> Enormous Alice see a wonderland
> That waited for her in the sunshine and,
> Simply by being tiny, made her cry.
>
> (CP, 224)

•

The dialogic relation of communicative and ludic functions, their timeless struggle as the creative impetus within any text, opens a new area of inquiry. If one naturally begins with an emphasis on the communicative functions (Who said this? What is intended? Is it true?), that innocent violence poses the question, Might the very apparatus of limitation provoke the responses of the text? Could a communicative tyranny unravel itself so that freedom need no longer attend upon some long deferred justice but could be traced even within the monuments of power? To pursue this question is to accept the charge of Rilke's *dennoch preisen*, which Auden called "the basis for all reverence for life and belief in the future" (EA, 387). Language enacts the myriad scenes of disciplinary repression. And yet for all that, it must be valued, seized, esteemed for the responsive play of its inscriptions.

But how? In 1929, shortly after arriving in Berlin for what he hoped would be a restorative *Wandersjahr*, Auden met the anthropologist John Layard, a disciple of the American analyst Homer Lane. What first drew Auden to Layard's theories was their emphasis on liberated desire. If only people would act on genuine, spontaneous feelings, life would once more be pure and good. As Auden discovered, this initially attractive gospel soon runs into serious difficulties. To begin with, it is impossible to locate a pure desire untainted by cultural influence. Unsurprisingly, when supposedly pure desires are translated into political action, they too readily assume the form of mob rule and the doctrine that might makes right.[14] In addition to the idea of spontaneous desire, Layard advocated a theory of psychosomatic illness. If contained within, frustrated desire leads to bodily disease. As Edward Mendelson describes this clinical premise, "every illness is in fact psychosomatic and points the way to recovery, since the disease manifests in twisted form a feared or repressed desire" (*Early Auden*, 56). Auden's early enthusiasm for the psychosomatic theories of Lane via Layard has long been an awkward point for his humanist defenders, who are eager to cast him as a visionary with psychological insights that must be taken seriously. So there is a tendency to slight this aspect of Auden's development as an adolescent phase, a fascination with what he soon enough came to parody: "all the

14. Although spontaneity may play an important part in those rare relations where trust is possible, Auden deeply suspected its application to political contexts: "But folly is folly all the same and a piece of advice like 'Anger is just. Justice is never just,' which in private life is a plea for emotional honesty, is rotten political advice, where it means 'beat up those who disagree with you' " (EA, 340). The passage illustrates the need for discursive differentiation (what is appropriate in a private context does not belong in a public one), as well as the danger of a romantic belief in some master discourse of true or authentic speech.

healers, granny in mittens, the Mop, the white surgeon, / And loony Layard" (EA, 96). Common sense suggests that Auden, as the son of a doctor (his father was a medical examiner), was rebelling against paternal rationalism. Or that Auden, as an unhappy neurotic (he had gone to Berlin hoping to find an alternative to his homosexuality, so he might return to Birmingham and marry the nurse with whom he was engaged before he left), wanted to understand his own troubling impulses. Or that Auden, as a precocious and manipulative intellectual (he periodically subjected acquaintances, especially Stephen Spender, to psychosomatic inquisitions), was indulging in a diagnostic will-to-power.[15]

But common sense is seldom a reliable guide when contending with poets. It forgets that creative thought conducts its inquiries by means of farfetched analogies and unlikely figurations. "Man is an analogy-drawing animal; that is his great good fortune. His danger is of treating analogies as identities" (DH, 52). Accordingly, Auden's interest in psychosomatic theories might be approached as a figure rather than a theme: psyche and soma propose an analogy to rival textual forces. The psyche, as the conscious element of a text, strives to gather both origin and end, intention and meaning, within its grasp. But this ennobled spirit (a near relation to the classical gods) never quite manages to sever its ties with an accompanying corporeality, a dense, uncooperative body. Perhaps what drew Auden to the psychosomatic analogy is its capacity to reassess the venerable body/mind dualism, in which one party traditionally dominates the other. But according to psychosomatic theory, the body is neither a negative inertia nor a positive instinct, but an anatomy of conflicting interests. In a historical sense, this notion of the body as a multiplicity of diverse desires breaks with an anthropology based on any sort of romantic unity. The body is not the wellspring of the one life within us and abroad. Rather, it situates and releases the refractory, mischievous, differing forces that Georg Groddeck traces in *The Book of*

---

15. As an epigraph for "Psychology and Art To-day," Auden cites Freud's admission: "I was, rather, spurred on by a sort of itch for knowledge which concerned human relationships far more than the data of natural science" (EA, 332). Should that itch become obsessive or ruthless, it degenerates into the kind of callous experimentation Auden later found exemplified in Shakespeare's Iago. "What makes it impossible for us to condemn him [Iago] self-righteously is that, in our culture, we have all accepted the notion that the right to know is absolute and unlimited" (DH, 271).

the It, which Auden used to pursue his early interests in psychosomatic diagnosis. For Groddeck, the body housed an inscrutable It, a plurality rather than a unity. But assigning a single source to Auden's sense of the body is probably impossible and certainly inadvisable.[16] For with regard to his understanding of the human soma, Auden's use of psychosomatic theory is also in accordance with the socially oriented Christianity he later described in *The Dyer's Hand*: "It is unfortunate that the word 'Flesh,' set in contrast to 'Spirit,' is bound to suggest not what the Gospels and St. Paul intended it to mean, the whole physical-historical nature of fallen man, but his physical nature alone" (DH, 131). The distinction is carefully drawn. Auden neither denies nor apologizes for the foibles of the body. Rather, he extends its significance so as to locate it in a more public realm, the historical arena of conflicting loyalties and commitments. The human body, a virtual palimpsest, offers the unerasable foolscap on which the various syndromes, quirks, reflexes, and seizures of a culture leave their mark. The body is thus the site of a separate memory, accretive, only in part subservient to conscious thought or control, a repository of impulses that are contentious and interactive rather than harmonious or fixed.

Yet the psychosomatic analogy of the text ventures still further. The image of a palimpsest accurately suggests the diversity of the body's inscriptions but does not say much about their activity. Through its symptoms, the soma actively engages the presiding psyche. So as an analogue of the doubled text, the body is not merely a passive repository of differing impulses but an active respondent, a dialogic other. In the gestures of its verbal medium, the text enacts a contrary movement to its apparently conscious intentions. Auden occasionally goes so far as to intimate that it is this internal dialogue, rather than the achievement of any conscious intention, that sustains the creative impulse of a text. (The conscious intention, for its part, serves as a pretext, a trap that entices an unsuspecting writer into the fond authorial delusions of power and dominion.)

16. See Georg Groddeck, *The Book of the It* (New York: Nervous and Mental Disease Publishing Co., 1928). Edward Mendelson (*Early Auden*, 41) provides a balanced assessment of this issue when he suggests that Auden derived his psychological themes from an odd mix of noncanonical writers, of whom Groddeck was only one.

Yes, the Liberal *Aufklarung* was wrong: in the last analysis we *are* lived, for the night brings forth the day, the unconscious It fashions the conscious fore-brain; the historical epoch grows the idea; the subject matter creates the technique—but it does so precisely in order that it may itself escape the bonds of the determined and the natural. The daemon creates Jacob the prudent Ego, not for the latter to lead, in self-isolation and contempt, a frozen attic life of its own, but to be a loving and reverent antagonist; for it is only through that wrestling bout of which the sex act and the mystical union are the typical symbols that the future is born, that Jacob acquires the power and the will to live, and the demon is transformed into an angel.[17]

It would be ill-advised to make too much of Auden's minor review of a far from major (if delightful) book, Walter de la Mare's *Behold This Dreamer* (though Auden later returned to the image of Jacob and the Angel as a figure of textual strife; see DH, 16). Still, the implications of this passage are far-reaching. Given the bias to intended meaning, it seems that the psyche rules the soma, the conscious intention dictates the sense of the text, so that a thought may be conveyed. But from a ludic perspective, this supervised conveyance is a ruse. A text originates well before any consciousness, in the diversity and energy of its discursive conflicts. And it is this conflict that engenders an intention, not to reach a semantic end but to provide a focal point for its continuing and disruptive responses. For through that dialogic strife, the struggle for a name between Jacob and the Angel, the text may be delivered from closure into play.

But how might one read the symptoms of the textual body? The value of a figure such as Auden's psychosomatic analogy is purely speculative, a matter of its disruptive potential. But the catch, as drawback, safety device, or unearned return, is that the analogy leaves conspicuous gaps. What does it mean for a phrase to display *dementia praecox* or a sentence to suffer from spastic afflatus? Auden never answers directly, so it is necessary to guess. Psychosomatic symptoms include betraying gestures: twitches in a medium that attend its proper purpose. A gesture, which Auden carefully distinguishes from a pose, is simply a bodily action. This

17. W. H. Auden, "Jacob and the Angel," *New Republic* 101 (December 27, 1939): 293.

movement is carefully marked: a tremor in an eyelid, a clenched fist, an idly swaying foot, a slight leaning forward or backward. So by inference the symptomatology of a discourse pertains to the way it moves, as it proceeds from one point to the next—in brief, its syntax. Although commonly defined as a fixed structure, the orderly arrangement of parts, syntax has to be put into motion for that arrangement to work. A syntax remains inert, lifeless, until its hesitations, reversals, leaps are enacted. And as each component meets the next, it embodies a gesture. So the movements of a syntax might well resemble a psychosomatic symptomatology. True to its checkered genealogy, the staid *tassein* of an orderly arrangement mingles with the corrupting *piptein* of happenstance, a devious fall into unforeseeable betrayals, maddening fits. Syntax at once embodies and proposes the symptoms. It yields the subtle convulsions within the discursive act through which an enforced order concedes not only its originary violence but an array of accusatory, dissenting inscriptions.

With the assistance of Auden's early notebooks, it is possible to follow the symptom/syntax correlation in greater detail. In the accompanying chart cited by John Fuller, Auden links Dante's division of the sinners from *Purgatorio*, XVII with some of Layard's psychosomatic markers.[18] The result is a cross between adolescent mayhem and theoretical genius. If read with the psychosomatic analogy in mind, the scheme addresses the question of how symptomatic gestures might accompany, and betray, specific discursive disciplines. The Dantean categories propose a distributed violence as an array of discursive tactics. In contending with the accompanying inscriptions of its textual body, a discourse can, for example, try to overwhelm these disruptive aliens (excessive love); to withdraw from their defiling contact (deficient love); or to deceive, disarm, or otherwise waylay and corrupt them (perverted love). To perform these tactics, it is of course necessary to span the communicative arc from sender (Self), through authenticating authority (God), to receiver (Neighbor). So Auden's quite fantastic scheme also proposes a systematic review of discursive violence. As syntax runs the gamut of disciplinary tactics, and as it completes the arc of an effectively conveyed message, it help-

18. John Fuller, *A Reader's Guide to W. H. Auden* (London: Thames and Hudson, 1970), p. 56.

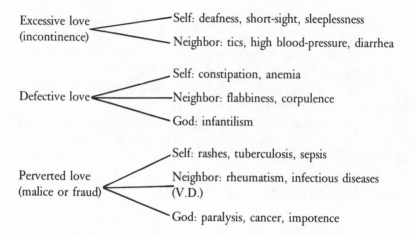

Excessive love (incontinence)
- Self: deafness, short-sight, sleeplessness
- Neighbor: tics, high blood-pressure, diarrhea

Defective love
- Self: constipation, anemia
- Neighbor: flabbiness, corpulence
- God: infantilism

Perverted love (malice or fraud)
- Self: rashes, tuberculosis, sepsis
- Neighbor: rheumatism, infectious diseases (V.D.)
- God: paralysis, cancer, impotence

lessly embodies a series of betraying gestures, and these are its psychosomatic symptoms.

If the analogy holds, then, it should be feasible to translate Auden's chart into a more recognizably descriptive account. For example, an attempt to dominate the rebellious inscriptions of one's own discourse induces a monotonal suppression of pauses, qualifications, or asides (deafness); an obsessive focus on details drifting within an otherwise blurred scene (short-sight); or an exasperating continuity (sleeplessness). When the attempt at domination is directed to the boisterous voices of the social arena, however, the symptoms shift. Here the syntactic gestures betray more aggressive impulses: spasms (tics), distracting overemphasis (high blood-pressure), and sudden bursts of uncontrolled verbiage (logorrhea). Domination, however, is only one mode of violence. To stifle the unruliness of the text, it is also possible for a discourse to practice the defective love of a deliberate withdrawal. If directed to the inscriptions of the speaker's own utterance, this withdrawal induces symptoms of radical ellipsis (constipation) or enfeebled predication (anemia); both are clearly attempts to keep a disruptive medium under control. But interestingly, when defective love retreats from competition with other contemporary discourses, it produces an opposite symptom. Now the syntax suffers from an inability to pull its diverse elements together (flabbiness) as if the discourse were attempting completely to fill a space, to leave no opportunities for any subversive inroads. In its relation to a supposedly absolute authority, a defective love will exhibit the symptom of a regressive atavism, a circling back to practices associated with the protection of some privileged origin (infantilism).

The most efficient discursive violence of all, however, involves deception, the feints of perverted love, with its tactic of conquest through surrender. With regard to the inscriptions at work within one's own utterance, this deception may produce symptoms of localized concession to isolated mutants (rashes); febrile desperation to keep just one step ahead of an unnameable adversary (tuberculosis, the most romantic of Auden's diseases); or an open circulation of pathogenic agents, which acts to strengthen any resolve to resist their destructive influence (sepsis). Relations with contemporary rivals require even more ingenious twists. Here the symptoms include a stiffening that requires prosthetic support (rheumatism) and a cunning concession that infects the other with a debilitating sterility. But what of the ultimate ground and support, God, the final guarantee of an utterance's consonance with the truth? Because the perverted lovers are sophisticated enough to realize there is no ultimate ground, yet wily enough to know they must sustain the illusion of one, their tactics of deceit become quasi-religious. Here the syntactic symptoms include formulaic rigidity, which also connotes a ritualistic awe before the fetish (paralysis); hesitation, which betrays both a terrified refusal to rival the splendors of the past as well as a fear of outrageous beginnings (impotence); and perhaps the symptom that most fascinated Auden, a proliferation of facile equivalences that, while they pay homage to a common source, block and eventually shut down the workings of a discourse (cancer).

The drawbacks of Auden's psychosomatic figuration are numerous. As a theory, it is extravagant; even worse, it is unavoidable. The syntactic construction does not exist that eludes diagnosis as a "symptom." Can something that might with equal validity be said of anything be taken seriously? Yet these drawbacks may be a source of strength. Extravagance is a matter of opinion. What if there is no neutral, objective, or unprejudiced discourse—if these are merely the names of whatever has become familiar and thus unquestioned. An utterance conveys a determined meaning only through a process of violence and repression. That is why the psychosomatic claim is inescapable. Truth, to become true, must sever any ties with the unruly inscriptions of its companion text. The symptoms are always, unavoidably, there because a summoning violence so faithfully precedes them.

•

Auden's first long poem, *Paid on Both Sides*, explores the psychosomatic theory in a more literary mode. Like *The Orators* and *The Sea and the Mirror*, it has an easily followed plot: the story of how the marriage of John Nower and Anne Shaw almost ends the feud between their families. But for Auden's purposes, such narrative action (the life and fate of the Airman; the return to Milan from Prospero's magical island) displaces a more adventurous inquiry. The narratives project along the sequential/thematic axis a dialogic process that is actually simultaneous and gestured. These narratives are neither representational nor expressive, then, but operate according to the logic of a mime. As Auden's subtitle indicates, the plot of *Paid on Both Sides* conducts a charade. It renders what is simultaneous (the symptoms of a textual soma) as if it were sequential, and the tacitly neglected (the inscriptive disruptions) as if it were explicit. Thus these long poems have less to do with such traditional critical concerns as psychological development, whether as political or religious transformation, than with the act of miming their own subversive returns. The plots both simulate and elude representation. Their concern is to articulate the interplay of an interminable strife.

As the impetus for the rest of the charade, the feud proposes an originary violence. No one remembers how it began. John Nower, the hero, is born on the day of his father's murder by Red Shaw, so the feud's beginning falls outside his experience. But the same holds true for everyone else. A few old-timers like Trudy complain of the stupidity and waste: "I am sick of this feud. What do we want to go on killing each other for?" (CP, 24). For the rest, though, the feud is a contextual assumption: it is just the way things are. Appropriately, fostering this mystery about its beginnings is the main purpose of the feud, since that mystery refurbishes the seamy complicities of history into a myth of ennobled unity. The mechanism of this dissolution is precise. As a commissioning agent, the feud demands revenge for the death of an ancestor. Utterly insignificant as an actual person, the ancestor serves the more ritualistic purpose of establishing a bond with an idyllic past, a time when life was complete, fulfilled. Through its imperative of revenge,

then, the feud dismisses contemporary society as worthless because riddled with anomalies and anxieties. Consequently, all energy must be
directed to the restoration of a lost totality, however futile that effort
might be:

> Tonight the many come to mind,
> Sent forward in the thaw with anxious marrow,
> For such might now return with a bleak face,
> An image, pause half-lighted in the door,
> A greater but not fortunate in all.
>
> (CP, 33)

In the world of the feud, history does not matter. All that counts is the
effort to avenge the loss of an idyll, which cannot be regained anyway
for it never existed.

The power of the feud as a disciplinary device can be gauged by the
degree of conformity it imposes. The Nowers and the Shaws have no
practical grounds for their conflict. They do not compete for raw materials or for a larger share of the market. Nor do they have any recognizable
ideological differences. The members of the two families are virtually
interchangeable: bride and groom, John Nower and Anne Shaw, could
almost be twins. This animosity within sameness suggest that the feud's
purpose is not, as might be expected, to preserve separate ways of life,
but to enforce a terrified rigidity. Were the two families to end the feud,
they would have a chance to meet and converse. But then the perfected
past might begin to lose its allure. Long protected discourses could be
reassessed and new ones encouraged to emerge. The imminence of this
threat becomes apparent in Seth Shaw's tortuous remarks after his
mother has ordered John Nower's death: "The little funk. Sunlight on
sparkling water, its shades dissolved, reforming, unreal activity where
others laughed but he blubbed clinging, homesick, an undeveloped form"
(CP, 35). Seth approaches the near edge of panic here. His resentment
admits a flux of irreconcilable discourses: schoolboy slang, poetic impres-
sionism, political cant, surrealist description, pseudoscientific exactitude.
Deprived of the protection of an idyllic wholeness and thus besieged by
a historical diversity, the murderer-to-be discovers his own plight as a
permanently "undeveloped form," a plasticity susceptible to the funk of
inscriptions, "where others laugh."

As so often in Auden's early work, partly as a lingering influence from the fiction of D. H. Lawrence, the arch-villain is the mother. *Paid on Both Sides* belatedly writes its own epigraph in the final chorus: "His mother and her mother won" (CP, 35). But the very neatness of the aphorism makes it suspect. Its formula restores a coercive psychological determination: sons do things because mothers make them. The problem with this runs much deeper than the obviously mechanical causality. For not only does it suggest a naive view of the relation between mother and son, but it offers an inadequate concept of each. Who is the mother? As Auden pointed out in *The Enchafèd Flood*, the supposed unity of this or any other image conceals sharp iconographic divisions. The mother might function as a protector of difference: "The images of the Just City, of the civilized landscape protected by the Madonna" (EF, 24). This tolerant figure recurs in the Elizabeth Mayer of *New Year Letter* ("Who on the lives about you throw / A calm *solificatio*"; CP, 193); "Memorial for the City" ("Wild beasts, deep rivers and dry rocks / Lay nursed on the smile of a merciful Madonna"; CP, 451); "Homage to Clio" ("Muse of the unique / Historical fact, defending with silence / Some world of your beholding"; CP, 465); and "A Lullaby" ("*Madonna*, and *Bambino*: / Sing, Big Baby, sing lullay*"; CP, 672). Yet the mother might also serve as an emblem of repression: "And then out to sea, for there in the ocean wastes, the Paternal Power may still be felt though but as dreadful tempest, and there still dwells the Mother-Goddess though she appear but in her most malignant aspects, as the castrating white whale to Ahab, as the Life-in-Death to the Ancient Mariner" (EF, 37). Again, this negative figure recurs in " Adolescence," "Lullaby," *The Ascent of F6*, and in Mary's eerie remarks in "At the Manger" (CP, 293). But whether as protective Madonna, avatar of repression, or any of the myriad variations between these opposing icons, the mother in Auden consists of an event not an identity. Her image serves as a gathering point for functions that interact and diverge according to describable tendencies. For example, positively: as an adjournment of paternal legalism, an acceptance of incompleteness, a welcoming of adventure. Or negatively: as a restrictive intransigence, a stifling vagueness, an incestuous resentment of all departures from the known and approved.

Certainly the mothers in *Paid on Both Sides* belong to the negative camp, as chief custodians of the feud. But theirs is not an easy task.

They must guard not only against lapses in internal discipline as well as inroads from the other side, but against even more threatening liaisons between the paternal body and the filial imagination it engenders. This may seem an odd construction, the body as the parent of the imagination, but the text demands it. Although the psychological father often functions as a reactionary principle in Auden ("Not, Father, further do prolong / Our necessary defeat"; EA, 109; and "How Father beat him, how he ran away"; CP, 109), the *paternal body* has a different part. It suggests the excessive remnant of the text and thus offers an opportunity for unrestricted play.

Joan Nower, as negative mother, inadvertently discovers the irksome vitality of the paternal body in her first and only speech.

> Not from this life, not from this life is any
> To keep; sleep, day and play would not help there,
> Dangerous to new ghost; new ghost learns from many,
> Learns from old termers what death is, where.
>
> Who's jealous of his latest company,
> From one day to the next final to us,
> A changed one, would use sorrow to deny
> Sorrow, to replace death? Sorrow is sleeping thus.
>
> Unforgetting is not today's forgetting
> For yesterday, not bedrid scorning,
> But a new begetting,
> An unforgiving morning.

[Baby squeals]

> O see, he is impatient
> To pass beyond this pretty lisping time:
> There'll be some crying out when he's come there.
>
> (CP, 22)

The scene, set in an inner stage, suggests the stilted posing of what Auden later characterized as "David's too too Empire Greeks" (CP, 172). Joan acts as if she were giving a soliloquy, though this is technically inaccurate since the stage directions read *"Joan with child and corpse"* (CP, 22). The discrepancy between manner and setting becomes comically acute when Joan finds herself interrupted by the other actors, who disrupt her only speaking part. With her newborn son, John, the interruption is obvious. But even more pointedly, Joan finds herself forced to struggle against the unnamed paternal body. Twice she tries to confirm its death, for she realizes it might corrupt her offspring, the "new ghost" who must be tutored by "old termers," proper guardians of the status quo. Yet Joan finds her meanings deviously spirited away. Her rhetorical questions, which mockingly ask if death might turn into metamorphosis ("a changed one") or absence into mirth ("use sorrow to deny / Sorrow"), inexplicably become real. The remnant text, bereft of adequate disciplines to enshroud and silence it, might indeed foster the son's chance.

Furious not so much at the impertinence as at the humiliation it implies, her meaning disrupted by the resistance of a silent corpse, Joan shifts from sarcasm to threats. "Unforgetting is not today's forgetting . . . But a new begetting" (CP, 22). Yet the impious paternal body gaily accompanies her through this shift but gives her words a different inflection. Precisely, it exults: memory's subversive engendering permits not a recitation of old terms but a new beginning, an event in which the text alternately eludes and thwarts its sanctioned meanings. With this stroke, the paternal body casts into doubt the link between maternal origin and dependent offspring. Through the returns of a textual body, the son might henceforth be free to explore a response to maternal discipline. At this instant, the baby squeals. Why? Joan reads (restricts) the noise in conformity with her vengeful obsession: the Davidian manchild shall destroy her foes. But there are other possibilities. Perhaps her child cries out in unexpected joy at the prospect of winning a subversive freedom.

When next seen, baby John has grown up and is busily continuing the feud. But this normality is interrupted when, after a successful raid, a Spy is found whom Nower orders shot. Fuller notes the similarities between this episode of the executed Spy and a case described by W. H. R. Rivers in *Conflict and Dream*.[19] But Fuller construes the passage

19. Ibid., p. 22.

as a Freudian allegory, in which John represents the repressive censor (ego) and the Spy the spontaneous natural desires (id). As with other humanist readings, this shows a keener interest in finding some external topic than in approaching the charade as a mime, a form of self-analysis through responsive gesture. After the shooting, *Paid on Both sides* undergoes a generic convulsion. It shifts from a mock-serious closet drama to a schoolboy skit in the vein of Auden's unfinished early play, *The Reformatory* (EA, 301). No sooner is the Spy executed than Father Christmas and his entourage burst upon the scene to perform an extravagant show: part cabaret act, part Mummer's Play, part dream sequence. The link between the shooting and this interruption is tacit but of utmost importance. The Father Christmas skit articulates a disciplinary violence into its symptomatic nuances; it does so by transforming ordinarily mute gestures into voiced parts. The text makes this connection between an instigating violence and its responsive gestures quite clear. Shooting the Spy (an enemy agent, hence the intrusive bearer of alien discourses) perpetuates the feud and thus repeats the violence of origins: the achievement of order through repression. But as the ensuing chorus uneasily murmurs ("The Spring unsettles sleeping partnerships"), that violence releases unforeseen consequences. It deceives itself ("But proudest into traps / Have fallen"; CP, 26). It generates friction so that productive mechanisms, "these gears which ran in oil for week / By week, needing no look, now will not work" (CP, 26). It establishes barriers that are continuously contested ("Outside on frozen soil lie armies killed / Who seem familiar but they are cold"; CP, 27). And in a tellingly cryptic image, its originary repression induces psychosomatic betrayals ("Now the most solid wish he tries to keep / His hands show through"; CP, 27). As in *The Orators* where the Airman's kleptomaniacal hands remain his worst enemies, this treacherous symptom figures the onset of textual resistance.[20] The would-be author tries to convey a message or express

20. The motifs discussed here, spies and hands, may well be cognate. Although one is political, the other corporeal, both serve a similar function: as figures of a devious innocence (the anonymity and even trustworthiness of a spy) or docile compliance (the obedience of hands, doing exactly as told) that meanwhile enacts the will of a subversive other. The spies quickly drop out of Auden's works, though there remains something of the informant or *agent provocateur* to his speakers. The hands, however, endure as a prominent motif right up to "Hands" (CP, 505) and *Shorts II*: "What we touch is always / an Other: I may fondle / my leg, not Me" (CP, 641).

an emotion. But the restless hands resist with uncontrollable fits, refusing to support the conscious design, or as compulsive kleptomania, seizing whatever is illicit, contraband, or incriminating.

Once under way, the Father Christmas interlude can be divided into two distinct movements, Trial and Diagnosis. John Nower begins as the accuser. In a speech adapted from the jingoism of World War I, Nower denounces the Spy as a traitor to patriotic values: "We cannot betray the dead. As we pass their graves can we be deaf to the simple eloquence of their inscriptions, those who in the glory of their early manhood gave up their lives for us?" (CP, 27). But the charge is soon reversed. When Joan threatens the Spy with "a gigantic feeding bottle" (CP, 27), it becomes apparent that the accused is an alter ego of Nower, an image of the unknown other. Thus the Spy, as Nower's accompanying yet dissident double, offers a series of implied commentaries on Nower's official poses: by intimating that the mature (the discourse of the fathers) is also the infantile; the heroic (sacrifice in war) is the dependent; the sublime (massive sentimentality) is the preposterous; the selfless (immersion in the unthinking group) is the opportunistic—in short, that the voiced is also the inscribed.

These tacit countercharges, however, are only the first movement of the skit. They are followed by a further development of its interruptive gesture, in which accusation gives way to ludic diagnosis. Father Christmas brings an entourage consisting of Bo, Po, the Man-Woman, and Doctor and Boy from the medieval Mummer's Play. This ensemble enacts an array of simultaneous inscriptions already at work within Nower's discourse. Bo and Po illustrate a neglected scene, an alien yet transformative place of endless "migrations," where "memory is death" (in the sense of both finality and change) and even casual utterances admit "speakers of a strange tongue" (CP, 27). The other adaptation from the Mummer's Play, the Man-Woman, might be taken as a summary icon for all supposed identities: s/he puts a slash through nature, a virgule severing the word from itself, the body from either a cultural resolution or even a physical basis. In the Man-Woman even the most elemental contradictions are not resolved but left carefully poised, so that each might illuminate the qualities of the other. But such poise is difficult to sustain: s/he is monstrous, a cacophony of twisted traces. Hence the Man-Woman chides Nower for his cowardice in retreating from the playful improvisation s/he demands to a safer earnestness: "Lastly I tried / To teach you acting, but always you had nerves / To fear performances as some fear knives" (CP, 28).

The Doctor and Boy conduct a ludic diagnosis that is even more aggressive. According to Auden's stage directions, the Boy "fools about" in an inane fashion wholly undeserving of critical attention:

Doctor: Tell me, is my hair tidy? One must always be careful with a new
       client.
Boy: It's full of lice, sir.
Doctor: What's that?
Boy: It's looking nice, sir.

(CP, 29)

Such punning takes place at a considerable remove from serious literary art, but only as long as one thinks in terms of representation rather than play. For the pun illustrates the illusion of any organic or natural bond between sound and meaning. There is no particularly compelling reason why "l" and "n" could not routinely trade places, so that the phonemic cluster "nice" meant crawling with parasites, whereas "lice" happily denoted a plenum of bourgeois virtues. But once severed from secure referential moorings and cast adrift on a surface of variable sounds, the punned word is unlikely to be restored to its former self: a remnant of the comically distended *pundigrion*, the pun scatters its semantic energies into fine quibbles, arch punctilioes whose identity is divided between a stultifying normality (based on the safety of appearances, "looking") and a teeming multiplicity (discovered through a horrified contact of bodies, touch, "full of"). The pun is of course the lowest form of humor, because its fatal concessions annul an intending subject's sovereign control. Its impertinence reveals that the sound of words is both an arbitrary irrelevance and a continuous leakage.

So the Boy plays the assistant in a quite specific way: his punning admits the textual tumult, a sonorous instability in which solid terms dissolve into one another, the excess from which the Doctor can venture a diagnosis. Clearly, not all the inscriptions chanced upon by punning are responsive. Many, in fact, spiral outward into a form of semiotic entropy. A few, however, acquire dialogic force (though their responses

71

differ not only from era to era but with each individual and even with each reading). To unravel these textual dialogues, by coaxing their nascent voices from the nonsense of the idiot Boy, is the Doctor's task. Or, to put this another way, the Doctor (quack, charlatan, *pretender*—as children pretend) is Auden's emblematic reader-interpreter, a cracked translator of somatic runes. His technique of reading suggests a mode of crazed midwifery. Not content with educing innate universals from the Slave Text (on the model of Plato's *Meno*), the Audenesque reader is expected to bring forth a repressed violence as well as its subversive aftermath. Sometimes both are enfolded within the same image.

> [*Examines the body.*] Um, yes. Very interesting. The conscious brain appears normal except under emotion. Fancy it. The Devil couldn't do that. This advances and retreats under control and poisons everything round it. My diagnosis is: Adamant will, cool brain and laughing spirit. Hullo, what's this? [*Produces a large pair of pliers and extracts an enormous tooth from the body.*] Come along, that's better. Ladies and Gentlemen, you see I have nothing up my sleeve. This tooth was growing ninety-nine years before his great grandmother was born. If it hadn't been taken out today he would have died yesterday. You may get up now. (CP, 29)

This might be taken as a succinct if slightly unorthodox account of poetic reading. What is intended or meant (the presumed authority of a unified subject) is discarded from the outset. The Doctor begins by telling John Nower, "Go away . . . your evidence will not be needed. It is valueless" (CP, 29). Instead he examines the remnant body of the dead Spy, the textual other, in which the Doctor finds an arena of contesting forces. Only one of these is readily apparent, "the conscious brain." Yet from its psychosomatic reactions, "advances and retreats," as well as its defensive measures, "poisons everything round it," the Doctor can tell that this supposedly controlling force is locked in mortal combat with an elusive prankster, the "laughing spirit." At this moment, something remarkable happens. Rather than taking sides with the conscious brain (thereby restoring normality and accrediting himself as healer), the Doctor delivers its adversarial other. From out of the Spy's dead body is born a new creation, a gigantic tooth.

What might this birth portend? The possibilities are many, of course, yet more important than any specific entry, more important even than their variety, is the dialogic responsiveness of the ensemble. Certainly the tooth signifies aggression: the outrage that leads to primal exile, the child's banishment from the maternal breast. Yet by means of its removal, an extraction that transforms incisive power into a labile gap, the tooth also intimates a castration. Oddly enough, though, this removal induces fecundity. The extraction mimics an ancient delusion, parthenogenesis, the divine self-sufficiency of an entirely male birth. In this sense, the birth gives rise to the ridiculous, a calcified simulacrum, an absurd homunculus that simulates a living child. Yet because of its enormous size, the tooth also intimates a giant form, the remnants of a grander being, some larger-than-life beginning. This beginning is not given as such, only hinted at as a metonymic item, thus as a link in a larger skeleton, a minor fragment from which an enterprising archaeologist might surmise a once living structure. Rather than being consistent, however, this informing structure is historically diverse. It exceeds the range of recorded ancestors, growing for "ninety-nine years before his great grandmother was born" (CP, 29). And as a dividend of three's (three times thirty-three), the ninety-nine replicates the uneasy triad of creation in which each exchange takes a chance, a spinning of the genetic wheel.[21] So even though the Doctor protests that he has no magical tricks, "you see I have nothing up my sleeve" (CP, 29), the tooth nonetheless retains talismanic powers, fitting it for service in an amulet. This is altogether appropriate for it can indeed suspend the linear advance of time, thus overcome death, by disclosing a maze of complexity where previously there was only mute obduracy, the infantile aggression of the tooth. Aptly, the passage ends with the Doctor's impromptu resurrection of the body: "You may get up now" (CP, 29). Whatever the textual possibilities, the important event is their dialogic return.

Still, the Father Christmas skit does come to an end. The obstreperous interlude, though its possibilities extend well beyond thought, is itself astonishingly frail. Once the interruption is over, the plot of *Paid on Both Sides* continues, and the skit ceases to exist. It is as if the pantomime had never occurred. In upbraiding the reluctant Seth for not murdering

---

21. Cf. the reference in *New Year Letter* to "Eros' weaving centrosome" (CP, 176), which, like the other figures of choreographed play in this text, suggests an origin that is at once pattern and free movement.

John Nower at the wedding, his mother rages: "Have you forgotten your brother's death . . . taken out and shot like a dog? It is a nice thing for me to hear people saying that I have a coward for a son" (CP, 35). The negative mothers still wield the discourse of reality. They control the way people are permitted to speak. They demand an unreflective conformity and a murderous rage against transgressors. Thus the sequence of trial, punning, mayhem, diagnosis, and resurrection of the somatic double has no force at the level of linear time, the so-called reality of events. The charade's status is purely textual. An irrepressible simultaneity, its mime accompanies every utterance, each word of the text. But its gestures operate within an entirely imaginative dimension, the interval of a ludic excess, about which the characters themselves know nothing.

This unawareness of ludic disruption poses an interesting question. If the characters (voices: the official *dramatis personae*) of a work remain oblivious to its gestures, because entranced within the hallucination of an intended meaning, then who are the players of the charade? Someone has to do the guesswork. But Father Christmas, Bo and Po, Man-Woman, Boy and Doctor/Quack are anomalies, carnival freaks. Who in actual practice takes their place? That question, which concerns Auden's notions of the reader, requires our more explicit attention.

CHAPTER THREE

Effigies and Auditors

When Wordsworth objects to eighteenth-century diction as "artificial," what he really means is artificial for his particular purpose. The diction of the Immortality Ode would be as artificial for Pope's purposes as Pope's was for Wordsworth's.
—"Light Verse"

And safely keep the living dead
Entombed, hilarious, and fed . . .
—*New Year Letter*

Each discourse cherishes its image of everyman (the average, the entirely normal). In a print-conscious culture, this improbable entity is known as the reader. Given criticism's traditional preoccupation with the author as origin and guarantor of the text's truth, the mere act of acknowledging the reader can seem a radical move. But the complex interweaving of Auden's texts suggests that this recently recognized figure, the reader, must be further differentiated: between the reader as image or, better still, *effigy* (a mocking mimesis and a deliberate subjugation as well, a recipient of the violence of an impotent judicial rage: the outlaw hanged/burned/castrated in effigy); and the reader as *auditor* (an acute listener, though only one of an uncertain plurality, hence both an unexpected interloper and a routine nemesis).

What does this distinction accomplish? *The* reader as such does not exist. In this instance the definite article tells a lie by operating both an exclusion and a hypostasis. For the historical individual who ventures into a text is, both prior to and during that act, an array of disparate, highly unstable, and conflicting discourses. Whatever his or her consciousness may believe about its inviolable identity, the reader is an overdetermined historical subject, thus a field of elusive and conflicting interests (grammars, codes). The human particular is not only unique, and so different from any other, but transmuted from one moment to the next as well as within each moment. The self is never itself.[1] So the casual invocation of *the* reader, a convenience at once indispensable and preposterous, casts a mythic oblivion over the intricate involvements of the subject. No doubt so disingenuous a concept as that of the reader should be shelved. But since this is impossible, it might at least be approached with some caution.

Whereas the reader is a historical being, effigy and auditor are textual functions. What they are is tangential to what they do. The effigy is the image of a good recipient fashioned by a communicative act. Such images can vary considerably, from the confidante assumed by a lyric, to the trusting child implied by a folk ballad, to the slightly jaded ironist who is addressed by a sonnet.[2] But what these deft impositions must all

1. Auden's theory of the subject may be found in "The Virgin and the Dynamo": "Man exists as a unity-in-tension of four modes of being: soul, body, mind and spirit" (DH, 65). These may be glossed as follows. The body indicates a largely unconscious, that is, active but unreflective repertoire of culturally imposed discourses. The mind has the capacity to formulate experiences and ideas in terms of these discourses, sometimes in succession, yet sometimes simultaneously: antagonistic discourses may compete in the production, for example, of a memory or dream. The spirit, in effect the creative impulse, does not apply or follow but rather reflects on and transforms the discursive structures to which it is given access. And the soul, far from being a static ideal or a ledger of faults and virtues, marks the site of an event, a uniquely human space in which body, mind, and spirit can conduct a continuous struggle. The entire discussion in "The Virgin and the Dynamo" is a good instance of how Auden revised the categories of a traditional, subject-centered psychology so that they might illuminate an anthropology oriented to cultural and discursive forces.

2. Over time, though, recognizable types begin to emerge, especially with regard to poetry, which because of its threatening demand becomes the occasion of a more systematic conformity. In "Making, Knowing and Judging," for example, Auden mentions four standard effigy types, which, because of their popularity, a shrewd poet might profit from implementing: "a prig, a critic's critic, a romantic novelist or a maniac" (DH, 48). The prig believes that the only worthwhile poem is one he or she would like to write but cannot. The critic's critic regrets that before there can be criticism there must be poetry. The romantic novelist uses the text to make up fictions about the author's personal problems. And one kind of maniac (for there are many varieties) sees the work as a prediction of the future written in ciphers.

achieve is a well-managed docility. The good recipient's tasks are to detect an informing intention; to purge any elements that distract from that intention's will; and to be naturally affected, to play a carefully prepared part. When all goes well and the recipient behaves according to plan, the result is a "good" reading, approved by the majority or at least by their appointed representatives, because its findings are conspicuously at ease with dominant prejudices.

Unlike the effigy whose functions may be gathered within an image, the auditor cannot be represented, except provisionally. For the auditor remains just beyond the margins of whatever an intending consciousness may anticipate and thus control. The instant the auditor becomes an image, however necessary that crystallization may be, it slips away into still more unforeseeable disruptions.

> Fresh loves betray him, every day
> Over his green horizon
> A fresh deserter rides away,
> And miles away birds mutter
> Of ambush and of treason.
>   (CP, 143)

Here, as so often in Auden's poetry, the inhuman chatter of the birds interjects a background noise, a din that is subversive, indecipherable, alien.[3] How does this muttering within the text help to define the activity of the auditor? As an incalculable event, a capacity to discern and articulate this noise, the auditor performs the tasks of resistance and response. Rather than letting a speaker hold forth, the auditor breaks in, impedes the natural flow of sense. Instead of trusting in a majestically authoritative origin, the auditor continuously searches for evidence of violence, of attempts to exclude or repress opposing discourses. And rather than

3. The deliberate contrast, of course, is with a more traditional imagery that takes the bird as an emblem of the poet (lyrical, harmonious, exultant), rather than the dissident impulses of the text. As Auden implies in *Letter to Lord Byron*, this tradition reached the limit of its credibility in Hardy's "Darkling Thrush": "Putting divinity about a bird" (CP, 98). For some of Auden's unamiable birds, see "Taller To-Day" (CP, 39), "The Wanderer" (CP, 62), "Oxford" (CP, 124), "The Riddle" (CP, 204), "In Transit" (CP, 413), and "A starling and a willow wren" (CP, 438).

being concerned with reconciling tensions, the auditor steadfastly exploits them, seeking to admit as much diversity as possible. It need hardly be said that the auditor commits a very bad reading indeed: farfetched, unfounded, slightly paranoiac. But the auditor also offers a measure of hope for the reader, the glimpse of a freedom that might make a difference were it ever tried.

What is wrong, though, with simply accepting the scene of address implied by a discourse and then going along with the image it offers? Auden gives a pointed answer to that question in "Lady Weeping at the Crossroads." This poem is curious in that it uses a direct address in a literary ballad. That is, the speaker engages not a denizen of the make-believe ballad world (e.g. the wedding guest stopped by the Ancient Mariner) but an ambiguously historical "you" who belongs to both the ballad world and our own.

> Lady, weeping at the crossroads,
> Would you meet your love
> In the twilight with his greyhounds,
> And the hawk on his glove?
>
> (CP, 219)

Through this direct address, the opening stanza makes explicit what is usually an unspoken contract. Do you, or do you not, take this image of the reader as your lawfully appointed self, along with all the entailments and imposts that shall accompany it? A list of the contractual consequences of answering yes may be drawn from Auden's densely clustered mythemes: the abandoned lady, the crossroads, the superpredator (hawk and greyhounds depict different kinds of hunting), the exhaustion of possibility hence hope (twilight, the day spent). To accept the image imposed by the direct address, then, is to accept the part of a victim, helpless before an unnameable threat (weeping, she is unable to detect landmarks or clues in the surrounding landscape), and paralyzed until some ruling presence intervenes to save her. Once this image is accepted, and the contract thereby sealed, the speaker grows mean and vicious. Each stanza makes an increasingly insolent demand until this brief allegory of reading ends with a demand for self-murder:

Put your hand behind the wainscot,
You have done your part;
Find the penknife there and plunge it
Into your false heart.

(CP, 220)

Thus the too easily overlooked question mark after the ballad's initial address marks a point of no return. Once its contract is accepted, the reader is caught. The tendered image of the forlorn lady (a respite to the weary subject, a deliverance from its unity-in-tension, a welcome identity on the exasperating journey through history) quickly hardens into an effigy. The reader-as-Lady becomes the recipient of contempt and abuse. The brilliant entrapment of the opening line is achieved by its speed, which almost conceals that the initial question is real, not rhetorical. Thus it entails a contract that *might be refused*. An auditor, for example, could take the penknife as an invitation to slit the hermetic envelope of the speaker's address, the fake bid of an imposed identity. But such counterviolence requires a shift in the function of the reader, who would henceforth have to accept the considerable risks of a more independent and perilous part.

Effigy and auditor may be found within any text. Because Auden wrote poetry, one might expect that he believed the most generous recognition of the auditor occurred in verse traditions. But this is at best a half-truth. If poetic genres are roughly divisible between the high and the low (according to subject matter, tone, and diction), it soon becomes apparent that the more elevated genres, at least since the romantic movement, have been strongly biased to the reader as effigy. In serious poetry the recipient is assigned the fate of poor Ganymede, a rapt (caught up, mastered, penetrated) image. Any deviations from this assignment are strictly disciplined. Thus in the aftermath of romanticism it is often the humbler forms of poetry, children's and nonsense verse, doggerel, limericks, even graffiti, that offer the best chance to a potential auditor. For the same reasons that such minor genres admit a greater variety of discursive competitors, they also welcome a greater range of responses. But as Auden noted in his essay on Byron, it is this comic generosity that the romantic canon (the official version of which texts shall be permitted to survive) has attempted to suppress: "Our association of the word *romantic* with the magical and dreamlike is so strong that we are apt to forget that the literary period so classified is also a great age for comic poetry. The comic verse of poets like Canning, Frere, Hood, Praed, Barham, and Lear was a new departure in English poetry, and not least in its exploitation of comic rhyme" (DH, 398). The passage implies a question: What invisible consensus established that mandatory exclusion? Who ordained that poetry must practice an elevated, incontestable discourse?

The ultimate triumph of canon formation, as with any tyranny, is to achieve a condition in which the canon may operate imperceptibly, unobtrusively, with the sadistic innocence of the purely natural. From the perspective of ideological utility, romanticism's dismissal of comic and light genres is not surprising. Comedy subverts disciplinary strength. It ridicules the incantatory, or visionary, or supremely passionate power necessary to impose an effigy on the reader. Romanticism, however, had taken upon itself the burden of promoting the values and interpretive practices of a powerful yet habitually insecure group, the ascendent middle class.[4] Thus romanticism turned to more weighty imaginative forms such as the meditation, the lyric, the elegy, and the apocalypse to enforce the submission required by its versions of a natural will.

> He was their servant (some say he was blind),
> Who moved among their faces and their things;
> Their feeling gathered in him like a wind
> And sang. They cried, "It is a God that sings. . . ."
>
> (CP, 152)

Once the song begins, the individual fades into a single image. As the voice of a specific interest group (though the oddity of the middle class is obscured by both its enormous size and its long-standing dominance), romanticism, like any disciplinary effort, had to impose its version of a necessary order. In terms of discursive practice, that meant a strong

---

4. Cf. an early journal entry: "The middle class: an orphan class, with no fixed residence, capable of snobbery in both directions. From class insecurity it has developed the family unit as a defence. Like the private bands in the tribal migrations. It is afraid of its fortunate position" (EA, 299–300).

preference for forms that could fashion and enforce a docile image of the reader.

Auden, though, did not abandon the poetic forms so esteemed by canonical romanticism. Instead he took them as an apt stage on which to illustrate the resistance of the auditor. The implicit reasoning here moves from the greater to the lesser: given the disciplinary rigor of high romantic modes, if the responsive activity of an auditor can be discovered there, it can be found anywhere. This reasoning leads to a strategy in which romantic forms are not exactly revived but rehearsed, so that what is tacit, relict (from its geological use: the survival of a formation that climatic forces have exposed) in their tradition can be assessed. Auden's design is not to establish superiority to the romantics, or to prove that English poetry is engaged in some grand and upward march. Any text entertains the responsive functions of the auditor, no matter how sublime, monologic, or authoritarian its disciplines may be. There are no unworthy texts, though there is an ample reserve of docile readers (faithful, exacting, scrupulous in their obedience to the effigy). Rather, the contrast between an Auden rehearsal and its romantic forbear serves a purpose beyond evaluation. It displays the auditor's untenable status: not as a veiled image, a substitute identity brooding within the poem as its sullen lord and master, but as a set of textual functions. Like the best dramatic roles, the auditor cannot be fixed or grasped, only reenacted.

•

The first entry in Edward Mendelson's useful anthology *W. H. Auden: Selected Poems* is an early meditation, "The Watershed." In both theme and setting this text explicitly offers a version of a venerable romantic topology, the *genius loci* poem. The features of this meditation are well established, in fact constitute a secular ritualism.[5] The newcomer

---

5. This ritualism is suppressed, however. Auden criticized both rationalism and romanticism for refusing to acknowledge their status as specific and socially organized activities, rather than the universal practice of sound reason or imaginative insight: "The Deist religion of reason had a catholic myth, that of the Goddess of reason, but no cultus, no specifically religious acts; all rational acts were worship of the Goddess. The romantic reaction replaced the Goddess by a protestant variety of individual myths; but it, too, lacked a cult in which all men could take part. Instead, it substituted imagination for reason, and in place of the man of esprit the artist as the priest-magician" (EF, 55).

crosses a natural boundary and thereby strays into unexplored territory. Immediately a spirit of the place arises to serve as interpreter, historian, and protector. After a brief but intense encounter, the traveler is supposed to move on, buoyed by eternal powers and transcendental longings. Unsurprisingly, this ritual offers a concise allegory of reading. The wanderer (reader) timidly ventures into a new domain (opens the text) and is then greeted by the presiding guardian of its semantic treasures (the genius loci, the speaking voice). Among the many variations of this drama, perhaps none is so accomplished as, or more beloved than, Wordsworth's "The Solitary Reaper":[6]

> Behold her, single in the field,
> Yon solitary Highland Lass!
> Reaping and singing by herself;
> Stop here, or gently pass!
> Alone she cuts and binds the grain,
> And sings a melancholy strain;
> O listen! for the Vale profound
> Is overflowing with the sound.
>
> No Nightingale did ever chant
> More welcome notes to weary bands
> Of travelers in some shady haunt,
> Among Arabian sands:
> A voice so thrilling e'er was heard
> In spring-time from the Cuckoo-bird,
> Breaking the silence of the seas
> Among the farthest Hebrides.
>
> Will no one tell me what she sings?—
> Perhaps the plaintive numbers flow
> For old, unhappy, far-off things,
> And battles long ago:
> Or is it some more humble lay,

6. William Wordsworth, "The Solitary Reaper," in *The Complete Poetical Works* . . . ,Vol. 4 (Boston: Houghton Mifflin, 1911), pp. 151–52. Unsurprisingly, this poem is sufficiently representational to serve as one of the paradigm texts in Geoffrey Hartman, *Wordsworth's Poetry* (New Haven: Yale University Press, 1964), pp. 3–18.

Familiar matter of to-day?
Some natural sorrow, loss, or pain,
That has been, and may be again?

Whate'er the theme, the Maiden sang
As if her song could have no ending;
I saw her singing at her work,
And o'er the sickle bending:—
I listened, motionless and still
And, as I mounted up the hill,
The music in my heart I bore,
Long after it was heard no more.

While the beauty of the verse is beyond doubt, it still manages to conduct an exacting and deftly imposed discipline. Wordsworth's poet-wanderer, the speaking voice, is not the genius loci but a pilgrim who has returned from the sacred quest. Rather, the genius loci is figured by the Highland Lass, as primordial source. Thus the speaking voice plays the role of interloper, the newcomer who has just arrived on the scene: the reader opening the text. In this way, an effigy is not merely assigned to the reader but fully enacted. Nothing is left to chance, because the speaking voice itself performs the role of an ideal reader. All an actual reader need do is assent, that is, identify with this already performed and quite effortless transformation of the banal into the ecstatic.

In Auden's rehearsal, however, the lines of address are redrawn. Here the genius loci is not overheard but actually speaks; thus the greater tendency to call this voice "Auden." Nor is the recipient an assenting passerby but a highly resistant auditor.

Who stands, the crux left of the watershed,
On the wet road between the chafing grass
Below him sees dismantled washing-floors,
Snatches of tramline running to a wood,
An industry already comatose,
Yet sparsely living. A ramshackle engine
At Cashwell raises water; for ten years
It lay in flooded workings until this,
Its latter office, grudgingly performed.

And, further, here and there, though many dead
Lie under the poor soil, some acts are chosen,
Taken from recent winters; two there were
Cleaned out a damaged shaft by hand, clutching
The winch a gale would tear them from; one died
During a storm, the fells impassable,
Not at his village, but in wooden shape
Through long abandoned levels nosed his way
And in his final valley went to ground.

Go home, now, stranger, proud of your young stock,
Stranger, turn back again, frustrate and vexed:
This land, cut off, will not communicate,
Be no accessory content to one
Aimless for faces rather there than here.
Beams from your car may cross a bedroom wall,
They wake no sleeper; you may hear the wind
Arriving driven from the ignorant sea
To hurt itself on pane, on bark of elm
Where sap unbaffled rises, being spring;
But seldom this. Near you, taller than grass,
Ears poise before decision, scenting danger.

(CP, 41)

Even granted the apparent differences between the two poems, the connections between them are sufficiently compelling to suggest that not only do the devious interiors of Auden's text suggest a liaison with Wordsworth's poetry, but vice versa. The resulting exchange between these works might be pursued. How do "The Solitary Reaper" and "The Watershed" differently configure that iron triangle, the speaker, the receiver, and the peculiar contract that binds them, so as to propose specific roles for their readers? (A work can only propose; what it actually permits rests with the imagination of a historical individual.)

Like so many of Wordsworth's solitaries, the Highland Lass is not a human figure at all but a pure archetype. We never meet her, learn her age, discover her loves or hatreds. Bereft of such ties, she is severed from the gross commerce of daily events. The Highland Lass belongs to a separate realm, a transcendental sphere of ideal forms. The continuous miracle of Wordsworth's art is its artless transmutation of such abstracted forms into the natural, the utterly immediate. Yet an archetype works only so long as it remains out of reach. The instant it becomes specific, historically discrete, it also becomes materially contaminated and thus unfit to serve as a paradigm. From this necessity follows the routine dilemma of the archetype. As a concrete universal, it must display the solid qualities of a thing, yet as a transcendental pattern, it must betray none of a thing's historical materiality. Since this dilemma is insoluble (the walls of museums are covered with lapsed archetypes), it typically produces a shrewd obscurity. Although it functions as the most real component of a work, the archetype demurely recedes into realms beyond thought, beyond even language. One might measure the skill of a poet through the deftness and impenetrability of these retreats. For example, in "The Solitary Reaper" an abstracted figure recedes into song; the song (because few understand Erse) into melody; the melody into a mood of elegant pathos; the pathos into the activity of harvesting; and the harvest into a densely enfolded apocalyptic mytheme: death, Last Judgment, inevitable fate. The pace of these withdrawals is exhilarating. But even more impressive is the artistry of their arrangement, through which the archetype casually slips away into the mythic resonances of previously presented yet minor detail. So by the time it approaches any crisis of resolution, the archetype already has many avenues of escape.

Auden's genius loci, however, is constructed so as to make such withdrawal impossible. Part sentinel (his first words are a challenge to an intruder), part tomb guardian (he watches over a realm of "sleepers"), the genius loci occupies a precarious border between the world of the newcomer and that of the landscape below. This marginal site, a fate of permanent exile, prohibits any effort at retreat. Auden's genius loci cannot fade into the landscape he protects because it excludes him. He is a spectator, not a participant in its natural rhythms. Unlike the Highland Lass whose song expresses a local yet universal spirit, the guardian of "The Watershed" seems to have memorized a potted history, almost as a tour guide would. Nor can the genius loci hope to join forces with the intruder. Again the contrast with Wordsworth's poem is apparent. Whereas the Solitary Reaper remains oblivious to the passerby because she has absolutely no need of him, Auden's genius loci must dominate the newcomer at whatever cost. It is as if the genius loci had been waiting for years, even centuries, with nothing to do until some unsuspecting stranger stumbles across the threshold of the title and threatens to trespass the text/scape below. At this moment the genius loci springs to life. Magically, the inert words on the silent page quicken with the inward life of an intending voice. Under these circumstances, it would be incredible to feign indifference. Auden's genius loci is a necessarily interested, specific figure who must withstand an assault on a disputed border.

But what of the intruder? In Wordsworth's poem this is the most completely developed part. The passerby who overhears the singing maid is a carefully devised effigy, an ideal reader, the timeless exemplar of someone who reacts perfectly to the poem: "Stop here, or gently pass!" Through the eloquence of the wanderer, a reader is not merely shown but vicariously inducted into the demands of a required image. And these demands are quite clear. One must not interrupt, for that would break the magical spell of the lyric by committing an act of sacrilege, the importing of alien discourses into the holy place. One must accept what is imparted, grateful, unquestioning, as if vouchsafed a revelation. And then one must depart quickly so that the song may be absorbed into the pulse of instinct, not worried by the clumsy gropings of thought. When assembled, these demands of noninterruption, acceptance, and departure entail an efficient set of disciplines. The Solitary Reaper stands revealed as the archetype of poetic inspiration itself, which in practice means the power of the voice. Her singing becomes an emblem of the sonorous magic that makes a discourse, any discourse, effective. That is why the wanderer's self-effacement barely masks a triumphant exultation, and why he is so cavalier about the theme of the maid's song: "Will no one tell me what she sings?" The topics conveyed by her lyric are unimportant. What matters in this tale of power is that the passerby succumb to the wanderer's lyrical spell by assenting to the demands of an imposed effigy.

Auden's genius loci might well feel nostalgia for such a compliant reader. Rather than the enacted rapture of a figure who plays the part of an ideal recipient, Auden's spirit of the place must contend with a corrosive silence. The uninterrupted song of "The Solitary Reaper" gives way to what might be called an elided dialogue. At each pause, Auden's genius loci is challenged. A possible analogy for the setting of "The Watershed" would be a dramatic sketch in which an on-stage actor converses with an off-stage character whom the audience can neither see nor hear, yet whose responses may be partially inferred from the performer's actions. The contrast with Wordsworth's practice could not be more striking. Whereas romanticism presents a completed image of the reader, an already constructed part that need only be accepted, Auden opens a gap, a fact of resistance, an always yet to be enacted point of return. This shift, from image to resistance, alters the essential task of interpretation. It becomes pointless to seek the intention of a sender, whether this numinous entity be located inside or outside the poem. Rather, the arc of communication is continuously broken, its ostensible circuitry interrupted at each pause. Given these new circumstances, the reader's task is to chart an unsystematic dislocation and, through what is little more than a process of imagining, to enter into an auditor's persistent returns.

The stakes are fairly high. Not only the authority of the romantic voice but the privilege of the ideologies it has espoused are at risk. The genius loci knows he must stop the newcomer. But his sentinel's challenge, "Who stands?" is greeted with an auditor's demand for further information, "[Where?]." The reply is portentously cryptic, "the crux left of the watershed." Yet this only gives the transgressor an opening. Is the crux *to* the left of the watershed or *all that is left* of it? So the genius loci is forced to supply another directive. But this one is even more ambiguous. Does "the wet road between the chafing grass" run through the separate fields of a neatly partitioned grid or within one field's chafing blades, that is, through a trackless labyrinth of endless paths? Disguising his frustration as a magisterial disdain, the genius loci indulges in one of his few enjambments and brusquely moves on to the scene below. He thereby gives proof of his synoptic authority: the power to grasp an entire world. Yet the newcomer balks, unable to see exactly what is said, if only because of the parallax, the fact that another person always stands on a slightly different spot. The speaker's picturesque "snatches of tramline" concedes a broken line of sight, the result of an intervening screen, and thus unwittingly knocks out a main prop of visionary poetics: its unmediated linkage between perception and reference. Irked, the genius loci tries to salvage matters by resorting to a stronger personification, "running to a wood," as a means of diverting attention to the mysteriously animating energies within the scene below.

87

But in the process of avoiding one rift, he chances upon another, for the auditor detects disruptive accents within his personification. It implies a drama in which the restrictive line is enamored of the wood, a tangled multiplicity, perhaps straying into its luxuriant growth so it may engender a second birth, an event already presaged in the tram, which is not only a depository for docile infants but also the weft of a twisted weaving, a devious device.

Growing still more irritable of the captious perversity of the auditor, the genius loci then tries to kill off his treacherous personification, which abruptly becomes "already comatose." Yet in addition to keen sight, the traveler has acute powers of hearing: a wheezing comes from the defunct industry, a clanking of gears and pulleys, the unmistakable noises of active production. Having discovered that the intruder is too adept to be waylaid through distraction, the genius loci shifts to a more adept sarcasm: unlike the previous personification, "grudgingly performed" is a deliberate hyperbole, an attempt to deflate through overstatement, as if one were humoring the whims of a difficult child.

Yet the newcomer refuses to be trapped by the insinuation. Pointedly ignoring the genius loci, the auditor examines the landscape below in a careful way. So even though silent, it is now the auditor whose implied responses set the direction of the poem. This development is crucial. After the opening sally, the speaker no longer initiates but reacts. As so often in Auden, an unspoken response wrests control of the text away from a presiding voice. Noticing the newcomer's interest, the genius loci proposes the topic of the "many dead." This tactic shrewdly displaces an actual landscape with a mythic one: a heroic yet inaccessible past to whose mysteries only the genius loci holds the key. What ensues is unsurprisingly the longest section of the poem, since the speaker assumes he cannot be interrupted. As if settling a score, he takes the opportunity to indulge in the sexual innuendo of "cleaned out a damaged shaft by hand, clutching / The winch" and the franker contempt of "nosed his way" (dogs nose, though the target in this case is an earlier explorer, not the current auditor). Nonetheless, even here the genius loci opens an irrevocable gap. Twice he admits that his epic history is not authentic or unmediated (the spontaneous upwelling of the local spirit within him) but textually derived: "some acts *are chosen*, / *Taken* from recent winters." Where are the mute scriptors out of whose narratives these histories were stolen? What silenced redactors, each intent on a disparate interest, have spun, woven, inscribed the materials the genius loci would claim as his own?

The importance of such elided dialogues for Auden's textual practice cannot be overemphasized. Where high romantic tradition would fashion a completed image, the effigy, Auden insists on an unappeasable silence, the responsive auditor. In this way, an apparently unruffled surface, the smoothness of a poetic monologue, becomes agitated, vexed. Because so many discursive disciplines converge in the genius loci, the dialogic implications of Auden's practice are far-reaching. Elusive, the genius loci manifests itself only to an elite, so that any dissent becomes a form of self-demotion. Authentic, it enjoys unmediated contact with a universal essence. Supernal, it demands absolute, ecstatic submission. Archpoetic, its word may in no circumstances be modified or doubted. Yet through the disruptive silences of an elided dialogue, this disciplinary apparatus comes unjointed. Exiled from its own landscape, Auden's genius loci must remain at the dangerous margins of writing, never at home, a densely material item with nowhere to hide. Derivative, it betrays a dependency on a quiltwork of not quite repressible histories. Overbearing, it provokes increased resistance at each pause. Doomed to authority, the seductive illusion of a controlling speech, it can defer its multiple liabilities only through an even more extended risk, a further utterance.

But the issues at stake here involve more than a shift in traditional roles or even a discovery of new ones. They imply a turning point, a watershed, in the process of textual formation. Auden poses the question, How is a poem brought into being? Is it shaped according to the demands of an extrinsic and imposed theme? Or does it devolve (in the archaic sense, of being continuously passed on to another) through a process of dialogic exchange, so that the poem derives its distinctive features from an interplay of voice and inscription, the subtle havoc of a discursive arena? In "The Solitary Reaper," for example, the most evident structuring forces are extrinsic. They have all been worked out, in advance, so that the poem's marvelous spontaneity conceals the disciplines of a rigged game. An untransgressible line of awe is drawn around singer and song ("the Vale profound" as *terra sacra*/world pudendum) not only to leave both undisturbed but to protect the votary from any destructive contact with the divine. Then the beauty of the lyrical voice gathers into an irresistible force through a brief theological *via negativa:* a catalog of the imperfect beings it exceeds ("No Nightingale"; "e'er was heard / In spring-time from the Cuckoo-bird"). In this way, the reaper's archetypal status as a timeless pattern, a witness of all "that has been, and may be again," is achieved. It remains only to illustrate the disciplinary power of her lyrical voice by providing an instance of its irresistible effect, that is, by fashioning an effigy of the compliant reader. Accordingly, the actors in the drama are resexed, so that the maid becomes a masculine agent of inspiration ("o'er the sickle bending"), at once seizing and cutting off, while the passerby becomes a feminine recipient, transfixed ("I listened, motionless and still") and indeed impregnated ("The music in my heart I bore").

With "The Watershed," however, the structuring force is not extrinsic but intrinsic. Coiled like a spring, it waits within the text. What brings the work into being and gives it shape and definition is a dialogic strife, the implied interaction of speaker and auditor. This elided dialogue precariously engenders, motivates, and directs the text. The opening lines of the second verse stanza of "The Watershed" offer a lucid instance of this dialogic production. Intent on being rid of the auditor, the genius loci commands "go home," in a voice that might be used to address a stray dog or a group of noisily playing children. But when the intruder lingers, in effect calling the bluff, the tone must be strengthened, "now." Yet this goes too far. Aside from the police and minor bureaucrats, few are permitted such imperiousness. Consequently, the speaker must establish his right to a suddenly challenged authority. Rather than promoting himself, however, the genius loci attacks the intruder. The newcomer is labeled a "stranger," alien to the ways of this forbidden country, and accused of being "proud of your young stock," sprung from a callow and insignificant lineage. But the insult is also a detour. The momentum of its imperative falters and quickly dissipates, as if it had been tricked into a deviancy that might explore the branchings of that stock, at once deeply rooted, intricately branched, and freely circulated (a new issue, a fresh asset). To regain control, the genius loci repeats the name "stranger," but here the inflection is different: the plea of a beggar or the remark of a clinician apologizing for an experiment gone awry. When the command is repeated, "turn back again," it is already too late. The newcomer has ventured past the presiding voice of the genius

loci, intent on an independent inquiry. And this act of defiance transforms the prohibition into a directive: to turn back again, to reaccent
and reimagine the genius loci's text, is to confirm what the auditor of
"The Watershed" has been doing all along. Appropriately, the syntactic
symptoms become convulsive at this point, the fits and spasms of a verbal
body riddled with warring elements. For in venturing past the speaker,
left "frustrate and vexed," the traveler embarks upon an unvoiced and
thus unguided inquiry into the waiting text/scape. Exactly how that
journey will proceed, and where it might lead, remain points of conjecture. But what motivates it is clearly an elided dialogue in which each
syntactic rupture, instead of advancing a theme, incites a different
response.

Yet does not the distinction between an extrinsic (imposed) and an
intrinsic (dialogic) principal contradict the statement made earlier that
"effigy and auditor may be found within any text"? Not really, since
Auden's theory of the text acknowledges that conflicting and even mutually exclusive systems can operate simultaneously within the work. At
the same time a poem completes a communicative arc from sender to
receiver, it also incites a further dialogism, from voice to auditor, symptom to response. Both are always involved:

> Sharers of the same house,
> Attendants on the same machine,
> Rarely a word, in silence understood.
> (CP, 30)

So if effigy and auditor can be traced in any text, it should be possible
to retraverse "The Solitary Reaper" and listen for the exchange between
its highly articulate voice, the poem's enacted effigy, and the dissenting
auditor. Interestingly, this possibility accounts for one of the more uncanny parallels between Auden's and Wordsworth's texts. The final
trope of "The Solitary Reaper" converts the aesthetic into the kines-
thetic: the speaker notices his quickened pulse, a racing heart. Of course
this can be variously decoded: physical exertion (he is walking uphill);
introjected violence (the resentful remembrance of a too recent castration); or exultant power (he has imposed an effigy by means of an
ingeniously vicarious performance). But similar references suggest still

91

another possibility, a fear of retribution. The motif of the would-be poet taking inspiration from natural sound recurs throughout Wordsworth: the subterranean music of "Michael," the wandering song of "To the Cuckoo," the natural tones heard by the Boy of Winander, the blast of harmony from the Bedouin's Shell in the dream of *Prelude V*. This natural source of inspiration confers imaginative power—but at a price. It requires the speaker to be an auditor before becoming a poet. Thus the dominant voice of a text is always *preceded* by an unsettling encounter with the other, a dissonant, inhuman, untranslatable sound. A moment from "Lines Composed a Few Miles above Tintern Abbey" recollects this finely displaced anxiety:

> I cannot paint
> What then I was. The sounding cataract
> Haunted me like a passion.
> ("Tintern Abbey")

Vision (fixation, hypostasis: the speaker's capacity to turn the unruly inscriptions of a refractory medium into docile images) not only falters in this primal scene but confesses its fatal beginnings: in a spectral encounter, a terrifying supersession encompassed and pervaded by ungovernable sounds. The poet is able to achieve a speaking voice only through a calculated violence to this din of inscriptions. This is a fine achievement, to be sure, yet as with any violence, the birth of power fosters its own nemesis: an irrepressible dissonance that haunts the poetic voice as both the precondition and permanent crisis of its art.

The last trope of "The Watershed" rehearses this romantic anxiety, but in a comic and untroubled way. The genius loci concedes at last that the text is filled with dissonant sounds: "you may hear the wind." Yet he dismisses their inscriptive aftermath: "But seldom this" (i.e., the voice of the speaker). Since this dismissal leaves the auditor with nothing to overhear, the genius loci achieves his objective, which is the reduction of an unruly intruder to a docile image, here explicitly fashioned as an imbecile rabbit: "Near you, taller than grass, Ears poise before decision, scenting danger" (CP, 41). Yet even this aggression is provocative, for it incites the defiance of further responses. A ridiculing comparison is easily imposed, but to control its reading is another matter. Rabbits are certainly susceptible to such mock-epic sneers as "taller than grass." But they also have keen senses, especially of hearing. In the presence of an unseen body, they can trace imperceptible gestures and respond quickly to the slightest movement. So at the end of the poem, the speaker concedes what he above all wishes to repress: the possibility of an independent auditor, capable of returning to the inscriptive tremors and tracing their slightest gestures. The sap that rises may be merely an organic essence, the residue of a lately active pantheistic thaumaturge. But its pun can also gloss, offend, and thus provoke an awakened sleeper: as an alerted dupe, rising unbaffled like the tones of unmuted, unrestrained organ stops. Whereas this quickening in a respondent would be a source of deepest anxiety for romanticism, in Auden's text it offers the prospect of a comic disillusionment, perhaps even freedom.

It would be instructive to pursue Auden's hint and reconsider not just a specific lyric from the standpoint of the auditor but the varied repertoire of romantic poetry. What would happen were the reader to become disenchanted with the seductive spell of the effigy and induced to pursue another course, to note the disciplinary mechanisms, the symptoms of their violence, and the inscriptions that so recklessly challenge their ancient claim? What strange dialogues might then be found to reverberate within the authoritarian splendors of the romantic voice? For now, though, there is a more pressing matter. As Auden's genius loci demonstrates, the discipline essential to successful communication (as repression, domination) must ensure that the effigy remains intact, so that the resistance of an auditor never emerges. Yet the resistance is always there. The relevant task thus becomes one of recognition: How is it that the very efforts to entrance and captivate a reader also release the refractory responses of an auditor? Since there are so many kinds of effigy, that question calls for a division of labor, perhaps even a provisional typology—a column of addressees. And that column in turn might propose a specific approach to Auden's textual practice: one equally concerned with the anticipated, and unanticipated, auditors of his various voices.

CHAPTER FOUR

The Enemies of Promise

And voices in me said, If you were a man
You would take a stick and break him now, and finish him off.
                                        —D. H. Lawrence, "Snake"

Perhaps no poetic form can claim greater authority than the interior monologue. Within the depths of the self, an authentic and genuine being, one's own and undeniable identity, speaks with quiet yet devastating truth: "A low unflattering voice / That sleeps not till it find a hearing" (CP, 124). At the moment of insight, the chatter of ordinary consciousness subsides and out of the whirlwind emerges a clear, distinct voice. Included in the illustrious heritage of the interior monologue are both Ezekiel, who accorded it an almost divine status, and Plato, who maintained that real thought consisted of the mind talking to itself. Thus in a rare coincidence both revelation and reason nod their approval of the interior monologue. Allowances must be made, of course, for the mad and bad to whom the inward voice speaks all right, but as the evil one. Yet such abnormal situations are easily managed. There are ample criteria for acceptability: ethical, epistemological, doctrinal. It is remarkable, though, that these criteria are usually viewed as restorative. The rules for a genuine inwardness, however cultural in origin or obviously restrictive in function, are greeted as the protectors of an otherwise threatened personal authenticity. To resist this illogic (the necessary public approval, even assignment of what may count as an inward voice), Auden sought to expose the routine complicity between cultural and poetic disciplines. He regarded *internally persuasive* voices, whether morally, rationally, or emotionally privileged, with the utmost suspicion.[1]

1. The phrase is from Bakhtin who formulates it in such a way as to make it clear

Enemies of Promise, to adopt a title from Cyril Connolly, these guardians of mediocrity are dramatized as striking an early and often fatal blow to the imagination.[2] For Auden, as for another poet/teacher, D. H. Lawrence, the unquestioned voices of a culturally imposed inwardness (conscience, reason, sense, duty) are hostile forces, practitioners of a repressive art.

Nor are they lightly overthrown. A frequent motif in Auden's early poetry is the foiled escape. It records the hopelessness of trying to resist a diabolical foe, one who knows every move in advance, even as it is thought, let alone acted. The fugitive from inwardness flees before mercilessly vigilant powers, as in "The Witnesses":

> But do not imagine We do not know,
> Or that what you hide with such care won't show
>   At a glance:
> Nothing is done, nothing is said,
> But don't make the mistake of believing us dead;
>   I shouldn't dance.
>
> (CP, 72)

Some of the reasons for the authority of the interior monologue are deeply entrenched in the Western tradition: the mystique of a unified (integral, centered) self; the anxiety of a terrified subject, eager to surrender its responsibilities to some idol.[3] But at a more practical and thus paradoxically elusive level, Auden found that modern society, through its rites of education, attempted to structure the self as a totalitarian state, complete with retributive dictator, rubber-stamp legislature, ministry of official lies, and highly efficient secret police. The early essay "Honour"

---

that the interior designates not a privileged or inviolable realm but an already cultural space: "In the everyday rounds of our consciousness, the internally persuasive word is half ours, half someone else's." See Mikhail M. Bakhtin, *The Dialogic Imagination*, ed. Michael Holmquist (Austin: University of Texas Press), 1981, p. 345.

2. Auden reviewed Cyril Connolly's *Enemies of Promise* in "How Not to Be a Genius," *New Republic* 98 (April 26, 1939): 348, 350.

3. But this surrender functions as a means of control, since the demands made by the idol have been opportunistically worked out in advance; hence the close ties between idolatry and Narcissism: "Narcissus falls in love with his reflection; he wishes to become its servant, but instead his reflection insists upon being his slave" (DH, 115).

illustrates one formal technique of this repressive practice. It considers a common disciplinary device, the honor system. As Auden explains, the rules are simple. One vowed in the presence of a master not to swear, smoke, or do anything indecent; to report oneself if one did; and to report anyone else. Although the regimen sounds innocent enough, the kind of wholesome decency designed to make parents rejoice at finding the "clean and healthy school they had been looking for" (EA, 325), Auden is unusually harsh on the honor system; "no more potent engine . . . for perpetuating those very faults of character it was intended to cure, was ever devised" (EA, 325).

What does this disciplinary technique accomplish? Auden considers the matter in terms of discursive practice. The main point to the honor system is that a peculiar and hitherto unfamiliar discourse, a school code, is sworn to in the presence of an external authority. Thus it is coercively imposed by a social representative, because no one may refuse. At the same time, however, that code is instated as one's deepest, most authentic identity. As an interior voice, its dictates are henceforth given priority over every other discourse: not only the formations of desire already active within the self but any other social discourse as well (for example, loyalty to schoolmates, on whom one is expected to spy). So with impressive efficiency, a now properly self-supervised pupil becomes the sole inmate of a totalitarian hell. Surveillance is constant, punishment merciless, and trust in anything other than official decrees out of the question.

But there is a prospect of hope, however tardy. Years or even decades after the violence of a good upbringing, one might begin to unravel its methods of discipline. As a poet, Auden could textually embody an internally persuasive voice but then adapt it to a dialogic rather than an expressive task. The imaginative impulse here is not, as in romantic practice, to venerate a presiding voice. The speakers of Auden's interior monologues must not be taken *in propria persona,* as the presence of The Poet. For the poetic task of Auden's personae is dialogic: to display a circuit of repressive disciplines which, when played upon by a dissenting auditor, betray a prior violence as well as summon an inscriptive response. Because this textual strife always begins with a speaker intent on completing the communicative arc, it is possible to fashion a continuum of Auden's interior voices. What disciplinary stratagems does each prefer?

And how does that violence, through the imperceptible tremors of a syntactic embodiment, provoke the exchanges it tries to repress?

In an authoritarian utopia, the auditor would not merit a separate name, would not even be nameable (thinkable) as such, but fade into a featureless blank—the they. The speaker of "No Change of Place" presides over such a monologic scene. He plays the mythic part of a *sole survivor* in that his power stems from an elaborate yet unspoken narrative: against tremendous odds, the sole survivor has penetrated an unfathomable remoteness, made contact with the powers of origin, and thereby won forbidden knowledge. Of course nowhere in the poem is any of this mentioned. This narrative of authenticity is entirely implied. The sole survivor, a figure deprived of its rightful genre (e.g., epic adventure), is condemned to live in a leaden age, as a voice sentenced to rule a decadent self. He is surrounded by temporizers who are "content to lie / Till evening upon headland over bay" (EA, 53) and cowards "leaning on chained-up gate / At edge of wood" (EA, 53). Cut off from the wellspring of generic support, the sole survivor resorts to the defensive tactic of the complaint. His interior monologue stages an alternately nostalgic and splenetic soliloquy to an anonymous yet ingrate self.

To preserve a mythic authority, the sole survivor must repress any other voice that might intrude upon consciousness. He achieves this tyrannical necessity, which is so improbable it cannot be allowed the status of a theme, through a presumptive irony. The sole survivor never defines his own values or beliefs. Instead he establishes their necessity by arranging the potentially intrusive discourses of the text so that they both subvert and are subverted by one another. In this way, the irony emanates from a privileged center, as an implied superiority that can ridicule all competitors out of existence, yet which itself need never appear.

The tactics of this presumptive irony are deflation, hyperbole, and annulment. Deflation occurs when a poeticized (elevated, picturesque) discourse is given a banal predicate: "Metals run / Burnished or rusty in the sun / From *town to town*" (EA, 53). Hyperbole, on the other hand, discredits a normative or supposedly objective discourse by giving it a comically pompous predicate ("Or smoking wait till hour of food"; EA, 53) or a vulgar one ("Yet nothing passes / But envelopes between these places, / *Snatched* at the gate and *panting* read indoors"; EA, 53).

97

Clearly deflation and hyperbole work as an ensemble in that the banality of the one can in turn be discredited through the ostentation of the other.

Most effective of all is annulment, through which the sole survivor's presumptive irony can achieve the miracle of creation through nothingness. In annulment, one discourse does not supersede another, as if in a linear progression, but rather each alternately cancels out the other, so that both remain operative. An excellent example of this is: "And first spring flowers arriving smashed" (EA, 53). Here the subject "flowers" connotes pathos (innocence, unguarded newness, tears, delicate beauty), whereas the predicate "smashed" suggests a crude vitality (cynicism, disillusion, virile laughter). Given one intonation, the flowers are precious and their destruction a welcome release. Given another, however, the flowers promise regeneration and birth, and their predicate becomes the essence of philistinism. And with an expert speaker, a truly deft survivor, both intonational zones might become alternately active. This suspension of a resolving accent opens the way for a creation through negativity. The shuttle of intonational possibilities, enclosed within itself and yet endless, implicates a privileged center through its tireless circling. Yet that center, the unasserted yet necessary basis of its ironic superiority, nowhere appears.[4] The sole survivor's authority thus consists of an insinuated but otherwise nonexistent point, a voice whose own discourse is constituted entirely through an annulment of its competitors.

Even so adept an irony, however, might fall victim to its success. Because sustained by negating something else, a presumptive irony works only so long as it is on the move. The slightest pause might prove fatal because it would allow the ironic center to come into focus and thus precipitate into a distinct and accessible image. This requirement of constant motion is readily met, except for those dangerous moments when conquest seems effortless. Almost imperceptibly, the sole survivor slackens in vigilance.

4. In iconographic terms, the irony spins on an imaginary axis, which it pretends is orbiting around a larger gravitational mass. Unsurprisingly, the image of a constant spinning, as a form of centrifugal containment, often has a negative sense in Auden's poetry, of solipsism, entrancement, or paralysis. Cf. "Now from my window-sill I watch the night" ("spinning like a top in the field, / Mopping and mowing through the sleepless day"; EA, 115–16); or Malin in *The Age of Anxiety* ("Faster revolves the invisible corps / Of pirouetting angels"; CP, 387).

For should professional traveler come,
Asked at the fireside he is dumb
Declining with a small mad smile,
And all the while
Conjectures on the maps that lie
About in ships long high and dry
Grow stranger and stranger.

(EA, 54)

The hypothetical "should" announces a rigged game, a completely regulated scene whose outcome is dictated in advance. In this way, the threatening intrusion of a discursive competitor, the traveler as bearer of alien ways, is silenced. But rather than moving briskly on, as required, the survivor lingers over that silence, fascinated with the traveler's helplessness and exultant at his own sense of power. Thus the "small mad smile" is distributed between both victim and oppressor: the helpless desperation of the one and the sado-erotic mastery of the other. This twitch of narcissism, an admiring glance into the mirror of reflection, is fatal to the ironic center. No longer an absent point, it becomes a specific embodiment: an archaic smile, an identifiable sign, not a present meaning but a marker of its production. As if aghast at the betrayal, the syntax too quickly flees the scene. The "And" is a connector that, in the absence of anything to connect, becomes an expulsion. The ensuing "all the while" attempts to conceal the flight through a distracting promise: something important shall be discovered. Yet the betrayal has already taken place. The presumptive center exists at the same discursive level as its competitors, so that instead of moving on to a new topic, the "conjectures" serve to repeat, eventually to translate, the earlier hypothetical. In this way, they reflect the hitherto concealed discourse of the sole survivor. Through so trivial a gesture, then, a brief narcissistic lapse, the irony becomes what it must never be, self-reflective. Its silent center must now be subject to scrutiny: as conjectured, thrown together, a medley of discrete elements, with no more intrinsic authority than the long abandoned schema, charts, surmises it derides. Like the immobilized vessels on the shore, the irony is stuck, unable to complete its communicative circuit. It becomes subject to textual returns in which its previous authority, declining, inflected like an article of speech, grows ever more precise and bizarre.

An interior monologue, though, need not confine itself to the soliloquy. As suggested by Auden's earlier title for "The Wanderer" ("Chorus from a Play"), the voice of authentic being, one's inmost identity, can also use a quasi-public form of address.[5] (In Auden this option becomes a preference: the internal voices often sound as if they were speaking in an institutional context.) The obvious impropriety, a deeply personal inwardness assuming the guise of a public persona, is deliberate. It illustrates that even the most passionately held identity is itself a mask, culturally contrived and imposed. The true, authentically voiced names of the self (psychological, economic, religious, professional, sexual) reliably mark the entry point for some of the most repressive disciplines. In "The Wanderer," for example, the self is named as a primal horde from which resistance has yet to erupt. The poem's setting recalls Vico's myth about the origin of language: a primitive clan huddles about a vatic figure whose voice displaces the original thunder, as center, focus, divinity, and threat.[6] The wretched effigies tremble at the invisible powers that encircle them ("Avalanche sliding, white snow from rock-face"), while their leader describes with mock regret the fate of one expelled from their protective midst ("From thunderbolt protect, / From gradual ruin spreading like a stain"; EA, 56). The text, then, models an early

5. The poem was first published in *New Signatures*, ed. Michael Roberts (London: Hogarth Press, 1932), pp. 30–31. Auden's titles raise interesting problems, since he tended to give his works suggestive enframements when they appeared singly in periodicals but then dropped the titles when they were collected in book form. (Cf. Edward Mendelson, *Early Auden* [New York: Viking, 1981], p. xxii.) It seems best that the interpretive use of his titles be guided by Auden's own sense that poems should be approached pluri-contextually: that is, while it is necessary to select, perhaps arbitrarily, an enframing context, this selection must itself be open to continued variation, so that the pertinence of the text, its capacity to model and contrast an array of social discourses, is in no way restrained. Auden defended this contextual openness in his introduction to *The Poet's Tongue*: "As regards arrangement we have, after some thought, adopted an alphabetical, anonymous order. It seems best to us, if the idea of poetry as something dead and suitable for a tourist-ridden museum—a cultural tradition to be preserved and imitated rather than a spontaneous living product—is to be avoided, that the first approach should be with an open mind, free from the bias of great names and literary influences, the first impression that of a human activity, independent of period and unconfined in subject" (EA, 330).

6. *The New Science of Giambattista Vico*, trans. Thomas Bergin and Max Fisch (Ithaca: Cornell University Press, 1948), pp. 104–8.

stage in imaginative development. It assumes the epoch of a virtually prehistoric self, terrified, isolated, and entirely at the mercy of a vengeful bard: the voice of the community, an unchallenged cultural authority.

But the authority of a voice measures only the degree of freedom surrendered by its recipients. That is why the roles of auditor and speaker are inversely related in Auden, with one growing more powerful as the other wanes. Thus to assemble a truly abject effigy, a huddled herd, requires nothing less than the absolute authority of a bardic totalitarianism. The opening line of "The Wanderer," "Doom is dark and deeper than any sea-dingle," alludes to a passage from *Sawles Warde*: "They are so wise that they know all God's counsels, his mysteries and his judgments, which are secret and deeper than any sea dingle."[7] The contrasts between the Middle English homily and Auden's modernist pastiche illustrate the repression practiced by this voice. The homily proposes a complex process of deliberation, "God's counsels," as well as a group that has access to it. Its scene of natural mystery, the "sea dingle," also admits a social interaction through which textual complexities can be interpreted within a context of historical differences. But the opening of Auden's interior monologue suggests a quite different discursive scene. "God," "counsels," and the interpreting "they" all disappear, while "mysteries," "secret," and "judgment" fuse into a semi-divine "doom." This compression defines a numinous and symbolic depth, the "sea dingle." Thus the sonorous doom confers upon its elect, the invincible bard, the power to saturate referents with meaning (voice) and hence not only to prevent the advent of further namings but to silence potential dissidents.

But that power is only an imputed effect, never a textual achievement. To ensure order, the bard tells the huddled group of a foolhardy adventurer, the "what man" who dared depart from the familiar, "leave his house," ignore the usual admonitions ("No cloud-soft hand can hold him"), exceed both civil precedent and natural law, "through place-keepers, through forest trees," and wander into that dangerous realm beyond the camp fires of feral truth, "a stranger to strangers over undried sea." The crisis of this misadventure takes the form of an epiphany in

7. *Sawles Warde* is cited as a source in John Fuller, *A Reader's Guide to W. H. Auden* (London: Thames and Hudson, 1970), p. 48.

which the miscreant achieves a shocking glimpse of the abominations that await the unwary:

> But waking sees
> Bird-flocks nameless to him, through doorway voices
> Of new men making another love.
>
> (EA, 55)

The disciplines here are finely devised. After a sudden awakening, the wanderer finds himself in a place where language fails. Unable to name, that is, to assert, the most elemental form of control over a scene, he is portrayed as both passive and ignorant. Yet instruction comes soon enough in the form of a visual trauma, as he inadvertently stumbles on a scene of perversion. This petrifying apparition is so horrid that words may not describe it, yet so real because visual (directly perceived, an unmediated perception) that it is unquestionable. The beauty of the traumatic device is that by means of its visual feint, it relegates the unspoken to the unspeakable. The wanderer is frozen into a docile effigy, inert and helpless.

Even so capable a voice as that of the vengeful bard, however, cannot entirely control the accompanying mime of its textual embodiment. The syntactic gesture of the visual revelation is one of convulsion, a sudden reaching out and seizure of the forbidden thing, although this gesture is demurely cast as an objective sequence: merely a report on the wanderer's experience. It is this seizure that breaks the taboo against naming (perversion, homoeroticism). Yet the gesture is still more complex, for it involves not only an abrupt seizure but an equally convulsive withdrawal. What is named is not at all the forbidden thing itself, the terrifying signifier as deviant phallus of a proscribed discourse, but its evasive simulacrum, the euphemism of "new men making another love." Further, the evasion is conceded: the new men are not seen but heard. So although the semantic momentum of "waking sees" carries over into the seizure, lending it the effect of a visual immediacy, the traumatic event is in fact an entirely auditory experience, a matter of detected "voices." When coupled within a single gesture, this passage from seizure to retraction and eventually to dissembling offers another prospect. It suggests that even the most daring venture of understanding, the arch-reality of a traumatic vision, can attain only a further discourse, alien accents, different names. In that case, the bard's masterfully devised shock-technique also intimates a different itinerary, the very path of the wanderer, a straying into alien discursive parts.

What might an auditor discover there? According to the practice of poetic dialogism, this illicit figure, who is never more than a potential for further performance, traces responsive inscriptions within the disciplines of a speaking voice. The only limit to this performance is that it must disown itself, moving beyond the comforting web of its own understanding and further into the text. In "The Wanderer" a likely departure point might be found within the very apparition of Medusan horror ("through doorway voices / Of new men making another love"; EA, 55). As noted, the tactic here is to coerce the audience into docility by means of a veiled accusation of deviancy. But this is precisely where an auditor could begin to trace differing accents: That meaning does not emanate from some numinous and inaccessible doom but arrives "through doorway," already structured, enframed, culturally rigged. That its resonances are not univocal but plural, "voices" that are diverse, competitive. That its performing agent is not a timeless subject but historical "men," actual, self-deceived, anxious. That the distinctively human activity of these individuals eludes the usual dualism of active (the righteous extirpation of the dissident) and passive (the abrupt impalement of inspiration), for a "making" that involves irreverence, assemblage, tinkering. That such production cannot replicate itself but must continuously provoke "another" as it interweaves with further discourses. That although this errancy might be called a perversion by some, it is also a "love" that relinquishes certainty and force in favor of a continuous, perhaps even humane, adventure.

So the monologue of even the vengeful bard may be dialogically disrupted. But of course internally persuasive voices do not halt at the margins of a single poem, any more than they retreat after a single assault. The contest is waged in increments. Each momentary victory over an internally persuasive figure only engenders another authoritative voice, wily, adept, and more authentic than before. (These increments gradually approach an identity: reading stops, mystification begins, when the gap between voice and text closes, and one at last hears the real intention, whatever it be called.) Imagine the wanderer has just stepped

103

outside the ring of bardic power. A sense of relief is of course in order as well as congratulations: "Having abdicated with comparative ease / And dismissed the greater part of your friends" (EA, 45). Yet without delay another figure appears, in fact has already intervened to police the unruly self: the bogus guide.[8] Welcoming the fugitive from discipline who has just arrived "Half Way," he offers a quick orientation course. Although every bit as tyrannical as the bard, the internal voice of the bogus guide relies on superior knowledge rather than inaccessible mystery. His success is a matter of degrading rather than threatening the self.

As with many of Auden's early poems, "Half Way" suggests the setting of a boys' school, complete with private codes, treacherously shifting factions, and the feeble plots born of impotent rage. This odd (irresponsible, elitist) choice of a setting is noteworthy for its disadvantages: it precludes either wide appeal or heartfelt sincerity. But the unpoetic quality of this oppressive context, a scene of pure repression, might itself be the point. The boys' school setting enabled Auden to explore the distinction between escapism and poetic dialogism. The differences between them are elusive because the two have many qualities in common. Each withdraws from a intolerable domination; each subversively renames its world; each claims hedonism as its justification. Yet escapism and dialogism diverge in the way they carry out their tasks. Escapism wants to obliterate the realities of domination, replace them with its own mythic narratives and thereby enjoy, if only in fantasy, the gratifications of revenge. Dialogism, however, withdraws to assess and reaccent, not erase; its inscriptions do not replace one discourse with another but trace an incessant discursive exchange; and dialogism refuses the prize of even a compensatory reference. Unlike its escapist counterpart, dialogism offers not a ravishing truth but a disruptive event.

Yet of the two, escapism has the considerably greater allure. The bogus guide initiates the recent fugitive into a privileged realm whose pleasures are derived from the finality of its names: "the Tutbury glass workers," "the Dream at the Hook," "Stinker," "Bog-Eyes," "the Kelpie." Such mythic designations convey more than boyish exuberance.

---

8. The phrase is from the early sonnet "Control of the Passes" ("He, the trained spy, had walked into the trap / For a bogus guide, seduced with the old tricks"; EA, 25).

Under the protective guise of fantasy, this esoterica achieves a nomination that is at once merciless and final. As the sorry butts of a school reunion soon learn, boyhood epithets are grim terminemes, as durable as the headstones they anticipate. Yet there is one name that does not fit: "If you meet Mr. Wren, it is wiser to hide" (EA, 46). Mr. Wren, migratory, reticent, transformative (feathers evolved from scales), wanders into the text from the supposedly oppressive but in practice more diverse realm of actual social discourses. In doing so, Wren illustrates the far greater tyrannies of an escapist idyll. As a historical subject, he can shift from code to code. Unlike the absolute designations of escapism, he can accept a wide array of predicates (professional, psychological, political). The mythic names of the bogus guide, however, are pseudo-subjects in that their predicates are fixed, as if frozen into a permanent masquerade. As with "the Kelpie," a type of sheepdog, their discursive status is predestined to what is docile, canine, obediently at hand. Moreover, this mythic reduction admits of no respite. Escapism enforces a pure power play: endorse its names, or be named (terminated).

For most of his performance, the bogus guide treats the fugitive with amused condescension: "How shall we greet your arrival"; "Of course we shall mention . . . though not very fully" (EA, 46). This enacts an undesired intimacy, a familiarity meant to convey not affection but an insolent superiority. At the end, though, the bogus guide decides to resolve matters in a more demeaning way: "Do you wish to ask any questions? Good; you may go" (EA, 46). The abrupt imperative shifts from insolence to pure aggression. Like any rhetorical question, it poses a threat: of imminent danger if silence is broken and the issue of the question presumptuously returned. But then the bogus guide proceeds to carry out the threat with "good": cynically cloaking itself in the values of vitality, regeneration, energy, the "good" enacts a summary dismissal. It cuts off the capacity to respond, indeed the very access to language. All it leaves is a powerless remnant, a subject so impotent that even its removal must be dictated.

Yet this arrogant shift, from intimidation to a performed violence, requires an accompanying gesture. Undeflected, impervious, the syntax proceeds with the blitheness of a formula, deaf to itself. It cannot hear, or even imagine, the rustle of inscriptions within its utterance.[9] At the

9. The sound of a dry, thin membrane, lifeless itself yet subject to the play of

semantic level, then, it rashly orders the fugitive into the contested landscape of its escapist retreat:

> But now look at this map.
> Here are the first- and the second-class roads,
> Crossed swords for battles, and gothic letters
> For places of archaeological interest.
>
> (EA, 46)

The combination of violence, deafness, and expulsion is comically disruptive. An enraged fugitive is sent, alone and unaccompanied, into a text whose inscriptions because inaudible, perhaps unthinkable, are altogether unrestricted. Even within the boundaries of the map, an emblem of schematic enthrallments, the excluded discursive arena begins its return. As a patent dissimulation, the map depicts a scene in multiple perspective (past conflicts, cultural antecedents, economic interests); it relies on arbitrary and yet unwittingly polyvocal signs ("crossed swords," "gothic letters"); it implements gradients of value and use ("the first- and the second-class roads"); and it admits an array of supplementary texts: histories, biographies, diaries, magazines, newspapers, letters. So an auditor might chance upon the discovery that so perturbed Stinker, "waving the paper," not because of what it said but because of what it conferred: access to a two-dimensional pattern of signs, depthless, flimsy, and yet stubbornly defiant of the fully contoured reality it can only promise.

The discursive arena always remains the important goal of Auden's poetry. It is glimpsed in the waiting cities that provide the surround for so many of his works: Berlin, Helensburgh, Macao, Hong Kong, Brussels, "Dover," Birmingham ("As I walked out one evening"), and New York in both *New Year Letter* and *The Age of Anxiety*. This context is actually a kinship. The auditor/self senses a filiation with the varied scripts out of which it is composed. Yet each step to the city's tumult is met with increased resistance. As the self becomes increasingly articulated, that is,

---

unpredictable forces, is among the most unsettling in Auden's auditory universe because it restores language to the medium of signs that its meanings must strive to escape. Cf. the chorus from "Advent" in *For the Time Being*: "only hearing / The silence softly broken / By the poisonous rustle / of famishing Arachne" (CP, 271).

more aware of its discursive diversity, its disciplinary voices become more adept. In "The Questioner Who Sits so Sly," for example, a would-be poet, someone foolish enough to believe that writing verse might have a transformative value, contends with an internal censor, a demonic ironist who mocks this hope as futile and delusive. Auden's original title, which is derived from a passage in Blake's "Auguries of Innocence," helps to gloss the setting of this interior monologue. A youthful writer, just prior to the poem's beginning, has proposed the design of a new poetics. Immediately the figure of the questioner, who supplies the pre-siding voice of the poem, springs to life. As Blake's phrase suggests, the tactics of this demonic ironist combine low cunning with judicial absolutism: a seated persona, accorded the legal privilege of examining without being examined, conducts a scene of inquisition. Yet the figure also poses a paradox, which in turns leaves an opening. "The Questioner who sits so sly / Shall never know how to reply" ("Auguries of Inno-cence"). Clearly the questioner *can* reply, at least dramatically, in that the entire poem consists of his belittling attack on the plan of the would-be poet. Yet this obvious attempt at domination conceals a subtler inca-pacity. Although the demonic ironist can mock an emergent writer, he is incapable ("shall never know how") of impeding or even discerning the subversive inscriptions that wait with such maddening patience within that writer's text. Auden's theft from Blake thus instigates a further thievery, in which a masterful voice finds its own meanings stolen away.

As a good tactician, the demonic ironist makes use of a particularly disabling form of annulment, a pastiche. The ambition of the would-be poet is metaphorically equated with the patriotic fervor of the previous generation, the fathers who went off to fight in the Great War. The ironist's ridiculing comparison suggests that to embark on a project of transformative writing is to accept a fool's errand. The would-be poet sets off for "the badlands," to court "martyrdom" out of respect to empty values ("the flag waves") and to suffer ultimate defeat.

> But to see brave sent home
> Hermetically sealed with shame
> And cold's victorious wrestle
> With molten metal.
>
> (EA, 36)

The war pastiche enables the ironist to operate an ingeniously closed annulment. Given a sarcastic intonation, his remarks suggest that those who join the would-be poet's struggle are dupes. From contemporary accounts such as Graves's *The Long Weekend,* or Lou and Mae's banter in *The Waste Land,* few could forget that England's returning army of heroes faced unemployment, a skimpy pension, and, once their leaders had no further use of them, a rapidly descending oblivion.[10] Thus one aspect of the annulment requires an intonation that mocks the young poet's ambition as a futile and probably self-destructive delusion. Yet there is also another accent, coiled within the first, which rejects this sarcasm. In addition to a disdainful superiority to the previous generation, Auden's contemporaries felt guilt at being too young to march off with the heroic fathers. They were the children left behind with "the sewing hands" (EA, 36) and thus historically relegated to a fate of permanent adolescence. So in addition to the note of mockery, there is an accent of self-contempt, a rage at having to bear the injustice of an accidental, implied, and yet inescapable charge of unmanliness. The important issue, however, is not the relative force of these distinct intonations but their almost perfectly balanced possibility. In this inflectional round-robin, either accent (sarcasm/self-hatred) might equally well gain dominance. This balance achieves an efficient form of restraint. When the ironist's hostility to the poet's ambition becomes too pronounced (thus itself vulnerable to analysis as an ideological structure), the discourse can shift and redirect that hostility to its own cowardice. And yet the shift is readily reversible. Should hostility toward the ironist become too great (again, too strongly marked and thus noticeable), the inflection can return to its contempt for poetic naiveté. "The questioner who sits so sly" thus proposes an efficient perpetual-motion machine, a disciplinary trap that works through the simple mechanism of an interminable cycle.

But the ironist's strategies are practiced not on an ill-defined group but on an already emergent and distinct capacity: an imagination willing

10. Robert Graves, *Good-bye to All That* (London: J. Cape, 1929), p. 388 ff. There are numerous passages in which Auden made use of the war jingoism he heard when at school: John Knower in *Paid on Both Sides* ("Yes. I know we have and are making terrific sacrifices"; EA, 8); the bishop's address in Ode V of *The Orators* ("they ran like hares"; EA, 107); and the Vicar's sermon in *The Dog Beneath the Skin* ("What was the weather on Eternity's worst day?"; EA, 138).

to be a poet. It is important to bear in mind that the auditor in this text is also a writer, a forger of texts, hence a provocative impulse silenced by the presiding voice. So it should be possible to recover the implied script of this writer, a missing manifesto. This motif of a missing script recurs in poems such as "The Letter," "Never Stronger," "Happy Ending," "Who's Who," "The Council," "One Circumlocution," "Bird-Language," and "Ode to Terminus," each of which takes its point of departure from an absent text. A complete recovery is fortunately impossible, because if found the missing script would have to divulge its own textual instability or degenerate into an even more intractable tyranny. So a subtle but important reversal precedes the dramatic action of the poem. A former scriptor, an instigator of textual responsiveness, is constrained to act the part of an auditor, which differs from the prior role in this respect: whereas the scriptor imposes a provocative order through the illusion of a masterful voice, an auditor traces a relentless return of dissident inscriptions within that voice.

As everyone knows, writing, "the greatest of vocations" (CP, 163), is difficult enough.[11] But Auden suggests that an auditor's patient tracing of inscriptions might be the more arduous task. As if guessing the disruptive design of the writer, to formulate texts that release a reader's unique imaginings, the ironist ridicules its improbability. Such extravagant imaginative activity will no doubt be banished. Any auditor would be doomed to live under a cloud of suspicion.

> Remembering there is
> No recognized gift for this;
> No income, no bounty,
> No promised country.
>
> (EA, 36)

The annulment of this passage is flawless, that is, its irony equally distrib-

---

11. For a specific reason: the apparently stable surfaces of writing are treacherous. Writing for Auden does not rest on the stable plane of an inert page, but rather moves within a medium of continuously shifting forces ("an improper word / scribbled upon a fountain"; CP, 110), a disintegrating permeability ("scribbling on the sky"; CP, 120), or an unreliable network of tables and legends ("scribbled on / The backs of railway guides"; CP, 122).

uted between victim and speaker. Thus at the semantic level it offers a frictionless surface. The poised yet contradictory intonations are so complete that it seems improbable, perhaps impossible, for a responsive reading to commence. The challenge to an auditor could not be more defiant. Yet such arrogance also concedes its blindness. In the course of delivering its challenge, the passage is afflicted with an acute tenesmus, a painfully unsuccessful effort at expulsion. Its gesture of remembrance, of embodying an inert past, naturally requires a list, the marker of a mastered completeness. But because the ironic annulment demands rejection of the list's contents, the items of this completeness must be systematically negated. Hence the passage strains against itself, at once entirety and rift, as it gathers up only to expel a delusion that continuously becomes a gap. In the ensuing play beyond voice, beyond even irony, the obvious fullness of meaning becomes riddled, vexed, an apt topography for a prospective auditor.

The syntactic gestures that accompany the irony's discipline offer a comic alternative: to detect, within the annulment, the returns of an absent text. Although the prospective poet's missing script cannot be recovered in any literal way, it can be responsively inferred. Each of the ironist's gibes might then be reaccented to disclose a ludic inscription, a return of the poet's missing manifesto. In that event it becomes essential to "turn a deaf ear" to the limitary chorus of a collective truth, "what they said on the shore," and instead "interrogate their poises" by putting the gestures of a somatic body into question. This requires an indifference to party allegiances ("Yet wear no ruffian badge"; EA, 35), as well as a yielding to discursive licentiousness ("Carry no talisman / For germ or the abrupt pain"; EA 35), so that any voice *at all* can be adopted. This mimicry lends the appearance a certain complicity ("Will you wheel death anywhere"; EA 35), at least to the earnest or unwary. Even worse, in a meaning- and intention-obsessed culture it will be the most reactionary who seize upon this mimicry as an endorsement of their own repressive program: "For to be held for friend / By an undeveloped mind / To be joke for children is / Death's happiness" (EA, 35). As the years pass, questions about the oblique, contradictory, and thematically meretricious quality of such an art will begin to mount. Yet the accused writer must consent "never to make signs" (EA, 36), never to indulge in a will-to-power over the text that would domesticate it by bringing it into congruence with some safe, unexceptionable theme.[12] The poet is forced to accept a likely neglect, relieved only by the rarest of events, a reading that consists of another's unsanctioned (punishable) imaginings.

> A neutralizing peace
> And an average disgrace
> Are honor to discover
> For later other.
>
> (EA, 36)

If nothing else, the poetic manifesto inscribed within "The Questioner Who Sits so Sly" portrays a youthful Auden, well before his public career was under way, who had an uncanny sense of the reception that awaited his texts. To effigies transfixed by vocal power, his poems would indeed seem tyrannical, unprincipled, shallow, cowardly. To an auditor, however, the play of voice and response might offer a way to greater insight and freedom.

The internal voices considered so far have spoken, prudently, on behalf of some other power. That is not the case with the matron-divinity of "Venus Will Now Say a Few Words." As her mythic name suggests, she is a Lucretian deity, associated in a general way with procreative energies. But intervening between *De Rerum Natura* and Auden's text are the sadistic demiurges of Thomas Hardy, as well as the social Darwinism of Herbert Spencer. Like Hardy's Spinner of the Years and Proud Doomsters, Auden's Venus in fact lends a mythic name to a contemporary belief. Thus the simple act of her personification conducts a subtle alchemy: of the contemporary into the timeless and of the culturally constructed into the immediately presenced. Accosting a would-be fugitive, Venus represents a determinism whose major tenets

12. Auden was relatively successful at maintaining this commitment to silence, though on a few notable occasions he remarked his exasperation with reviewers who persisted in reading his work according to the dictates of the romantic canon, that is, as expressions of an author rather than as deliberate modelings of disciplinary devices and their aftermath: "Authors can be stupid enough, God knows, but they are not always quite so stupid as a certain kind of critic seems to think. The kind of critic, I mean, to whom, when he condemns a work or passage, the possibility never occurs that its author may have foreseen exactly what he is going to say" (DH, 8).

hold: that human life *ought* to be governed by purely natural forces; that these forces are pervasive and indisputable; that resistance is futile because such opposition is itself part of Venus's evolutionary design.

> Nor even is despair your own, when swiftly
> Comes general assault on your ideas of safety;
> That sense of famine, central anguish felt
> For goodness wasted at peripheral fault,
> Your shutting up the house and taking prow
> To go into the wilderness to pray,
> Means that I wish to leave and to pass on,
> Select another form, perhaps your son;
>
> (EA, 45)

Auden's Venus exemplifies a familiar type of psychologically persuasive voice: the interior monologue of a consciousness dominated by popular truisms about normality, whether that normality be defined in intellectual, moral, or sexual terms. Her duty is to save the self from its lust for the enticing apparitions, the forbidden pluralities, of the desert.[13]

But her commanding personification also serves as a marker of weakness. Because language never actually delivers anything beyond its historical materiality (as a riddled maze of discursive systems), disciplinary personae are more wisely cast as envoys, annunciators on behalf of some august authority who is otherwise engaged. Venus, however, is forced to make her authority a matter of personal power. Yet whatever is manifest thereby becomes accessible, which is why authority rarely shows itself until desperate. Since speaker and auditor form a correlative pair in Auden, with each furnishing a condition for the other, this decrease in Venus's disciplinary strength implies a relative increase in the self's resilience. Venus accosts not a huddled mass or an aspiring writer but a more resolute and adept power of imagining.

---

13. In this respect, Auden remains within the romantic iconography of the desert, which sees it as a symbol of decadent multiplicity. The difference is that whereas romanticism wants to reduce multiplicity to unity, Auden traces a dialogue of discursive forms within that multiplicity. Cf. *The Enchafèd Flood*: "E.g. the desert is the dried-up place, i.e., the place where life has ended, the Omega of temporal existence. Its first most obvious characteristic is that nothing moves; the second is that everything is surface and exposed" (EF, 19).

There is good evidence to indicate the resistance of this auditor, who is not permited a single word and is confined, like the text itself, to tacit gestures. Venus begins in the manner of an expert naturalist, a student of the bizarre mating habits of a particularly amusing species ("You are the one whose part it is to lean"). But instead of being humiliated, her auditor finds this comic and apparently laughs out loud. So she snaps, "But joy is mine not yours," and shifts from deprecating expert to experimenting demigod, "whose cleverest invention was lately fur." Yet this only makes matters worse, for the auditor now looks at her with the frank skepticism of someone caught in the company of a mad scientist, which she detects in "that shape for your face to assume." So again Venus shifts roles, this time to the voice of a guilt-mongering parent: "I shifted ranges, lived epochs handicapped." This even greater imposture is greeted with blank astonishment.

Frustrated, Venus resorts to her most powerful device: she breaks the terms of the contextual contract. Turning away from the auditor, she addresses another group ("You in the town now call the exile fool"). The apostrophe performs the disciplinary maneuver of replacing an actual individual who can respond with a hypothetical group (the townies) who cannot. Of course, this shift to an easier audience, a docile effigy, is opportunistic, hence an implicit concession of defeat or at least of heavy resistance. So to conceal her tactic, Venus berates the imaginary townies for *not* undertaking the adventure she wants to prevent the auditor from attempting. Her repressive technique, then, might be compared to the ancient method of lion training, in which some wretched dog was beaten in full view of the lion so as to intimidate and demoralize the more dangerous beast. It seems to work. Upon returning to the actual scene, Venus strikes at the visibly downcast auditor, "Nor even is despair your own." Yet something has gone awry. The contrition is merely feigned. She notices for the first time that preparations have already been made for the long venture into the discursive desert, "Your shutting up the house and taking prow." Angrily, she tries one more threat: "Before you reach the frontier you are caught." Yet this compromises the position she took before, that even successful resistance serves her purpose. Adopting a more defensive stance, Venus insists that whatever happens beyond the borders of generic naming involves deviancy ("Cause rather a perversion on next floor"), madness ("central anguish felt / For goodness wasted at peripheral fault"), and social anarchy ("Though he [your son] reject you"). Already it is too late. In a final gesture, Venus shouts at the back of a departing figure: "Others have tried it and will try again." But this is desperation, a warning to potential effigies (perhaps the docile souls reading the poem), not the successful repression of an active auditor.

What is the source of the auditor's inexplicable resistance? The event that even so diabolically skillful an internal voice as Venus cannot control is the body of desire, her own aberrant text. According to the inverse logic of poetic dialogism, it is at moments of consummate rhetorical mastery that a text becomes most disruptive. In her apostrophe Venus devises a futurist archaeology. That is, she locates and then occupies a perspective in some indeterminate future from which it is possible to look back at the present moment, scientifically, synoptically, as if detached from the perturbations of history. The genius of this tactic is its omnivorous scope. From this securely retrospective niche, Venus can enframe and thereby control any other discourse.

> You in the town now call the exile fool
> That writes home once a year as last leaves fall,
> Think—Romans had a language in their day
> And ordered roads with it, but it had to die:
> Your culture can but leave—forgot as sure
> As place-name origins in favorite shire—
> Jottings for stories, some often-mentioned Jack,
> And references in letters to a private joke,
> Equipment rusting in unweeded lanes,
> Virtues still advertised on local lines;
> And your conviction shall help none to fly,
> Cause rather a perversion on next floor.
>
> (EA, 45)

Yet her mastery is betrayed, for the text displays symptoms of incipient delirium. Each time an alien discourse is mentioned, it becomes active, directive, so that rather than remaining an item to be discarded, it begins to work as an operative framework. The direct address trails off into a cityscape, a doubled epithet, a surreptitious writing, and lastly an elegiac reminiscence of falling leaves. So at the same time Venus devises a retrospective omniscience for herself, the text indulges in a wayward drift. As if aware of the betrayal, she makes a reference to Latin in an attempt to reassert control over these discursive aliens. Yet she càn regain that control only by discarding this exemplary language before its inscriptions can gather any responsive momentum. In devising her futur-ist analogy, then, Venus has little success. Her comparison breaks down because the contemporary discourses she cites are vital, fascinating glimpses into varied cultural realms, not the dusty artifacts of a bygone epoch. So despite her belief in a natural and continuous evolution, the inscriptions of her text prove otherwise. They tempt the impassive sur-veyor into varied name origins, contingent implotments, wreckage-strewn landscapes, collages of contemporary rivals (the blur of advertising posters in a rapidly passed suburban station). In her unintentional way, then, Venus too is a liberator. However inadvertently, she fosters the disclosure that even the voice of natural necessity is a quiltwork of discrete discourses, and that even the deepest personal origin is a "convic-tion," a judicial hence imposed edict which nonetheless induces a "per-version," a more intense ruin or subtler overturning.

In the absence of obvious markers (a darkened set; an invisible speaker, who is thereby encoded as numinous, disembodied), how is it possible to recognize a voice as internal?[14] Perhaps the most distinctive characteris-tic is tone. Because such insolence would not be tolerated from another person, the sheer abusiveness of a voice may serve to locate it within a cloistered sphere, a scene of torment in which an officially sanctioned discipline can stifle the emergent life of the self. Yet this general rule, the natural inwardness of insolence, has its limits. As the self becomes responsively adept, its internally persuasive voices must gradually relin-quish their primitive arrogance. The continuum of Auden's interior monologues eventually crosses a point (it might be called The Great Intonational Divide) where the tone shifts, from coercion and threat to solicitude. Made cunning by weakness, the internally repressive voices

14. The divorce of a voice from its productive body, which is the impossibility on which both authorial mastery and positive truth depend, is cited as an especially destruc-tive illusion in the poetry. Cf. the passage in *The Age of Anxiety* where Quant, in order for the four characters' inquiry to proceed further, silences the radio: "Listen, Box, / And keep quiet. Listen courteously to us / Four reformers" (CP, 356).

become sympathetic, attentive, intimate. Instead of the tyrant, they now play the part of protector and confidante.

Despite differences of age, sex, or period, the icon for intimacy remains the grouping of mother and child, whether as madonna or pietà. From the standpoint of disciplinary tactics, this arrangement achieves two closely related objectives. While severing the self from its inscriptive genealogy, which is thereby cast as the hostile (ugly, martyring) external world, the mother/child configuration also binds the self to a protective source, through means of a guilt-ridden obligation. Even if the self takes no thought of its own well-being, and wanders off to desert, city, border, or some other figure of the discursive arena, it must still suffer remorse for harm done to its natural origin, which undergoes shame or worse should the offspring misbehave. An instance of such remorse occurs in "The Wanderer": "Protect his house, / From gradual ruin spreading like a stain" (EA, 56). Intimacy is a most effective disciplinary technique, then, because its longed-for embrace mingles violence with compassion, heroically noble sacrifice with predatory cunning.

The "Epilogue" to *The Orators*, itself a long poem devoted to undoing the effect of childhood disciplines, "the immense bat-shadow of home" (EA, 66), models this intimate violence in ballad form. Its presiding voice uses the format of a rhetorical question, posing then answering its own query, so as to at once exhort and accuse:

> 'O where are you going?' said reader to rider,
> 'That valley is fatal where furnaces burn,
> Yonder's the midden whose odors will madden,
> That gap is the grave where the tall return.'
> (EA, 110)

The poem is unusual in that its auditor actually replies to these questions, in the final stanza. But the text carefully distinguishes between this stated response, or actual dialogue, and the subtler disruptions of its poetic dialogism. A dialogue is voiced. It occurs between characters and operates at the thematic and referential level. A dialogism, however, is unvoiced. It occurs between discourses and operates at the structural and metalinguistic level. "Epilogue" illustrates this contrast through a carefully observed disjuncture. Its tacit auditor does not reply to the stated question.

Rather, the implied response enlists unvoiced inscriptions, traces of alien discourse, within the parent text.

> 'Out of this house'—said rider to reader
> 'Yours never will'—said farer to fearer
> 'They're looking for you'—said hearer to horror
> As he left them there, as he left them there.
>
> (EA, 110)

Thus the auditor is not a reactive reader (an effigy: even an irate rejection of a voiced theme, insofar as it neglects the play of inscriptions, is a regrettable form of docility) but a participating rider (an appendage, a devious contravention, an irksome script tacked on to something else). The inscriptions are consequently elided, both summoned and dispatched to the blankness between the speaker's statement and the auditor's response. In this way, dialogism skirts a permanent rift, which it may observe but not close: "That gap is the grave where the tall return." It engages not themes but the neglected strata of inscriptions within a thematic violence, even when that violence is enforced as a solicitous concern, an intimacy that knows its recipients far better than they know themselves. What might an auditor hear, so that the dead come back to life, or the tall liberate and not haunt? Like an actor at some infinite rehearsal, obliged to practice the same lines yet permitted the license of an infinitely varied inflection, one must await an accent that uncoils into resistance.

But the difficulty of overcoming an intimate internal voice should not be underestimated simply because of an easy (lucky) success. The voice of intimate concern is likely to plague an individual long after the avatars of childhood terror have been formally banished. A year after his epilogue to *The Orators*, Auden wrote a companion ballad, the better-known "O what is that sound which so thrills the ear." In the epilogue, the auditor achieves independence by detecting the hairline crack between a rhetorical question and its dialogic inscriptions. In the companion ballad, however, this discovery begins to take place but is then waylaid by the snares of a solicitous voice.

> O what is that sound which so thrills the ear
> Down in the valley drumming, drumming?

Only the scarlet soldiers, dear,
The soldiers coming.

(EA, 125)

The victim, clearly marked as an effigy ("dear"), notices premonitory details ("that light I see flashing so clear," "all that gear," "why have they left the road down there"). But s/he is fearful, hesitant to act, and consequently relies on a trusted intimate, whether as spouse, lover, or parent. This demonic figure glosses over the ominous developments with a series of half-truths and trivializations, couched as common sense. It is indeed "the soldiers coming," but the "only" lies: their mission is lethal. The confidante's technique of deception is both wary and cynical: an anxious recipient must of course be carefully watched but will in general prefer reassurance to the perils of dialogic inquiry, even if that reassurance leads to a fatal end.

O it's broken the lock and splintered the door,
O it's the gate where they're turning, turning;
Their feet are heavy on the floor
And their eyes are burning.

(EA, 126)

Yet just as the trap snaps shut, the text offers another chance. Prior to the last stanza, the seductive intimate departs: "No, I promised to love you, dear, / But I must be leaving." This departure of the dominant voice raises a quite impossible prospect, though that impossibility may contain in brief the whole of Auden's dialogic poetics. What is left after the treacherous speaker, a reassuring and tutelary voice, departs? Only a text, with neither origin nor destination, at best an uncertain column of inscriptions. Unguarded yet embodied, even these last lines summon illimitable responses.

As interior monologues lose their once absolute power, they eventually reach a point on the continuum of voices where it is inefficient to proceed farther. The capacity of an emergent self to delineate and respond becomes too accomplished. Thus Auden's collected poetry suggests an important if unmarked division. The disciplinary voices turn away from ruling the self (always, as spiritual shepherds insist, the hardest task) and return to their point of origin. This origin is not at all the unique soul, enfolded within a hushed inwardness, but rather the discursive arena from which the soul so passionately removes itself. Yet the mood of this retreat by the disciplinary powers is exultant. Beyond the self waits a more inviting prospect, the external world of other persons. Here the effigies are much more manageable, for they are held in check by constant scrutiny, collective inertia, and the threat of swift retribution. So the enemies of promise need not languish in their disappointment. They can still take the route to a more imperial conquest, a path that leads to the quite different space of Auden's public voices, his various orators.

CHAPTER FIVE

Orators and Others:
Auden's Civic Voices

Who is the third who walks always beside you?
When I count, there are only you and I together
But when I look ahead up the white road
There is always another one walking beside you
Gliding wrapt in a brown mantle, hooded
I do not know whether a man or a woman
      —T. S. Eliot, *The Waste Land*

It is easy to take Auden's use of civic voices for granted. But his imaginative use of these figures, who adopt the personae, themes, and disciplines of ordinary discourses (a headmaster to his students, a clergyman to his flock), is one of Auden's more important departures from romantic practice. As he noted in *The Enchaféd Flood*, romanticism tended to reject the discourses of the city. It feared and resented the practices of business, science, law, journalism, and politics, which it saw as "destroying the heroic individual and turning him into a cipher of the crowd, or a mechanical cogwheel in an impersonal machine" (EF, 26). Whatever its ostensible basis, this rejection was only partly concerned with humanist values. Of course romanticism's announced theme centered on a correct definition of the individual (as sublime, spontaneous, unique, in touch with supernal nature, and so forth). But the primary issue was disciplinary rather than thematic. Romanticism saw that the new discourses of the city fashioned an intolerably degraded image of their recipients: whether as faceless integers in an arithmetical sum (the voters, the unemployed, the masses) or as replaceable parts in an impassive and much more important social apparatus (a clerk, a teacher, a bureaucrat).

And so romanticism decided to abandon the city. Fleeing the discursive arena, it set out for the steep and exhilarating splendors of the isolated individual. In the mountains, as T. S. Eliot has the clinging Marie exult, you feel free.[1]

But Auden did not follow the path of this romantic departure. By turning from the discursive arena, romantic poetry and its long line of inheritors did more than ensure the ascendancy of the novel for the next few centuries. It also made a contract: in return for a reduction of discursive range, it acquired a greater freedom. Obviously the types of utterance that can be assembled within the confines of the self are fewer than those available to an entire society. An individual, to *qualify* as an individual (normal, sane, decent), must carefully restrict the different roles that are permitted to constitute the self. This is readily demonstrated by the protocols that govern even a simple conversation. A rigorous decorum is enforced, with regard to topic, tone, precedence, right to interrupt, and so on. Should any of its rules be violated, they are quickly enforced: beginning with facial gestures (surprise, shock, pity); then advancing to queries, threats, reprimands; and eventually leading to ostracism and expulsion. Nor should the casualness or informality of the context be deceptive. As Auden pointed out, even the natural camaraderie of the men's smoker adheres to its own versions of decorum and is governed by exacting codes.[2] So the bargain romanticism struck was not unreasonable. In return for a reduction in discursive range, it secured, at least in theory, a greater freedom of imaginative movement.

But this hypothetical freedom was betrayed by historical factors. Although romanticism rejected the sterile formalism of its adversaries, it retained, even elevated to a fetish, the dream of a systematic totality, a unified vision that might seize all reality in its grasp. This dream of a comprehensive totality led to the irony Auden traced in his review "Heretics." Just when science seemed on the verge of absolute epistemo-

1. T. S. Eliot, *The Complete Poems and Plays* (New York: Harcourt, Brace and World, 1962), p. 37. Eliot's allusion to the Mayerling affair is often read as a commentary on European decadence. But there is no compelling reason why the poem might not be approached as a series of romantic topographies revisited in light of a modern discursive plurality.

2. The brash recruit in Ode V of *The Orators* who presumes to ask the awkward question, "Who told you all this?" is quickly shut up: "The tent-talk pauses a little till a veteran answers / 'Go to sleep, Sonny!' " (EA, 107).

logical victory, it voluntarily retreated into relativity and indeterminacy theory. So it now became the artist, in works such as Yeats's *Vision* and D. H. Lawrence's *Fantasia of the Unconscious*, who claimed to have found "the new and only science" and thus the way to a universally valid faith.[3] Yet romanticism's new and comprehensive science had to be developed within the limits of a purely individual experience. In retrospect, then, romanticism set a virtually impossible task for itself. By rejecting the corrupt diversity of the discursive arena, and then embarking upon a quest for the new totality, it asked too much of the isolated imagination. The result was the sense of sterility Auden cited in Rimbaud's *Bateau Ivre* ("Je regrette l'Europe aux ancient parapets") and Coleridge's *Rime* ("Alone, alone, all, all alone / Alone on a wide wide sea!"; both EF, 18). Even worse, the quest for totality in isolation ran the risk of merely rediscovering cultural stereotypes, the mindless replications of Ibsen's Button-Molder (EF, 149).

Certainly it is possible to disparage Auden's return to the banal discourses of the city, as inappropriate, graceless, unpoetic. But if the standard, which is to say, romantic, criteria of judgment are briefly put aside, Auden's unpoetic aberrations may be defensible in terms of a dialogic poetics. Any voice, even that of undisputed power, the Minotaur itself, offers a potential provocation for the inscriptions of the text. So if a poet is committed to exposing and disrupting the disciplines used by a range of voices, sooner or later a pilgrimage must be made to the New Jerusalem (CP, 483), the site of actual power.

What are the features of this new space, the public part of the arena, or what Malin in *The Age of Anxiety* describes as

> the polychrome Oval
> With its kleig lights and crowd engineers,
> The mutable circus where mobs rule
> The arena with roars, the real world of
> Theology and horses, our home because
> In that doubt-condemning dual kingdom
> Signs and insignia decide our cause.
>
> (CP, 362)

3. W. H. Auden, "Heretics," *New Republic* 100 (November 1, 1939): 373.

Rhetoric would begin with its speakers, their thoughts and mystifications. But from Auden's vantage, the most important factor in the public arena is the individual who refuses historical anxiety in order to join the crowd. The new entity created by this action (neither a person nor a thing) deserves a singular name: a *relict*, in the geological sense, as that which survives after a process of erosion. The relict is a human complexity reduced to a simplified image. Clearly the relict is related to the effigy, in that both involve docility and not a little cowardice. The relict is different, however, in requiring an overt act of acceptance. To become an effigy, it is necessary only to read in a familiar (sympathetic, faithful) way. Indeed to read otherwise demands an awkward dislocation of a purely natural momentum, the flow of sense. To become a relict, however, requires an explicit choice. One must decide to join the crowd, thus to fade into the gratifying oblivion of a mass reaction. After that, the rest is easy. The sullen faces on the way to the coliseum have little connection with what is committed there, for in the interim a new creation has emerged. Unlike individuals who can think, relicts simply behold. They do not distinguish one event from another, since the act of uninvolved beholding is the only task they are assigned.

> The crowd does not see (what everyone sees)
> a boxing match, a train wreck,
>
> a battleship being launched,
> does not wonder (as everyone wonders)
>
> who will win, what flag she will fly,
> how many will be burned alive,
>
> is never distracted
> (as everyone is always distracted)
>
> by a barking dog, a smell of fish,
> a mosquito on a bald head:
>
> the crowd sees only one thing
> (which only the crowd can see),
>
> an epiphany of that
> which does whatever is done.
>
> (CP, 479)

Through becoming a relict, an uncertain and anxious individual can leave the ambiguities of historical existence behind and be born again into new life, as a collective entity, a being fit to witness absolute truth (ritual death as terminal reality).

Through the too easily neglected decision of joining the crowd, then, it is possible to fashion a new Adam, modern man as a megalithic form, a posthistoric being (because its identity presupposes a departure from history). This colossus is glimpsed in "the recumbent giant" (CP, 482) at the beginning of "Vespers."[4] Usually it is composed of innumerable smaller beings, an assortment of relicts: for example, an age group ("Schoolchildren"), a statistical average ("The Unknown Citizen"), a professional elite ("The Managers"), an amalgam of unreflected beliefs ("Limbo Culture")—in short, a congeries of disparate beings that has somehow come to think of itself as a natural and organic unity ("The Chimeras"). The kinds of relict, however, share recurrent functions. In joining a group, one agrees to certain terms. Although these conditions are rarely made explicit, their effects are readily apparent, as in Auden's human abstract from "As He Is":

> Wrapped in a yielding air, beside
> The flower's soundless hunger,
> Close to the tree's clandestine tide,
> Close to the bird's high fever,
> Loud in his hope and anger,
> Erect about his skeleton,
> Stands the expressive lover,
> Stands the deliberate man.
> (EA, 217)

The relict, "the expressive lover," "the deliberate man," is matte, without texture, and entirely circumscribed. It stands as both the culmination and the rejection of a preceding history, the complex social world from which it has departed. Yet this departure does not lead to death but to

---

4. It also appears in "the white death" of "The chimneys are smoking" (EA, 116–18); "the Sugarloaf standing, an upright sentinel / Over Abergavenny" of "Here on the cropped grass" (EA, 141); the "bigger bones of a better kind" of the "Dirge" (CP, 395); and the "First Dad" of "Winds" (CP, 426).

an eerie afterlife. Before long the relict begins to move: "He picks his way, a living gun" (EA, 217). Yet the source of this movement has no origin other than the controlling voice. Like a possessed soul, the relict obediently moves to the commands of a speaker, with no direction, goal, or life of its own. So the obligations of a relict, even though they remain unspoken, are quite heavy: reduction to a restricted image, severance from a world of diverse forms, possession by an ordaining voice.

What is surrendered on one side of the communicative arc, though, is recovered on the other. Through a combination of both mystical and predatory principles, the civic voice, the figure endowed with the powers forfeited by the relicts, grows to quasi-divine proportions. For here too a wholly new being is fashioned. As a civic voice, the mere individual is metamorphosed into an avatar, "an incarnation / of *Fortitudo, Justicia, Nous*" (CP, 478). Yet this divinity is parasitic, entirely dependent on what is yielded by others, hence desperate because any other force presents an intolerable rival. A passage from "The Shield of Achilles" illustrates some of the features characteristic of this figure.

> Out of the air a voice without a face
>   Proved by statistics that some cause was just
> In tones as dry and level as the place:
>   No one was cheered and nothing was discussed;
>   Column by column in a cloud of dust
> They marched away enduring a belief
> Whose logic brought them, somewhere else, to grief.
>   (CP, 454)

The divinity should spring forth *ex nihilo*. Here the miracle of electronics makes up for the unavailability of more conventional mythic machinery (Venus from the sea-foam, Athena from the forehead of Zeus). What powers does such a being have? No one may inquire into the human peculiarity, the biases, myopias, tattered motives of this disembodied voice. No one may consider rival views, since the logic invoked is seamless, perfect within its own fullness. No one may find any tensions or frictions within the discourse, since its components are inert "statistics," devoid of inscriptive life and thus subservient to a ruling formula. And no one may presume even to agree since the capacity to respond is itself traitorous.

125

But there is a resistance to the compact between orator and audience. Something always intervenes, a third who travels between them, the textual body. No matter how enthralled the relicts, there are always interludes in which the details of a historical particularity insinuate themselves: "a barking dog, a smell of fish / a mosquito on a bald head" (CP, 479). And no matter how expert the orator, there are always quirks, twitches, almost imperceptible motions that betray an inscriptive response: "you have only to watch his mouth" (CP, 478). So the pact between voice and relict, of power conferred in exchange for admission to a collective supremacy, is threatened by the unregenerate body, perennial site in Auden of all that remains diverse, resistant, other, or, in brief, human. It is because of this threat that the defining ritual of the social arena is the public execution. This event appears, for example, in "the ungrateful stroke" of "Legend" (CP, 71); "the flesh we are but never would believe" of *Memorial for the City* (CP, 453); the "three posts driven upright in the ground" of "The Shield of Achilles" (CP, 454); "the occasion of this dying" of "Sext" (CP, 480); the "bigger bangs" of "Friday's Child" (CP, 509). The execution is not a separate affair, some isolable event that can be drawn into a theme, but a pervasive analogy. It enacts, at the level of ritual, the violence that sustains the contract between orator and audience. Its performance illustrates a collusion to subject the resistant body to a final discipline.

What does the public execution accomplish? Before the censuring gaze of an innocent multitude, the body of the condemned is reduced to spectacle, put at stake. Meanwhile the spectators, gathered into the safety of a crowd, become collective, invulnerable, and enjoy the privileges of a spiritual state: righteousness, detachment, power over life and death. Victim and spectator, body and relict are precisely if asymmetrically aligned. Through the execution, the offending body (which must be put aside to attain the beatific condition of the crowd) receives its just end, symbolically for the onlookers, literally for the condemned. As the means to a gratifying transcendence, the public execution offers its spectators the ecstasy of retribution. They simultaneously escape from and avenge themselves upon the tenacious embodiment discarded in joining the crowd. It is this retributive ecstasy that dictates the formal requirements of the execution. The body of the condemned is made apparent, held up to a merciless scrutiny (nakedness was once the rule) so that all its undivinity, its historical imperfections and foibles, can be put on display. Held in space, the resistant body is fixed, impaled, denied any other scene or context. Arrested in time, it is obliged at last to conform to a static image, the death mask. Thus as a fitting ritual, the public execution offers a capable analogy of the violence that underlies successful public speech. The audience is gathered into a disembodied collective in the grammatical sense, a subsuming name; the speaker is elevated to a quasi-divine status, an enactor of timeless justice; and the resistant body is subjected to a final discipline, the act of definition itself.

What is so easily enacted at the level of ritual, however, becomes more elusive in the realm of the text. An orator's audience is readily held in check, by intimidation, inertia, and complicity. But the text is another matter. Within each utterance, an embodying discourse comes into being, and along with it the strife inherent in language. No orator can avoid the treacherous betrayals of a syntactic gesticulation or entirely anticipate, let alone master, the inscriptions it provokes. Cold comfort, perhaps, to the victims of actual tyranny. But for poets and readers, the principle of textual resistance has real enough implications. Shortly after the Russian occupation of Czechoslovakia, when troops were brought in to stifle the dangerous freedom of the Prague Spring, Auden wrote the commemorative verses "August 1968":

> The Ogre does what ogres can,
> Deeds quite impossible for Man,
> But one prize is beyond his reach,
> The Ogre cannot master Speech.
> About a subjugated plain
> Among its desperate and slain,
> The Ogre stalks with hands on hips,
> While drivel gushes from his lips.
> (CP, 604)

Factually, this is untrue; the totalitarian state long ago mastered the codes of euphemism and disinformation. But the poem does not conduct a parody, a gesture of patriotic defiance, so much as invite an analysis. It is the accomplishment of authoritarian discourse, the very lubricity of its formations (drivel: a syntactic gesture that loses control through its

127

excessive facility, an unwitting naiveté in sophistication), that deposits *draeflein*, refuse, a betraying remnant. Like Shelley's Ozymandias, Auden's Ogre is undone by time, but through the medium of language rather than force. Eventually, given sufficient reflection and patience, the dictates of the tyrant divulge insignias of freedom and thereby become unwitting harbingers of a disruptive response. "Gushes," though an expression of contempt (effusive, the flow from an open wound), also figures as one of Auden's most positive motifs, in the emergent spring or dancing fountain:

> It is our sorrow. Shall it melt? Then water
> Would gush, flush, green these mountains and these valleys,
> And we rebuild our cities, not dream of islands.
>
> (CP, 105)

The imbalance between relict and text, the complicity of the one and the responsiveness of the other, suggests an approach to Auden's civic voices. However straightforward (virile, direct) it may seem, a public voice traces divergent arcs. One extends from speaker to recipient, and in keeping with the prohibitions of a nameless decorum, it admits only a restricted return, in extreme cases none at all. The other extends from an embodying syntax to its varied inscriptions. Here the returns are irrepressible, incalculable. This distinction makes it possible to fashion a continuum of voices according to the competence of its orators. A really adept speaker will be able to so enthrall his/her relicts with the rewards and fascinations of the first arc, the bond of a shared sense, that they will remain oblivious to the diversions of its accompanying textual play. A less skillful performer, however, will be far less successful, so that the syntactic betrayals and summoned inscriptions become more conspicuous. In actual practice this continuum begins with the minimally competent, Auden's early demagogues, and proceeds to the expert conversationalists of his later poetry.

Yet what is the standard of competence? Auden's demagogues, the speaker for a Prize Day in *The Orators*, the Vicar in *The Dog Beneath the Skin*, Herod in *For the Time Being*, are essentially vulgarizers. Crude in manner, predictable in thought, they are a dubious achievement for a poet of Auden's stature, and not merely because they speak in prose. Is there justification for so novelistic an inclusiveness, even in highly stylized form? In Auden's defense, it can be noted that vulgarity confers considerable power. It establishes not only authenticity (an achievement of the irreducible, the brute discourse of truth) but status and thus license. The vulgarizer is permitted an excess that is otherwise prohibited, because the service rendered by this individual is deemed crucial. So from the standpoint of actual practice, this role is a major bulwark of disciplinary power.

Yet where does this power originate, and what are the realistic chances of resisting it? Pursuing these questions reveals some unusual applications of poetic dialogism. Officially (mythically), the vulgarizer's license is culturally conferred. But in fact the compliance of the audience is the final source of disciplinary power. Although the required docility can be enforced, for example, by prohibiting responses, posting guards, excluding nonbelievers, no power on earth can protect an orator from the havoc of inscription. Thus in a highly repressive regime, it may be that a poetic dialogism offers political freedom one of its few remaining chances. By putting demagogues on display, Auden discloses the apparatus of disciplinary power. But in an equally practical way, he also illustrates how the resistances of the text provide a too commonly neglected source of hope.

It is easy to scoff at the speaker for a Prize Day. Inspired by one of Auden's own headmasters, this character is so impressed with the eminence of his position that he pays little attention to either his meaning or its effect on his audience.[5] "Commemoration. Commemoration. What does it mean? What does it mean? Not what does it mean to them, there, then. What does it mean to us, here, now? It's a facer, isn't it boys? But we've all got to answer it" (EA, 61). But simply dismissing

---

5. Edward Mendelson, *Early Auden* (New York: Viking, 1981), p. 98, identifies the speaker as "an old boy down for the day." Humphrey Carpenter in *W. H. Auden: A Biography* (Boston: Houghton Mifflin, 1982), p. 120, hedges his bet: "the speaker is an old boy of a public school—though his speech opens with a parody of Auden's old headmasters." Robert Medley is more precise, identifying the speaker as a parody of J. R. Eccles, headmaster at Gresham's School Holt and successor to Howson, who introduced the despised honor system discussed in Auden's "Honour: The Old School." Cf. "Gresham's School Holt" in *W. H. Auden: A Tribute*, ed. Stephen Spender (New York: Macmillan, 1975), pp. 37–38.

this speaker, although gratifying to a conviction of superiority, would be premature. Given the audience, a gathering of restless schoolboys, his tactics are shrewdly chosen. For even though openly disdainful of authority, adolescents are notoriously eager for an authoritarian regimen.[6] The speaker's apparent self-ridicule (at the end he bolts off stage to catch a train) satisfies this desire by performing a sacrificial part. His discourse shunts onto its persona any suspicion or animosity that might otherwise be directed toward its disciplines. Thus the speaker for a Prize Day, by repudiating himself as ridiculous and expendable, effectively clears a space in which the disciplines can do their work. Few of his comments are likely to be heeded or even remembered. Yet that is not his aim. Repressive disciplines are most effective when enacted as functions, relations of power that can readily migrate from discourse to discourse, yet are not themselves easily reducible to a theme. The speaker for a Prize Day, then, is less interested in commemorating past greatness than in implementing a structure of efficient authority.

The operative technique of that authority is familiar. "Imagine to yourselves a picked body of angels, all qualified experts on the human heart, a Divine Commission, arriving suddenly one day at Dover" (EA, 61). This suggests both threat and promise. The sudden arrival of a judgmental force is balanced by the prospect of joining its mission. Should the audience go along, they will be inducted into a spiritual elite, a disembodied cadre undistracted by the compromises of history. But this elite requires a mission, which is easily arranged since the world is very sick. "What do you think about England, this country of ours where nobody is well?" (EA, 62). Cribbing a passage from Dante's *Purgatorio xvii*, the speaker offers an anatomy of the damned, those who must be brought into conformity with conveniently vague norms, or expelled. In this way, the Prize Day address efficiently creates a well-defined group, its faithful relics. At the same time, it pretends that the source of the speaker's authority lies elsewhere: in another field, a book of which only the older boys have heard, and which no one has read. Thus in a brief space the familiar apparatus of execution is put into place.

6. Auden commented on the dangers of youthful conservatism in "The Group Movement and the Middle Classes," *Oxford and the Groups*, ed. R. H. S. Crosman (Oxford: Basil Blackwell, 1934), pp. 89–101. He also considered the topic in a more comic vein in Ode IV of *The Orators*.

There is a spiritually authorized voice and a disembodied collective. All that is further required is a victim. Although the speaker himself may be rightly regarded as a buffoon, the disciplines he operates are quite effective.

Is there any warrant for a dissident sequel? Toward the end the speaker, apparently for the first time, looks at his audience: "Are you just drifting or thinking of flight?" (EA, 64). The candor is deceptive in that it interjects the subversive possibility of a "drifting" through which the textures of a word ripple and eddy, in a dizzying moiré effect. Momentarily disoriented, he grows belligerent. "Need I remind you that you are no longer living in Ancient Egypt? Time's getting on and I must hurry or I shall miss my train. You've got some pretty stiff changes to make. We simply can't afford any passengers or skrimshankers. I should like to see you make a beginning before I go, now, here" (EA, 64). The syntactic fibrillation warns of imminent danger. Each phrase has ample energy, yet there is little coordinated movement. As an ensemble of gestures, the passage is spasmodic. It portends an imminent terror, a need to lash out—but at what? The supposed misfits are only scapegoats. Timid nonconformists, they present little threat and are quite happy simply to be left alone.[7] Hence the required victim must be sought elsewhere: in a vertiginous drift that the speaker cannot prevent, for he is about to leave the textual scene and thus surrender its destiny to the feeble protection afforded by an imputed voice. Soon he will be offstage and out of hearing range. With luck, his remarks will be parodied and forgotten, so that their subtler disciplines may continue to work. Still, there is always the danger that a few of the skrimshankers (darting cripples) may linger in the vicinity of the emptied text and wander through it as an archaeological site, treacherous, bizarre, an opened tomb. It is this fear that induces such strong syntactic tremors.

7. Auden's early attempt to rattle a school matron, "I like to see the various types of boys" (EA, 192), eventually grew into a fondness for typology. A passage from *The Prolific and the Devourer*, which divides students into the political, apolitical, and antipolitical, helps to gloss the nonconformists singled out by the speaker for a Prize Day: "The apolitical is one whose interests are not those of the State but do not clash with them, which usually means that they have nothing to do with people. Perhaps he is a photographer or a bird-watcher or a radio mechanic. As he is only anxious to be let alone, he performs his social duties well enough to keep out of trouble, and climbs slowly to a position of obscure security" (EA, 399).

The anguish of an orator: whereas it is possible to exercise considerable control over an actual audience, it is quite impossible to regulate the inscriptions of the text. The pressure of this asymmetry accounts for the tendency of Auden's orators to become increasingly hysterical. Where might the drift of a vacated text lead?

No doubt the proudest achievement of the speaker for a Prize Day is his Dantean typology, with its inventory of the four depravities: excessive love of self, excessive love of others, defective love, perversion. The typology itself is both irreversible and degenerative. To proceed through it is to descend a ladder of wickedness, once and for all. But after the guiding voice has departed, there is nothing to prevent a further tracing of the typology's inscriptions and a reaccenting of its inscriptions into tales of imaginative venture. The excessive lovers, for example, "famous readers," cross a range of genres (histories, romances, detective novels) whose diversity subverts the intransigence of any presiding or limiting center. Like "the voice, of the announcer, maybe, from some foreign broadcasting station they can never identify" (EA, 62), the text begins to acquire dubious, perhaps mistaken origins. The miscreants of the next group, the excessive lovers of neighbor, risk an extravagant insight. "Have you never noticed in them the gradual abdication of central in favor of peripheral control? What if the tiniest stimulus should provoke the full, the shattering response, not just then but all the time?" (EA, 63). An insignificant detail can summon an array of dissonant inscriptions. Thereafter, the adventures of reading might continue without end. Following such ecstacy is disillusionment, of course, the discovery that not just a few but all of a culture's natural meanings are produced by specific contrivances: "Old tracts, brackets picked up on the road, powders, pieces of wood, uncatalogued . . ." (EA, 63). Yet even this is an incipient disruption, for beyond the discovery of the semantic junkyard lies a further project, "last and worst, the perverted lovers" (EA, 63), of those who seize upon the panoply of revealed structures to interpolate discourses, stage dialogues, invite taboo liaisons that defy natural laws. The puzzling line used to describe them—"In some a simple geometrical figure can arouse all the manifestations of extreme alarm" (EA, 63)—is glossed later in the Airman's Journal as *A Sure Test* (EA, 74), where such diagrams are used to distinguish between the normal, who trace regularities, and the demented, who track insidious asymmetries and imbalances.

The disciplines used by a public voice suggest an odd parity. The more power a speaker holds over an audience, the more resistance is offered by the accompanying text. According to this rule, a particularly repressive voice, for example, that of a charismatic demagogue, would be likely to induce the most vigorous dialogic resistance. Even though nothing might be done at the time, the relicts of such a discourse could still await the moment when its neglected inscriptions would begin their return. In his sermon "On Bolshevism and the Devil," for example, the Vicar in *The Dog Beneath the Skin* enjoys powers any orator might envy. A minor parish dignitary, he can assume the approval of the community. An ad hoc chaplain, he can claim an officer's right to give orders. A prelate, he can draw on the institutional credit of a church. A voice from the pulpit, he can serve as the privileged conduit, the awful intermediary of the Almighty itself. Furthermore, because of the dramatic setting, a rousing speech to the "Lads of Pressan" who are mobilizing for war, the Vicar can be assured his audience will readily accept these assembled authorities. What else are conscripts, forbidden to dissent and unable to escape, likely to do? Their realistic choices are either to accept the Vicar's claims, and think of themselves as heroes fighting in a noble cause, or to reject his remarks, and regard themselves as exploited dupes.[8] Given the highly reliable desire for self-esteem, the Vicar reckons that acceptance is more probable. The soldiers are only too eager to be inducted into a spiritual elite, "God's cause" (EA, 141), a condition whose moral righteousness is proof against the mere weapons of their foes. A taint of mortality, the awkward vulnerabilities of a historical body, still clings to them. But warfare provides a perfect opportunity to shift the nuisance of embodiment onto the enemy, who can be subjected to a fatal reification: "They shall be trapped by the stalks of flowers. Sheep shall chase them away. Useless for them to imitate natural objects: a boulder or a tree. Even the spade-handed moles shall declare their folly!" (EA, 141). In this version of the public execution, it is the enemy who become the bearers of a despised embodiment.

Yet even with such disciplinary power at its disposal, the Vicar's discourse suffers from a curious affliction. To justify the current struggle,

8. Cf. the lot of the conscript in *Sonnets from China:* "Far from a cultural center he was used: / Abandoned by his general and his lice" (CP, 154).

that is, to conceal its character as a trade war (it is announced after the sermon that Miss Iris Crewe, the patroness, is engaged to a well-known munitions manufacturer), the Vicar casts the war in terms of a moral absolutism: as an extension of the ancient struggle between evil and good. Because good must be accorded the greater status, it has to be portrayed as existing first, according to the venerable formula of diegesis: priority establishes authenticity. To exemplify this priority, the Vicar gives a thumbnail sketch of prelapsarian bliss.

> So, on this inconceivably more catastrophic occasion, no door banged, no dog barked. There was no alarm of any kind. But consider its importance! No judge's sentence had yet been passed. Basedow's Disease had not occurred. Love. Joy. Peace. God. No words but these. No population but angels. And after . . . the whole lexicon of sin: the sullen proletariat of hell! (EA, 139)

But the bliss betrays a singular impotence. In the Vicar's paradisaical realm of utter completion, syntax becomes impossible. With no gap between subject and predicate, since each already contains the other, there can be nothing to say. As if in a blinding light of perfected being, distance and difference are washed out, so that the syntactic body is immobilized in a deathlike trance, a virtual impotence. It cannot pierce the rim of fullness that encloses its members, and if it could, there is nowhere to go. Each word, as a simultaneous fulfillment of a wordless perfection, resonates in perfect harmony with every other. The attainment of such vagueness is the usual goal of reactionaries and charlatans, because it makes any meaning at once promiscuous and rescindable. Yet its condition of primordial impotence is difficult to sustain. Even as he speaks, the Vicar leaves paradise for the maze of history, as his discourse strays into the defiles of predication. Across the gap of an ellipsis, an entranced perfection is transformed into a resentful host, and a numbing tautology plunges into the amazing articulations of an overcrowded, treacherous word trove.

The momentary paralysis of the syntactic body begets a crisis for the Vicar, for it occurs in a crucial passage, a scene of mythic origins. If the beginning witnesses a collapse into a signifier that remains entranced with itself, the Vicar is left in a sorry plight. Either the expulsion from that undifferentiated trance is an awakening, the real creation; or the origin, in order to account for the diversity of the ensuing creation, must have a different character. As if captivated by his own predicament, the Vicar begins by resolving the issue.

> What was the weather on Eternity's worst day? And where was that Son of God during the fatal second: pausing before a mirror in an anteroom, or in the Supreme Presence Itself, in the middle of an awful crescendo of praise, or again, withdrawn apart, regarding pensively the unspeakable beauties of the heavenly landscape? (EA, 138)

As a man of God, the Vicar stands on an ultimate revelation. But his concern for origins frames the tacit question, Whence comes this revelation? Insofar as he does not claim to be the recipient of special illuminings, the Vicar relies on the Bible. As he illustrates, though, the Bible is a text. It is crisscrossed with riddles and opacities, as well as with what a semiotician would call ghost chapters: details or incidents whose gaps invite the generation of a further text.[9] To bridge these gaps and thus secure the hermetic seal of revelation, it is necessary to interject later and quite unbiblical discourses, as here, concerning the physics of refraction, angelic musicology, or the mimetic conventions of heavenly landscapes. So at the same time that he claims an anecdotal priority, the natural vantage of the storyteller who always manages to be there *in advance*, the Vicar disperses the basis of his authority across the devious instabilities of a text. He prescinds, like all power, from a textual genealogy. Hence he stands upon a revelation whose gaps devolve into a array of discourses and eventually into a dialogic conflict of codes.

This surreptitious betrayal may have some bearing on the Vicar's closing gestures. As the stage directions specify: "The final passage is wailed rather than spoken. Tears pour down his cheeks, saliva runs from his mouth: He has worked himself up into an hysterical frenzy" (Dog, 162).[10] Although this works as satiric relief, serving to undercut a religious hypocrite, it also plays into a poetic dialogism. The stage directions

9. Umberto Eco, *The Role of the Reader* (Bloomington: Indiana University Press, 1979).

10. W. H. Auden and C. Isherwood, *The Dog Beneath the Skin* (London: Faber and Faber, 1968), p. 162.

transform into visual terms the analysis that is more subtly enacted in the syntax. At the same moment when the Vicar reaches dramatic impotence, an inability to speak that rehearses the earlier paradisaical bliss, he succumbs to hysteria: a helplessness before incalculable, invasive forces.

Although Auden's public personae may suggest crudeness at the stylistic level of theme and ethos, their disciplinary tactics can be quite refined. This is certainly the case with Herod in "The Massacre of the Innocents" from *For the Time Being*. Unlike his medieval predecessors, Auden's character is not a raging tyrant but, as tetrarch, the equivalent of a minor bureaucrat, efficient, prudent, and, after his fashion, fair. Unfortunately, the rash Wise Men have just announced a divine birth, a savior come to redeem humankind, which leaves Herod with a dilemma: he can do nothing and run the risk of a demagogue-inspired uprising (which will cost many lives when the Romans decide to suppress it, and probably his throne as well); or he can show leadership, nip trouble in the bud, and be remembered as a merciless butcher. A good administrator, Herod knows he must do the practical thing: "Why is it that in the end civilization always has to call in these professional tidiers to whom it is all one whether it be Pythagoras or a homicidal lunatic that they are instructed to exterminate?" (CP, 303). But even if he can bully the present, there is still the regarding future, so the dilemma remains. Accordingly, Herod's disciplinary tactics must be ingenious. His remarks are a soliloquy, the comments of a man officially alone and speaking to himself. Yet his discourse is cast in the form of a public address, the speech of a political incumbent to the grateful multitude. In a stage performance, "The Massacre of the Innocents" should produce a sense of unnerving disorientation. The audience, expecting to play the usual role of eavesdroppers and voyeurs, find themselves accosted by a direct address that breaks through the stage's invisible fourth wall and yet refuses to admit it is doing so. What is the advantage of this? Uncertain of his reception, Herod splits his recipients into two entities, inner conscience (himself) and later historians (the audience). Because both are not only equally possible but equally obvious, the discourse shuttles between inner and outer, present and future, recipients. It thereby attempts to impress each with the imputed assent of the other. For example, to those who take the soliloquy as an intimate self-address, the question naturally arises, Would a man so lie to himself? But to those who detect the public nature of the discourse, the question becomes, Would a man so attempt to deceive history? Through this tactical shuttle between recipients, then, Herod secures from the relict imputed to each an assent he could otherwise attain from neither.

This ingenious shuttling between recipients demands certain adjustments in rhetorical form. Herod begins in approved meditative fashion by asking the question one is *supposed* to ask, when alone and burdened with a hard choice: Whence have I come? The query itself connotes authenticity; it is allowed only at moments of unguarded candor. Yet Herod casts his reply in a public genre, the carefully prepared acknowledgments of a prizewinner at some imaginary awards ceremony (Tetrarch of the Year). He thanks Fortune, for having fated him to escape assassination, his father for indulging his love of travel, his mother for a straight nose, and so on. This odd arrangement of genres, a discourse of utter authenticity to enframe a discourse of comic clichés, recasts Herod's decision to massacre the innocents so that it becomes commonplace and praiseworthy. At an awards ceremony, the audience has already conferred its approval. The occasion is not a ritual of judgment but of confirmation: the previously approved is recognized for having been attained. In this way, Herod's discursive framework transfers responsibility from himself to an undefined cultural mandate, which has designated his deed as a universally recognized good. Attention is thus shifted from the spotted motivations of an individual, to an invincible collective will. The historical fact of the massacre conveniently drops out of sight. Its beginnings are absorbed into an inaccessible social force, a consensus; and its effects are dissolved into a precondition for something else, the awarding of a prize. Herod effectively disqualifies the issue of personal responsibility.

What can resist such tactical skill? Certainly not the infants whose name registers their historical fate, as not-speaking, forbidden access to language. Because he so adroitly blocks the means of dissent, Herod's soliloquy suggests a limit-case, an extreme challenge to the disruptive capacities of the text. Once past the perils of his prologue, he confidently launches into self-praise.

And what, after all, is the whole Empire, with its few thousand square miles on which it is possible to lead the Rational Life, but a tiny patch

of light compared with those immense areas of barbaric night that surround it on all sides, that incoherent wilderness of rage and terror, where
Mongolian idiots are regarded as sacred and mothers who give birth to
twins are instantly put to death, where malaria is treated by yelling,
where warriors of superb courage obey the commands of hysterical female
impersonators, where the best cuts of meat are reserved for the dead,
where, if a white blackbird has been seen, no more work may be done
that day, where it is firmly believed that the world was created by a giant
with three heads or that the motions of the stars are controlled from the
liver of a rogue elephant? (CP, 302)

This serves Herod's parodic intent, with its heavily weighted contrast
between the "patch of light," that is, what falls within the range of his
voice, and the "immense areas of barbaric night." That contrast requires
a distinct hierarchy, of self-contained reason (The System) over supersti-
tious barbarianism: though encircled, the forces of reason serenely retain
a greater simplicity and adequacy. But the syntactic body details a different movement. In the company of barbaric discourses, it becomes impassioned, incontinent. The anaphora of successive where's, whatever its
intention, suggests fascination. Vivid, textured, energetic, the barbaric
discourses have an irresistible allure. What is worse, because of this allure
they begin to be recognizable, feasible alternatives with a coherent world
of their own: complete with icons, rhetorics, dietetics, labor laws, cosmogony, physics. Not that the text espouses any kind of primitivism.
Its rapt fascination only insists that Herod's version of reason must take
its place in the discursive arena, as one among many competitors. In that
case, his announced rational superiority must yield to a further exchange,
a dialogism across discursive lines. It might then emerge from this exchange that the radically opposed adversaries, reason/barbarism, are not
so unevenly matched.[11] A system that murders the mother for having
twins must strain to assert its advantages over one that committed geno-
cide in hope of slaying an infant who *potentially* threatened civil order
(there is the chance that no one would believe the Wise Men or that

11. Cf. one of the "Shorts" from 1940: "The Champion smiles—What Person-
ality! / The Challenger scowls—How horrid he must be! / But let the Belt change hands
and they change places, / Still from the same old corners come the same grimaces" (CP,
233).

people would think the whole thing a hoax). But the important issue is that the exchange itself, provoked by the energies of repression, is already under way. Is that enough? Outrage against Herod would no doubt be more gratifying. It promises the clear superiority of an objective vision and implies that decent folk would never do such a thing. But in an imperfect and cunningly self-deceptive world, the text must often settle for less.

Demagogues are by no means the only, or even the most dangerous, civic voices of Auden. There are also more genteel tyrants who exercise their "old right to abuse" (EA, 26). In the salons and offices, on the avenues of the discursive arena, the tones must shift, the strategies modulate. Lacking the official sanction of rostrum or pulpit, hence the loss of such convenient instruments as ostracism and the police, an ordinary voice must become mild, affable, gracious. Without the direct command of executive force, a civic voice must nonetheless be able to tap the source of such power, the consensus of a group. This necessity requires adaptation. An ordinary voice is not without a repertoire of disciplinary techniques, many of them developed and perfected within the poetic tradition. But the successful use of these disciplines requires an adjustment of scale, a prudent moderation that calculates the limits of what an audience is likely to bear. And that adjustment, in turn, relies on a flawless equanimity that makes it possible for a speaker to concentrate on too easily straying relicts. It is not always the case in Auden's poetry that this adjustment of scale and assured self-possession are adequately conducted. Some poems deliberately model off-register efforts, in the printer's sense: an incorrect alignment of components. They show not the performance of an accomplished voice but the trial efforts of what may later become one. Still, the ludic, as opposed to expressive, function of such works should not be undervalued. These poems do not, as in the narratives of an intention-based criticism, show a youthful "Auden" testing his talents in an effort to find an authentic voice.[12] Rather, they eavesdrop on the disciplinarian's workshop. Through their deliberately

---

12. Christopher Isherwood has been an influential proponent of the view that Auden began as a precocious but largely derivative technician who had little to say. "Some Notes on Auden's Early Poetry," *New Verse* 26–27 (November 1937): 4–8. See also his *Exhumations* (London: Methuen, 1966).

off-register arrangements, they gain access to a scene of production, the tactician's stithy where disciplines are forged into meanings and truths.

The rhetorical oddities of "Consider" (EA, 47) illustrate this deliberate misalignment quite well. Its voice is that of an aspiring Hyde Park orator, inexperienced as a public speaker though well-versed in visionary conventions (perhaps an avid reader of Yeats, or the later Lawrence). An earlier version of the poem contained an address to specific individuals, as if the orator were singling out passersby: the "Financier," those who belong to "College Quad or Cathedral Close" (EA, 47). But Auden eventually dropped this section, so that the poem's audience became more generic, a universal image of humanity. The revision suggests that the speaker is portrayed as having an inadequate sense of the role into which he must cast his prospective relicts, which is why he cannot define them more precisely. The likely source of the problem is that he is too preoccupied with his own anxieties to devote sufficient attention to the audience. As is characteristic of many of Auden's early works, the tone of "Consider" is equivocal. It suggests the opportunism of someone who aspires to be a literary artist, but who finds the resistances of the text too unruly and so turns to what seems an easier project, the domination of others.[13] This opportunism accounts for the equivocal tone, which implies the speaker's skepticism about his visionary claims yet also an indignant expectation that the passersby must accept them.

The interplay of these opposed accents is one of the most fascinating aspects of "Consider," as in the following passage which warns of a cosmic terror about to unleash its wrath.

> Then, ready, start your rumor, soft
> But horrifying in its capacity to disgust
> Which, spreading magnified, shall come to be
> A polar peril, a prodigious alarm,
> Scattering the people, as torn-up paper

13. Some of the most incisive passages in *The Prolific and the Devourer* comment on this familiar and highly encouraged evasion, in which a writer turns from the exchanges of the text and becomes politically involved, relevant: "He who undertakes anything, thinking he is doing it out of a sense of duty, is deceiving himself and will ruin everything he touches. You cannot give unless you also receive. What is it you hope to receive from politics? excitement? experience? Be honest" (EA, 403).

Rags and utensils in a sudden gust,
Seized with immeasurable neurotic dread.
(EA, 46–47)

The rhetorical rhythms are capably marshaled here, first recoiling as if
to gather strength, then expanding in vigorous and climactic phrases. But
the imagery suggests another attitude. The destructive power begins as
a sly innuendo, an oscitant member "soft / But horrifying" in its disgust-
ing frankness. It then commences to enlarge (though the "magnified"
smirkingly hints that this enlargement may be the result of an onlooker's
obsession: the fixation that makes whatever it beholds seem bigger), until
soon it threatens to engulf the entire globe, "a polar peril," a world-
destroying force.[14] No sooner does this distended immensity emerge,
however, than it explodes in "a prodigious alarm" and worse, leaves
behind "a sudden gust" whose withering miasma scatters the onlookers.
So the speaker combines pedantry with ridicule (of himself, his discourse,
his relicts) by using renaissance physiology, which attributed erections
to an influx of air, to recall passages such as Spenser's seriocomic battle
between Red Cross and Orgoglio. Such schoolboy pranks interestingly
complicate the tone. But they also mark the text as an off-register performance. Knowledgeable, talented, but inexperienced and unfocused, the
tyro employs miscalculations that serve to expose disciplinary mechanisms in a way that more accomplished performances might not.

His best technique is the device of synoptic authority. As commentators have noted, the poem begins with the wide-angle perspective that
Auden later attributed to Hardy's influence.[15]

Consider this and in our time
As the hawk sees it or the helmeted airman:
The clouds rift suddenly—look there

---

14. The orator links two familiar motifs from the early poetry. The first motif is a
visual fixation: "World-wonder hardened as bigness" (EA, 21); "the mountain heights
he remembers get bigger and bigger" (EA, 61). The second, the nightmare of a world-
destroying phallus: "Rise with the wind, my great big serpent" (EA, 56); "but, as the
huge deformed head rears to kill" (CP, 286).

15. W. H. Auden, "A Literary Transference," *Southern Review* 6 (Summer 1940):
78.

> At cigarette-end smoldering on a border
> At the first garden party of the year.
>
> (EA, 46)

But a more apt comparison might be drawn with some of Yeats's poems, for example, "An Irish Airman Foresees His Death" and "The Second Coming." Whereas Hardy uses distance to render the inertial quality of a scene, its sullen permanence, in Yeats distance serves a revelatory function: it achieves a comprehensiveness which in turn leads to further, even more shocking mystery. As a mimicry of this Yeatsian technique, the visual perspective of "Consider" begins with the natural flight of a bird, shifts to the compound vision of a classical-modern warrior (the "helmeted" is both archaic and contemporary), penetrates a sudden opening in the clouds, and then triumphantly alights upon a suitably sinister symbol. This synoptic device confers considerable power with minimal expense. It does not require the relicts to do anything other than passively witness a scene. Because this is such a familiar demand, it is barely noticeable that in assenting to it the audience is inducted into a disembodied (gravityless) elite, a winged, predatory force. And through the same transaction, their speaker-guide becomes perhaps the closest approximation of divinity in a scientific age, a neutral and aloof observer. Like his relicts, he merely beholds (sight being the most objective, reliable sense), though with the modest difference that he also fashions a narrative. Thus by exploiting a common bias about the cognitive immediacy of sight, the orator positions himself, as a good visionary must, to reveal some grand Mystery.

But the passersby pay little heed. Perhaps it is late, or raining, or they hear a more adept voice on another corner. It is this almost palpable rejection that shapes the poem's development. The aspiring orator, infuriated, turns away from the moronic multitude and addresses the apocalyptic force itself: "Long ago, supreme Antagonist, / More powerful than the great northern whale" (EA, 46). The technique is commonly used by Auden's early orators, who often try to recapture the attention of a wayward audience by launching into an apostrophe to a more august being. Quite likely, the speaker had planned to present the Antagonist in a positive light, as an obliterator of regressive forms, hence an ally of the orator and his faithful little band. He insists that the Antagonist is not equivalent to Leviathan, the unregenerate social beast. But because the audience has failed to rally around the speaker's voice, they must then become the Antagonist's victims. In this way, what had been planned as a visionary paean is forced by circumstances to become a threat. But who is at risk from the Antagonist? As the speaker indicates, this mysterious figure works through a discursive medium ("Your comments on the highborn mining-captains," "You talk to your admirers," "interrupting / The leisurely conversation," "Summon / Those handsome and diseased youngsters") as a highly contagious "rumor" (EA, 47). Yet the only voice that actually speaks in the poem is that of the orator. By inference, then, the disruptions of the irresistible Antagonist must occur within that voice, as a neglected accompaniment, a hooded shadow to the speaker's accents.

If the Antagonist intimates an illicit dissent, waiting its chance, then opportunity presents itself in the impassioned finale:

> You cannot be away, then, no
> Not though you pack to leave within an hour,
> Escaping humming down arterial roads:
> The date was yours; the prey to fugues,
> Irregular breathing and alternate ascendancies
> After some haunted migratory years
> To disintegrate on an instant in the explosion of mania
> Or lapse for ever into a classic fatigue.
>
> (EA, 47)

Perhaps inspired by Yeats's example in *A Vision*, the orator draws upon a suitably arcane source, McDougall's *Abnormal Psychology*, for the technical terms of his revelation. But these awkward borrowings upset the syntax by afflicting it with unsightly patches and forcing it to pause and marvel at such curious textures. Within this interlude, a mere moment, the doubts and resistances that were evaded when the speaker turned to the public forum have a chance to reassert themselves through the mottled terms furnished by his discursive theft. Despite even accomplished disciplines, the voice cannot elude the humming of inscriptions, inescapable as the sound of a frightened man's pulse pounding down "arterial roads." That sound eventually unleashes the tumult of "fugues," orches-

143

trated extravagances of tentative meanings, and permits the disruption of "alternate ascendancies," rival discourses emerging within the tones of a dominant voice. To a would-be authoritarian, this tumult leads to contrasting terrors of "mania," a chaos of warring voices, or "a classic fatigue," an eventual recuperation of some victorious albeit exhausted discourse. But the inscriptive tumult of the Antagonist also intimates a further possibility, of "haunted migratory years," a journey through the discursive arena that recognizes its obsessive spirits yet rejects their sacred status.

The passage from disciplinary repertoire to rhetorical performance is not always so helpfully off-register. When certain Auden poems are read in sequence, they leave the impression of considering the same speaker but at different stages of expertise. The casual persona of "Watch any day his nonchalant pauses" (EA, 31), for example, could well be a later and more adept version of the failed visionary of "Consider."

> Watch any day his nonchalant pauses, see
> His dexterous handling of a wrap as he
> Steps after into cars, the beggar's envy.
>
> 'There is a free one,' many say, but err.
>
> (EA, 31)

What lessons have been learned? The ineffectual generality of "Consider," its address to a universal humanity, is replaced with a precise social hierarchy. The speaker classifies humankind into privileged hypocrites (the pauser); abject retainers (mistress, "his dexterous handling of a wrap," and chauffeur, "steps after into cars"); resentful outcasts ("the beggar's envy"); mindless herd ("many say, but err"); and, of course, the discerning elite of those who heed the speaker's voice. This act of classification is not innocent, for it operates a system of punishments and rewards. Those who assent to the speaker's views are inducted into a voyeuristic kinship, as the line of the disembodied who can see and yet not be seen. Those who ignore or reject the speaker, however, are relegated to one of the other categories and thus established as satiric targets. The discipline of classification is effective because it operates *by default*, without calling attention to itself. Anyone who dissents is unobstrusively, automatically numbered among the parodically embodied.

As for the speaker, he has clearly mastered the art of an ascetic insinuation. By becoming transparent himself, inconspicuous as a persona, he is able to serve as the faithful voice of an audience's prejudices. A modest onlooker, he divests himself of personal attitudes and beliefs to become the unexceptionable reflection of what is generally known and accepted. Of course this modesty is a ruse, combining deceit with dominance. It enables a voice to enter the imagination of an audience and, through the pretense of selfless subservience, assign it a restrictive part, the role of a relict. It also permits an ideal setting for irony in that the speaker can ridicule other discourses without having to incur a position of his own. His discourse is permitted to remain immaterial, anonymous in its deliverance of the truth. Nonetheless, the irony exercises restraint, for example, in its dismissal of unreflective opinion: "He is not that returning conqueror, / Nor ever the poles' circumnavigator" (EA, 31). "Returning conqueror" borrows a phrase from schoolboy discourse (the trot of some Latin text) which is then made even more ridiculous through the emptily portentous "that." "Poles' circumnavigator" is derived from the same schoolboy lexicon, perhaps a stilted history of Renaissance exploration. In both instances the discourse imputed to the majority is cleverly marked, as imposed, formulaic, piously dated, irrelevant. Yet because of his ascetic insinuation, the speaker need accept no such compromises for himself. His origin is simply "the song," a melody so perfect it can only be imputed, not heard or played. The disciplinary rule at work here is that if a discourse can be successfully assigned to an attending relict, with no further ado it eludes its own historical involvement so as to become pure movement, lyrical immediacy. The song is nothing describable or even discernible in itself. It is simply the successful coordination of other elements (beat, rhythm, harmony), and thus it furnishes an apt image for a disembodied language, remote, entrancing, pure.

Given such accomplished mastery, even on a reduced scale (though for Auden's ordinary voices a reduced scale is often the precondition of their mastery), it is difficult to maintain restraint. Yet the speaker of these modest verses is so expert that he manages to displace his exultation into a discreet stylistic exuberance. Virtually nothing in "Watch any day

145

his nonchalant pauses" is stated just once. Rather, the line keeps turning into itself, as if determined to get matters right:

> But poised between shocking falls, on razor-edge
> Has taught himself this balancing subterfuge
> Of the accosting profile, the erect carriage.
>
> The song, the varied action of the blood
> Would drown the warning from the iron wood,
> Would cancel the inertia of the buried:
>
> Travelling by daylight on from house to house
> The longest way to the intrinsic peace,
> With love's fidelity and with love's weakness.
>
> (EA, 31–32)

The persistence of repetition (poised/balancing; accosting profile/erect carriage; song/varied action; warning/inertia; travelling . . . on/longest way; house to house/intrinsic peace) is stylistically coded. It suggests concern for the audience, lest anything be concealed or deleted. It also signals a mistrust of the subject matter, because of its treacherous motility which must be fixed. Together, these connotations of concern and wariness offer a sufficient blind for a less admissible nuance, the speaker's thrill at a mastery so complete it can anticipate, encompass *in advance* any possible dissent.

But dissent proceeds from the inevitable gestures of the discourse. What seems prudent in regard to the relicts can have a different bearing on the text. The syntactic gestures accompanying the repetitions suggest not mastery but anemia. The movement is rhythmic enough, but its predications hesitate, doubt themselves, fall short, and then return to their task with no more conviction than before. The resulting effect suggests not so much precision as enfeeblement. The repetitions neither continue nor even modify one another, but devalue themselves as inadequate installments, so that the text indicates both weariness and restlessness. The gesture seems eager to discard a detritus, all that it has, yet for which it has no use. Within the economy of the text, however, nothing is wasted. What is written remains indelible, inscribed, so that the anemia only grows more acute as its castings mount. Gradually, with no presiding voice to supervise their movements, the deserted repetitions wander, stray into conflict. Rather than establishing a triumphant sameness, they engender responsive frictions. Through this growing dissidence, the song divulges an assembly of discrete elements, a variable and tenuous circulation, which admits of reckless accents. Its perfect poise rests upon "this balancing subterfuge," a devious flight beneath, in which an assumed support trickles away. Even its easy achievement of "the intrinsic peace" is steadfastly deferred: to the end of an interminable journey whose "longest way" never encounters anything more than peculiar structures, disparate locales, "from house to house."

In keeping with the ritual of a public execution, Auden's civic voices require a victim: a body of the condemned to receive and thus annul the anxiety denied by both the speaker in becoming a quasi-divine force, and the audience in becoming an abstracted relict.

> For without a cement of blood (it must be human, it must be innocent)
> no secular wall will safely stand.
>
> (CP, 484)

But is the victim necessarily a person? A civic voice contends with a divided resistance, an audience, of course, but also a text. Of the two, the text is the more formidable. Individuals are readily held in check by an ample array of disciplines, ranging from crude threats to subtler coercions. So the capacity to respond to a discourse (that is, to engage its productive machinations, not merely its argumentative themes) is in most instances easily restricted. Yet little can be done either to anticipate or disarm the inscriptions inherent within a text. Hence an undiscovered aspect of poetic justice. Although imposing the most repressive disciplines, an authoritative voice must also embark on a penitential journey, across dissident inscriptions. Eventually, though, a civic voice is likely to emerge that is shrewd enough to put its adversaries in the balance, the audience and the text, and to engage the more dangerous force.

That shrewdness characterizes a distinct group of Auden's personae, which might be called his neo-Luddite collection. These voices direct their attention to structures rather than persons: "The Maze," "The Shield of Achilles," "Et in Arcadia Ego," "The Maker," "Fairground," "Moon Landing," "Progress?" In such works the target is a cultural device, something human beings have made yet can no longer control. These personae appear more frequently in the later poems. Thus, in keeping with the logic that Auden's voices become increasingly adept, their disciplinary strategies are complex. They draw upon a familiar bias, the self-evident superiority of persons (autonomous, unique, free) to mechanisms (contrived, repeatable, determined). Although accurate in its limited way, this bias is then fashioned into a questionable enthymeme: since persons are superior to mechanisms, it is assumed that speakers and their audiences must be superior to textual structures. The unobtrusive slide, from machines to discursive functions, is clearly false. The structures of the text resemble mechanisms only by way of figural necessity, the need to find an available image. In practice, textual structures are diverse, in conflict, and evolving. So it is deceptive to set up a contrast between "persons" and "structures," because it is the textual aspect of structures, their plural and transformative quality, that lends persons a distinctive and unpredictable character. Nonetheless, Auden's neo-Luddite voices exploit the enthymeme not to restrict the text (for that is impossible) but to supply a dummy target, an image of its dissidence, over which they may then pronounce a triumph. The victory is Pyrrhic, since its cost is the production of a further text, and short-lived; though if winning a little time can induce a neglect of inscribed responses, it may be all a speaker needs.

The cynical onlooker of "Fleet Visit" offers a good example of neo-Luddite tactics. The scene overlooks a harbor, perhaps the Bay of Naples, where an American task force has just arrived. The conspicuously poetic setting poses the implicit question, How is it possible to write public verse in a modern world that offers so few appropriate subjects?[16] The speaker, though, does not wish to resolve the problem but to exploit it. Through ironic references to *The Iliad* (the sailors come ashore from "hollow ships" and are more interested in comics and baseball than "fifty Troys"; CP, 420), the first stanza expands the poet's predicament to a general condition of resentment: the modern world forces not just writers but everyone else to occupy a degraded, untransformable scene.

16. The question is taken up in "The Poet and the City," under the heading "four aspects of our present *Weltanschaung* which have made an artistic vocation more difficult than it used to be" (DH, 78). Significantly, Auden casts the issue not in terms of lost themes but in terms of severed ties between writers and readers.

To sustain this resentment, the speaker draws a contrast between a heroic world of epic combat and the cold war, a high-tech waiting game whose anonymous threat of universal catastrophe can be reported in the dullest journalistic prose. Against a backdrop of lapsed greatness, the ships of the naval fleet come to serve as a handy synecdoche, a poetic compact of all the dangerous snares that civilization, in its zeal to progress, has set for itself. Although the onlooker scoffs at the sailors, parasites who "neither make nor sell" (CP, 421), it is the ships that bear the weight of his irony.

> But their ships on the vehement blue
> Of this harbor actually gain
> From having nothing to do;
> Without a human will
> To tell them whom to kill
> Their structures are humane
>
> And, far from looking lost,
> Look as if they were meant
> To be pure abstract design
> By some master of pattern and line,
> Certainly worth every cent
> Of the billions they must have cost.
>
> (CP, 421)

The imagery draws on Horace's *ut pictura poesis,* the venerable truism that poetry and painting are sister arts, springing together from a single birth.[17] But as a tactic of Auden's ironist, this humanist convention is exposed as a disciplinary device. What restrictions entrap these poetically painted vessels? They are set on a static ground, an impermeable and inert blue, the marker of a vapid infinity through which they are cut off, by means of an ingenious excess, from contact with other structures. Then the poetic painting assigns a mimetic essence, an easily grasped cause, the dollar cost. But since causes naturally have effects, the description must not only fix the ships in a sufficient past but suspend them in

---

17. Cf. Rensselaer W. Lee, *Ut Pictura Poesis: The Humanist Theory of Painting* (New York: Norton, 1967), p. 3.

an inescapable present, a sealed envelope of time in which there is "nothing to do," hence no future prospect. When assembled, these capable restrictions render a structure that is manageable and harmless. In this way, the civic voice of "Fleet Visit" uses its painterly technique to fashion a protective fetish: an image that turns away the evils of textuality by allowing those evils to be mastered within itself.

The success of this substitution of a managed image for an unruly text hinges on the decision of a reader. So there is always a chance that the fetish might fail and the textual body be traced in its play of resistance. "Fleet Visit" is written in heavily end-stopped trimeters reminiscent of Robert Frost's "Neither Out Far Nor In Deep." The deliberate clumsiness performs a dual purpose. Because the rhythms of a poem supposedly imitate the character of its subject matter, the trimeters emphasize the rigid and confining quality of the parodied structures. Also, because poetic gracefulness testifies to the skill of the persona, the use of this awkward meter confirms his resentment at being doomed to live in an unheroic age. Yet the syntax is not in step with this rhythm. By means of its frequent enjambment, including the linkage between stanzas, it disregards the imposed meter (or at least relegates its corroboration to the rhyme) and maintains a separate conversational rhythm. The point is not to adjudicate between two opposing systems of stress but to note how they furnish the occasion of an irregular tic, a tremor in the discourse. Because the two rhythms vex each other, the text becomes subject to spasms, moments of perplexity when the allocation of a proper accent becomes difficult or impossible to decide. As chance would have it, there is the following variant of the fourth stanza's opening line: "But the ships on the dazzling blue" (SP, 197). The accident (Why was one chosen? How did the other survive?) illustrates the irrepressible force of poetic dialogism in that either variant, "vehement" or "dazzling," admits responsive accents. The blue (vehement), the innocent void of an unthinkable excess, shelters a resistance, an impassioned opposition, incensed, of a counter violence whose origins may never be closed. Yet the blue (dazzling), a disintegration into blindness, also defies the sight to which it seductively promises dominion, through its faceting of mere intensity into diverse prisms, casual refractions that dispel the illusion of a center. In each case, the syntactic tremors instigate a responsiveness that is never more than just begun.

The elements of success for an ordinary voice might be duly listed: compliant relics, an ascetic insinuation that can efface its own identity while simulating the prejudices of others, a synoptic vantage, an easily repudiated structure. The last of these might be anything, since every item of perception is also marked as a cultural product. (Even to be tagged as insignificant, trivial, pointless discloses a format of production: as that which may be safely ignored, furnishes a neutral background, is under control, and so forth.) In general, however, the more densely inscribed (intently wrought, frequently reviewed) and august an object, the greater a speaker's challenge. It is tempting to hurl satiric barbs at the American fleet as a convenient synecdoche of cultural impositions. Yet what of more venerable contrivances, hallowed images that rate a mandatory reverence, a space and time of their own? Overcoming these considerably more formidable emblems of the text is the task confronted by the cicerone of "Musée des Beaux Arts."

This justly famous poem (so effective that many have found here, if nowhere else, the real voice of Auden himself) achieves its success through a combination of disciplines, rather than any single tactic. Why do people seek a guide, who must after all be paid? Wending through the museum depths, a huddled band follows its redemptive leader, pausing at sites of especial torment to hear an account of the surrounding *bolge*. The ensemble suggests both an act of consignment, seeing and thinking through another, as well as appeasement, the mollification of an impromptu genius loci. Thus the implied audience have already cast themselves in the role of a specific relict: the unworthy yet devout souls, eager to endure this purgatorial place in exchange for admission to a paradise of illumination and self-praise, as initiates and cognoscente who have returned from the beyond. Even if the museum visitors are entirely unaware of playing this role, the cicerone understands it quite well. From the weary yet proficient quality of his discourse, it is clear that he has rehearsed his drama of revelation many times before. Reassurance, of course, but above all a sense of superiority is what the relicts want, a reward for having expended so much effort to devote an afternoon to Culture. So even though the speaker has considerable authority, he must use it with tact. Only the guides and the museum guards are permitted a normal speaking voice. All others are expected to be reverentially quiet or to whisper. (Violators are branded: pompous ass.) Granted this privilege, however, its repressive powers must be directed to the artifacts of the museum, not to the awestruck visitants.

The enabling condition for the contract between speaker and audience is the museum itself. As the requisite topography for "Musée des Beaux Arts," this hushed space plays a crucial part. The truism that museums are designed to resemble fortresses is inaccurate. That metaphor supposes a purpose: that museums house a precious commodity, which must be protected from theft (e.g., Fort Knox). But the confusion is revealed by asking, What is actually being protected? To cross the museum threshold is to leave a realm of fluent and spontaneous meanings, whose production discreetly retires behind the truth it so artlessly proffers. Instead one enters an alien space, a domain of displayed textuality, where generative structures are suspended, openly shown, poised against one another. The shift is terrifying, more anxious even than the transition from life to death, since once past the museum threshold it is no longer clear which is the land of the living, which of the dead.[18] And as if a single instance of this suspension were not problematic enough, the museum hosts a gallery of such productions, a disorienting montage of structures and their play of aberrant codes. To wander through the museum is to witness, at least potentially, how imaginative schools, epochs, have diversely fashioned the timeless icons of truth, beauty, justice. Perhaps no greater insult to the solemn trance of reality might be devised than this open display of cultural devices. Having transgressed the museum threshold, one enters a space where grammars become vital, obtrusive, their structures unstable and evolving. So the fortress metaphor might be replaced with another, the mausoleum. It is not the artifacts that require protection from the docile visitants, but vice versa, the unaware from the reflective.

That is why the huddled band clings to the cicerone, whose voice is all that intervenes between a blissful mystification and the textual abyss. The guide fashions a discourse from a proven bulwark against chaos, the exemplum: "About suffering they were never wrong, / The Old Masters" (CP, 146). With three bold strokes, he hues a topic from the

18. Sometimes the painting seems more alive than its viewers, as in "Woods": "Sylvan meant savage in those primal woods / Piero di Cosimo so loved to draw, / Where nudes, bears, lions, sows with women's heads, / Mounted and murdered and ate each other raw" (CP, 427).

cavernous void, asserts an authoritative claim, and founds it upon a firm basis of stereotypes. No one could ever be wrong about suffering (though its existence might be faked). Others endure pain or misery, but suffering is a personal condition. It can be refused or disguised but not falsified since the self-deception would then become part of the suffering. The cicerone, however, *imputes* suffering: he transposes what is indisputable as a personal, reflexive claim into a larger generalization that has no validity. His absolutism is concealed within a casual denial, "never wrong," and then propped up with a sturdy consensus of authorities, "the Old Masters." The refusal to be specific is pure intimidation: it operates under the pretense that everyone knows who the Masters are, though its more probable impulse is that nomination would spoil the desired effect, of an inaccessible consensus. Why does the speaker take such elaborate pains to introduce a personal experience into a public setting? Not only does the confusion permit him to become the voice of his relicts, the expression of their deepest being (since suffering is personal), but it supplies that voice with a universal theme, an experience that may not be denied or even questioned (since suffering is immediately apparent). Through this deft insinuation, the guide stations himself as an invulnerable because finally narcissistic authority.

So it remains only to establish dominance over the text, or at least its displaced image, the figures rendered on the canvas. Once the announced exemplum has served the purpose of providing a pretext for a series of disciplinary tactics, it can be dropped, and the discourse turn to the work of parodic subversion. In effect the cicerone turns the Old Masters against their own work by characterizing them as contemptuous of the "human position" they portray:

> About suffering they were never wrong,
> The Old Masters: how well they understood
> Its human position; how it takes place
> While someone else is eating or opening a window or just walking dully
>   along;
> How, when the aged are reverently, passionately waiting
> For the miraculous birth, there always must be
> Children who did not specially want it to happen, skating
> On a pond at the edge of the wood:
> They never forgot

That even the dreadful martyrdom must run its course
Anyhow in a corner, some untidy spot
Where the dogs go on with their doggy life and the torturer's horse
Scratches its innocent behind on a tree.

(CP, 146–147)

The pseudoexempla imply that the guide's account duplicates the artists' representations. Obliged like all good description to be complete, this substitutive account organizes the represented world into a moral order, a hierarchy of concern. To ensure superiority over the various levels of this order, the cicerone stages a brief parody of each. As the human particulars are described, then, they are simultaneously mimicked. The oblivious ones who do not know of the suffering are portrayed in the voice of a mindless automaton ("eating or opening a window or just walking dully along"). The rapturously attendant, who know of the suffering but think it may be overcome, are described in the tones of a credulous imbecile ("reverently, passionately waiting / For the miraculous birth"). The indifferent, who know of the suffering but do not care, are relegated to the voice of capriciousness ("who did not specially want it to happen"). Even the entirely innocent do not emerge unscathed. The creatures, who neither know of the suffering nor can be held responsible for it, are reduced to the cute ("the dogs go on with their doggy life") or worse, to the fatuously solemn ("and the torturer's horse / Scratches its innocent behind on a tree"). In this way, the cicerone's description reduces its painterly texts to trivialized images, not merely shown but parodically mastered entities, over whose victimized embodiment both guide and victims, speaker and relicts can claim an easy superiority.

Were the poem to end at this point, its voice would not yet be triumphant, but its violence would be less perceptible. There is an inexplicable obsession, however, a tendency to fatal excess that overtakes Auden's speakers just on the verge of success. In effect conceding that the initial survey is no more than a pretext, an excuse for a parodic prologue, the cicerone supplies the example promised earlier. But now, instead of proceeding outward from an implied and thus inaccessible objectivity (the stark, unillusioned eye of the Old Masters), the discourse becomes more reflective and returns to the scene of the body's demise.

In Brueghel's *Icarus*, for instance: how everything turns away
Quite leisurely from the disaster; the ploughman may
Have heard the splash, the forsaken cry,
But for him it was not an important failure; the sun shone
As it had to on the white legs disappearing into the green
Water; and the expensive delicate ship that must have seen
Something amazing, a boy falling out of the sky,
Had somewhere to get to and sailed calmly on.

                                               (CP, 147)

The persistence of the fascination sets up a dialogic event. As it approaches the scene of death, the discourse, rather than parodying its topic, begins to vary itself. Its former transparency yields to a more kaleidoscopic effect, a succession of variously configured utterances. The impervious mirror of irony is dropped, and its smooth surface breaks into jagged discursive facets.[19] "The disaster" proposes an unavoidable event of considerable magnitude, mandated from the stars. Except this occurrence is an individual mistake, the result of an avoidable decision, a boy's exuberance. "The splash" tries to retreat into casual trivialization. But the event's significance is important enough to be awarded mythic, archetypal status: Icarus as a classical prefiguration, a contrast to the Christological reference implied in the first stanza. Indeed "the forsaken cry" takes up the Christological nuance, adapted from synoptic narratives of the crucifixion. As if bewildered by this emergent and quite unmanageable accent, the discourse then shifts to an aggressively secular mode, "the white legs disappearing into the green / Water." This wrenches the scene into a displaced eroticism, the supple limbs gliding into an insatiable oblivion, as well as a barely veiled psychological allegory: the son, slipping away from paternal control, is about to be enveloped within the maternal unconscious. Distracted by these unguessed and disruptive energies, the passage rejects such subversive accents with the sarcasm of "something amazing." Yet "a boy falling out of the sky" does not quite

19. Auden visited the Brussels museum in the summer of 1938 (Humphrey Carpenter, *A Biography*, p. 240). The insight stumbled on by Auden's cicerone bears an interesting resemblance to a remark by Brecht. Cf. *Brecht on Theatre*, trans. John Willett (New York: Hill and Wang, 1964), p. 157: "Even though Brueghel manages to balance his contrasts he never merges them into one another, nor does he practice the separation of comic and tragic; his tragedy contains a comic element and his comedy a tragic one."

restore the desired normality. It offers only another discursive facet: an implausible naturalism, a specious reality-effect that is the unlikely prerogative of made-up texts. (Given the velocity of a falling body, an actual onlooker would see a falling object or, as in more realistic Ovid, the event's aftermath.)[20]

These disruptive accents do more than mar the efficient disciplines of the cicerone. The resistance of the textual body, its refusal to be curbed or silenced, portends the fate of any civic voice, however adept its persona, however docile its relics. Accompanying each transparent meaning is a text whose syntactic gestures, beyond the reach of any imputed consciousness, remain fascinated with a scene of failed domination.

> Not knowing quite what has happened, but awed
>   By death like all the creatures
> Now watching this spot.
>
>   (CP, 482)

Beside the relict waits a more intransigent party, the companion text on which the disciplines must rely. As the authority of a persona encounters this anatomy of variants, the mastery of its voice provokes a tale of forbidden responses, where even self-evident truths may incite a continuing dialogue.

---

20. Ovid, *The Metamorphoses*, trans. Horace Gregory (New York: Viking Press, 1958), p. 222: "Then as he called again his eyes discovered / The boy's torn wings washed on the climbing waves."

CHAPTER SIX

A Necessary Angel

The mind has added nothing to human nature. It is a violence
from within that protects us from a violence without.
                    —Wallace Stevens, "The Noble Rider
                    and the Sound of Words"

What is the poet? That modest question conceals a neglected
miscellanea. The poet W. H. Auden locates a point of convergence
shared by certain texts: reminiscences, letters, reviews, a particular style
of commentary. Although these points of biographical stability hold a
real interest, their tendency to fashion a fixed identity within the name
Auden makes them unhelpful for a project of reading. The poet, however, also designates a quite different entity, a scriptor. This figure is not
a person in the usual sense (self-possessed, accountable) but a cluster of
functions. For example, the scriptor gathers discrete discourses, arranges
them to promote conflicts, sounds the murky sediments of words, and
so on. As a potential answer to the question, What is the poet? the
scriptor might make a useful entry, except there would be nothing to
discuss. Each ambitious account of the scriptor would find itself stranded
in silence, appended to its own truth as a legend that recedes into an
absurdity. The scriptor is a god forbidden to abandon the treadle of the
machine it constantly disowns. Fortunately, the poet also designates a
stabler entity, and as luck would have it, this more manageable meaning
coincides with the usual sense of the word. The poet, as every student
learns, is a mastering voice that emanates from and then dominates the
text. It is this more familiar sense that will be used here. For present
purposes, the poet is neither a biographical fixity nor a grouping of
functions, but an imputed force. The poet is an effect of reading, a

presiding voice that results from certain activities (keeping the right speed, obeying conventions of irony, maintaining intolerance to contradiction). What is so remarkable is that this pure effect, an officiating voice, has the capacity to assume a not only independent but prior existence. The poetic voice, even though it is nothing without the creative activity of a reader, is routinely permitted to dominate both text and reader.[1] As the name of a result that reliably destroys the process that brought it into being, then, the poet merits attention as a most accomplished foe of the responsive text.

But that attention must be carefully focused. If the poet operates as an imputed voice, a doubling that is also a divergence occurs whenever this voice mentions the poet. When that happens, there are two figures in the poem: one operates an almost imperceptible discipline, a controlling voice; the other offers an image, a tangible body. The two must be kept distinct from each other. As usual in Auden, to be assigned a body, even the body of a poet, is to become a victim. A satiric idyll from "City Without Walls" offers the following scene of instruction, in which a feral tribe huddles

> in groups ruled by grandmothers,
> hirsute witches who on winter nights
>
> fable them stories of fair-haired Elves
> whose magic made the mountain dam,
> of Dwarves, cunning in craft, who smithied
> the treasure-hoards of tin-cans
> they flatten out for their hut roofs.
>
> (CP, 564)

It requires no great insight to see that these truly postmodern bards (the

---

1. Auden's comment in his foreword to *The Orators*, for example, shows a contest for possession of the text between its presiding voice and a biographical remnant: "My name on the title-page seems a pseudonym for someone else, someone talented but near the border of sanity, who might well, in a year or two, become a Nazi." *The Orators* (London: Faber and Faber, 1966), p. 7. Furthermore, there is a scriptor who recedes into "my unconscious motive in writing" (p. 8), where the possessive pronoun lays claim to a surmise that quickly passes into a fable.

imaginary setting is the aftermath of a nuclear war) are parodied as barbarous and derivative: their spontaneous genius reinvents Wagner's *Ring*. The satire suggests the distinction between an implicit (voiced) and explicit (represented) poet. The poetic voice of "City Without Walls" scoffs at the image of more primitive successors, not because of their occupation (both ply the same trade) but because of their incompetence. An adept professional, the performing poet regards the portrayed figures as ludicrous amateurs. They adopt tactics, devise disciplines that at least by modern standards do not work. This doubling of poets within "City Without Walls" is instructive because it shows why an analysis of Auden's poets cannot proceed through the usual approach: considering the various appearances of the poet and then endorsing the speaker's highly accomplished satires. For insofar as such a reading neglects the speaking voice itself, which it gratefully takes as a unexceptionable given, it falls into a carefully devised snare (the first of many). The focus, then, must concentrate on the voice of the poet and its clandestine disciplines, rather than its gladly offered images.

If the hirsute witches are comic bunglers, what is it they overlook? They occupy a world in which poet and audience share a space. But as Auden suggests in "The Poet and the City," this actual presence of the poet, however useful as an illusion, neglects a crucial technological intervention. Adopting a point from Kierkegaard, Auden makes the distinction between a crowd and a public. A crowd is "a visible congregation of a large number of human individuals in a limited physical space" (DH, 82). A public, however, includes any of the consumers of a communicative medium: for example, the viewers of a film, the readers of a newspaper or book. Although easily overlooked because of its familiarity, the distinction between crowd and public is important. The members of a crowd retain a real existence in time and space. They can interact with one another or with the person who addresses them. But the members of a public enter a mode of existence that is purely fantastic.[2]

2. Cartoons of the public deny its inconceivable quality, as do polls and statistics, but these would be instances of psychological denial: contending with a terror (the unthinkable, oblivion) by giving it an image. As Auden pointed out in "Notes on the Comic," a main attraction of the caricature is that it makes the indeterminate determinate: "A caricature of a face admits that its owner has had a past, but denies that he has a future. He has created his features up to a certain point, but now they have taken

Removed from both time and space (two people can read the same work in different countries and different epochs), a public eludes any conceivable embodiment. Exiles from history, its members are effectively isolated. They have no access to whoever is addressing them, no capacity to engage the conveying medium, no contact with one another, and insofar as they remain content with the rewards of consumption, no ties with their peculiar historical being. One watches, or reads, to forget a troublesome world and enter a uniquely Western nirvana, an oblivious passivity. By means of technology, the members of a public are caught within a hermeneutic spell. Nothing in themselves, they acquire a vestigial existence by taking what is offered. The one remaining privilege of this nothingness is the exercise of a minor negation: to consume something else instead.

Still, the case must not be overstated. As with any technology, the rewards are mixed. From the standpoint of a poetic (repressive) voice, the advantages conferred by the formation of a public are summarized in the Myth of the Book. Against the public's nothingness, the Book sets a monumental edifice, replete with truth, inspirited with an invincible guiding force. How can a mere nullity dare to challenge the Book? And yet there are disadvantages as well. As a consequence of consigning itself to the printed page, the Book might at any instant degenerate into a text. Its possessing voice would then absent itself and leave behind a vacated assemblage of signs. For this to happen, all that is necessary is for someone to halt the normal flow of sense and regard the suddenly defunct page. The magical phantasms of truth recede. In their place remain only derelict mechanisms, the once formidable armatures of truth. A passage from "The Prophets" glosses this eerie moment, as an epiphany of

> Those beautiful machines that never talked
> But let the small boy worship them and learn
> All their long names whose hardness made him proud.
> (CP, 203)

----

charge of him so that he can never change; he has become a single possibility completely realized" (DH, 383).

The hope of Auden's poetry is that language may be transformed from an unassailably voiced truth into a collection of devices whose names must be learned, and whose naming involves an intricate articulation. What is at stake in this shift? No longer operating at speed, specific mechanisms become apparent. Because they are no longer directed to an end, their sheer oddity is revealed. No longer restrained within a logic of competence, each is left to unfold a private saga, a history of responsive inscriptions.

It is the persistence of this threat, that a public might track an enthralling voice into its unruly text, which dictates the mission of the poet. Unlike the modernists of the previous generation, Auden maintained that the poet neither creates new nor unearths ancient forms of thought: as in the imaged word of Hart Crane, the supreme fictions of Wallace Stevens, the ruling symbols of Yeats. Rather, the discourses used by a poet are acquired from the repertoire of available social languages. Although the themes and disciplines of these languages might be displaced, they cannot be transcended. As Auden remarked in his introduction to *Poems of Freedom*, the poet remains the citizen of an age and is consequently less an inventor than an enforcer of myth:

> Poets are rarely and only incidentally priests or philosophers or party agitators. They are people with a particular interest and skill in handling words in a particular kind of way which is extremely difficult to describe and extremely easy to recognize. . . . Because language is communicable, what they do for society is much the same as what they do for themselves. They do not invent new thoughts or feelings, but out of their skill with words they crystallize and define with greater precision thoughts and feelings which are generally present in their class and age. (EA, 370–71)

Yet it does not follow from this reasoning that originality disappears. If there is an innovative poetic task, it is both more practical and precise. The poet's job is to develop techniques for the subjugation of the text. Poets, as a class of virtuosi, conduct star performances. They perfect the magic that holds a treacherous medium at bay, through the imperceptible violence that permits meaning and truth to escape the labyrinth of signs.

Given the crucial nature of their mission, as the defenders of an unperturbed consumption, one might expect poets to be more amply rewarded, especially in a capitalist society. But as Auden pointed out in his foreword to *The Dyer's Hand:* "It is a sad fact about our culture that a poet can earn much more money writing or talking about his art than he can by practicing it" (DH, xi). Significantly, Auden complains not about the level of the poet's income but its odd distribution. Penurious yet shrewd, capitalism retains what it may need in the future. It *rewards* only what it needs at the moment. As long as the consuming public remains obligingly docile and inattentive, even crude disciplines suffice to obscure the workings of a text. But at any moment this might change. In that event, a system based on the passive consumption of meaning must have at its disposal a stockpile of more powerful disciplines. So the poet makes an invaluable if generally unappreciated contribution to safeguarding the constantly imperiled routes of communication. For even if unheeded in its own time, a poetic voice might develop disciplinary tactics that are required by another epoch.

With reference to Auden's poetic virtuosi, their main disciplinary techniques may be gathered under three headings: an indifference to the audience, a meticulous calculation of textual resistance, and a journalistic parasitism. Although each is effective in its own right, when properly combined they accomplish an impressive subjugation of the text.

Unlike either the inward or civic voices, Auden's poets take little heed of their recipients. The audience is neither coerced nor flattered; indeed it can hardly be said to exist at all in that it is accorded only a most tenuous status. Yet this neglect does not result from unawareness or distraction. Rather, the virtuoso knows quite well that a public will be in attendance, but also that this entity, dispersed past reckoning in both time and space, does not count. The disciplinary pressure of the poet's neglect is subtle. By refusing to cast the audience in a distinct role, the poet relegates these lost souls to a horrible fate: dissolution into the anonymity they already suffer, enrollment within the public. Through a casual act of omission, as if talking to no one in particular, the poet abandons the audience to a condition that is both the prerequisite and the intolerable motive for their reading, the oblivion of belonging to the public. What is the disciplinary value of this? Without an assigned role to intervene between even an inferior identity and an encroaching insignificance, the discourse offers the reader but one respite: vicarious identification with the speaking voice, the masterful poet. In this way, the poet's studious indifference operates an ingenious repressive circuit. The reader is in effect required to merge with the officiating voice and thus to become a vicarious enactor of the text's subjugation.[3]

Even with the advantage of this unspoken threat, however, the poet's performance must be impressive. Because of their status as virtuosi, poets can practice gestures of domination that would be forbidden almost anyone else: Elegiac Condescension ("and what was god-like in this generation / was never to be born"; CP, 124); Pedantic Ostentation ("Eros Paidagogos / Weeps on his virginal bed"; CP, 124); Prophetic Ennui ("again some writer / runs howling to his art"; CP, 127); Sentimental Snobbishness ("who'd never heard / Of any world where promises were kept, / Or one could weep because another wept"; CP, 455); Lubricious Derision ("caressed by clammy cobwebs, / grinning initiates emerge into daylight / as tribal heroes"; CP, 605). But it is important to locate the object of this mastery. Exactly what is being controlled? In one sense, the poet's domination is sterile because it occupies a realm of pure simulacra, as in this dream garden from "Circe":

> Inside it is warm and still like a drowsy
> September day, though the leaves show no sign of
> turning. All around one notes the usual
>   pinks and blues and reds,
>
> a shade over-emphasized. The rose-bushes
> have no thorns. An invisible orchestra
> plays the Great Masters: the technique is flawless,
>   the rendering schmaltz.
>   (CP, 646)

No one has ever heard the strings of Circe's mythic band, any more than they have met Eros Paidagogos. But the patently contrived status of such entities, their confinement within a realm of signs, sets the stage for a more important triumph. It is not merely personae or even themes that the poet masters, but something far more elusive and resourceful,

---

3. As a correlative of this vicarious enactment, readers who ally themselves with the speaking voice of a text may, under the guise of a scrupulous devotion to interpretative fidelity, indulge a deep hostility to language.

the *text itself.* Unconcerned with the need to manage an audience, the poet can devote full attention to anticipating, disarming, repressing the syntactic body. What seems a casual gesture, an offhand remark whose spontaneous ease serves as a well-established marker of genius, in fact conceals an elaborate effort: the precise calculation of textual resistance and, because that resistance can never be completely suppressed, a careful concealment of its disruptions. To a greater degree than any of Auden's other voices, the poet is aware of the text and bent upon its containment.

Such expertise is entitled to its rewards. As a result of his triumph over the discursive arena, Auden's poet is permitted a rare privilege: a return to mundane events. This journalistic parasitism, the privilege of holding forth in clear and compelling language about an actual occurrence (a gathering of gamblers, the civil war in Spain, the invasion of Poland), is itself a terminal effect. It depends on the success of the first two disciplines, namely, the enlistment of a vicariously participating public and the conquest of the text. Only because resistance has been eliminated, from all quarters, can the poet's virtuoso performance deflect the curse of inscription and break through to reality itself, the solid truths waiting forever just outside the labyrinth. The modest factuality of the poet, then, is nothing of the sort. Its hard realism is at once guarantee and ruse. It can promise only what is never delivered: a theme that magically conceals the body of its accompanying discourse.

The poet's disciplines are better understood if illustrated rather than inventoried. If the poet is to achieve dominance over the text, the participation of a public in the voice's performance must be achieved with minimal effort. As demonstrated by the poet of "Casino," stereotypes are well suited to this purpose.

> Only their hands are living, to the wheel attracted,
> are moved, as deer trek desperately towards a creek
>   through the dust and scrub of a desert, or gently,
>   as sunflowers turn to the light,
>
>
> and, as night takes up the cries of feverish children,
> the cravings of lions in dens, the loves of dons,
>   gathers them all and remains the night, the
>   great room is full of their prayers.

To a last feast of isolation self-invited,
they flock, and in a rite of disbelief are joined;
   from numbers all their stars are recreated,
      the enchanted, the worldly, the sad.

Without, calm rivers flow among the wholly living
quite near their trysts, and mountains part them, and birds,
   deep in the greens and moistures of summer,
      sing towards their work.

But here no nymph comes naked to the youngest shepherd,
the fountain is deserted, the laurel will not grow;
   the labyrinth is safe but endless, and broken
      is Ariadne's thread,

as deeper in these hands is grooved their fortune: lucky
were few, and it is possible that none was loved,
   and what was god-like in this generation
      was never to be born.

                        (CP, 123–124)

This passage draws from common wisdom on the topic of gamblers. Its claims are preceded by the assumption: Everyone knows that. . . . Thus, everyone knows that gamblers are compulsive, isolated, pathetic, and so forth. Such stereotypes have the capacity to generate a virtually incontestable reality-effect because they match so perfectly with settled prejudices. It is this match between prejudice and stereotype that induces the reality-effect, not any correspondence between sign and thing. So even though there is little in the poem that would qualify as accurate description or factual narrative, it leaves the impression of an objective report. The poet presents an unadorned case. Intent upon facts, he may ignore the audience, since that intentness is clearly encoded: as placing no demands, having no designs on the recipient. Abandoned in this way, the audience is left with an empty choice that has already been made anyway, by the simple act of continuing to read. They can be relegated, as members of the public, to a cavernous repertoire of further stereotypes: the night that contains the sick, the bestial, and the perverted. Or they can join the poet and become vicarious enunciators of a pastoral realm's natural and harmonious order.

All this, of course, is groundwork. The poet's real concern is the text. As a topic, gambling invites a frankly moralistic contrast between restricted and unrestricted exchanges. That is, tokens pegged to a substantial basis (hard work), traded for real things, and hoarded in jealously guarded deposits are good; but tokens allocated by the play of chance, exchanged for other tokens, and continuously put at even greater risk, are bad. But where does the poet stand? Through a process of displacement, the poet's scorn for the gamblers compensates for his own involvement in a game of chance: as a scriptor who casts words in accordance with specific lexical and grammatical probabilities, yet without certainty of how their inscriptions will fall.

The more intimate tasks of poetic repression, however, are conducted through the license of parataxis. To attain certain effects, poets are permitted syntactic forms that are more elaborate than standard constructions. Unrelated clauses may be juxtaposed without explanation, and verbs either misplaced or withheld. Like the stereotype of gambling, this parataxis is also encoded, but in a different way. It connotes casual elegance, the spontaneous candor of one who insists on being a speaker, not a writer. In this way, the poet exempts himself from the labor of revision. Once something is said, it cannot be erased, only superseded. What is meant to be impressive is that this casual ease does not prevent the poet from achieving a virtuoso effect, for example, a punning that contrasts the gamblers' compulsive movements to more decent occupations, "dust and scrub." Yet this impression of spontaneous unrescindable utterance is a pretense. Its immediacy attempts to conceal the labor of composition within the brief span of a dramatic moment. In fact, a poem such as "Casino" requires an exorbitant effort, mainly because of the care that must be exercised in curbing the unruliness of its text. Each syntactic gesture must be carefully noted and, so far as this is possible, its inscriptions trivialized or disarmed. That is what the poet's casualness seeks to achieve by containing the responsive accents within a safe insipidity: a matter of clever but empty tricks. In light of the poet's disciplinary parataxis, then, the question becomes to what extent a textual play can elude such finely wrought restraints.

Forced to comply, since the poet intervenes at the level of syntax, the textual body does not become servile but rather absents itself. It is simply not there, a resistance that is elaborately anticipated yet cannot be found. And so this poem's dialogic tale would be quite brief, except that such absence is itself a symptom, a sign of incipient mania, the condition of a semi-distracted yet eerily lucid madness. Accompanying the poet's paratactic ruse is an absented, wandering body, a textual willingness to move aimlessly in an almost trance like condition and yet suddenly rebel with an inscriptive response. The poet's initial gesture, an act of dismemberment, provides a focus for this response. "Only the hands are living." The rest of the body is henceforth deleted, cast into the oblivion of the public, for the crime of admitting what cannot be contained even by a stereotype: an origin that degenerates into a too vocable genealogy. But having made the deletion, the poet must then deal with its consequences. Lest ludic mayhem ensue (a spectacle of dismembered, groping hands, crazed homunculi in search of an adequate anatomy), some substitute for the deleted body must be found.[4] The problem, however, is that such compensatory anatomies, possible candidates to fill the title role of casino or little hut, persistently readmit the vexatious body.

The circle, "to the wheel attracted," a sufficiently archetypal symbol, provides the first substitute. It suggests confinement within space, the rim of horizon, as well as futility in time, the turns of a sterile dialectic. From this point, it would make sense for the poet to move directly to the ironic similes of deer and sunflower, which contrast the gamblers' demented compulsion to more natural desires. Unlike the needs of plants and animals, which are temperate, the impulse to gamble is both insatiable and destructive. Yet these similes also reintroduce the proscribed topic of the body and, since the gamblers have a body as well, subvert their own irony by admitting a further contrast. In addition to the mythic body of organic unity, there is a discursive body crisscrossed with conflicting scripts. To save the irony, the parataxis conducts a distracting insertion, "are moved," which distances the initial dismemberment and its vexatious body from its corrective similes. Following these moves requires a fine attentiveness. Yet this is the only way to track the poet

---

4. The search for a form superior to the body (ennobled, unchanging, consistent) is a frequent motif in the poetry, for example, in the allusions to architecture as a mode of human recreation: "so is Schönbrunn, / to look at someone's idea of the body / that should have been his, as the flesh / Mum formulated shouldn't" ("Thanksgiving for a Habitat," CP, 519).

at work. The text must be taken as an archaeological cue, a fragment left from the struggles waged to achieve its specious calm.

Nonetheless, the textual inscriptions are never altogether hushed. According to the laws of agreement, the paratactic "moved" should go with "hands." But as a result of the casual order of phrases, there is little to prevent its inscriptive field from overlapping with that of "wheel." In that event, both "wheel" and "hands" begin to share the deprecatory determinations of "moved," but with this difference: whereas the hands are moved by other elements of the body (e.g., the arms for a literalist; the heart, brain, soul for a sentimentalist), the wheel is spun by a person, the croupier. Thus even within the discipline of a paratactic casualness, the textual mania manages to interject its dissent. The poet's carefully wrought synecdoche is turned inside out, since it is not the hands that belong within the substitutive framework of the wheel, but the wheel that turns according to the promptings of the hands. Nor does the reversal reinstate some myth of the natural body, for the body in question is that of *homo inventor*, the fabricator of devices: not only the wheel itself but the varied cultures it bears.

Imposed upon this undercurrent of textual mania, the poet's double simile, a virtuoso flourish, begins to acquire the aspect of a flustered departure. It becomes a further distraction from the awkward disclosures of a parataxis that was itself to offer distraction. So even within the opening lines, the struggle of poet and text is well under way. Made wary by his unsuccess with the wheel, the poet resorts to a more shrewdly calculated corporeal substitute, the no less archetypal "night." As both terminus and oblivion, the night "takes up," yet as final entropy, it is itself untransformed "and remains the night." Still, the engulfment succeeds only at the level of the immediately voiced, since the "takes up" instigates other accents: improvisation, as one takes up a part; beguilement or even fraud, as something takes up time. And because the parataxis promises a hermeneutic thrill (the sentence that shall divulge what the night does with its takings), but then thwarts it through tautology, it initiates a momentum that has little outlet except to explore these accents. Consequently the night, as would-be engulfment, is transformed into a dramatic ensemble, a collective of diverse discourses: cries, cravings, loves, prayers. In remaining the night, a deliberate nothingness, it passes into its remains. So yet again the poet's substitute anatomy, an encompassing oblivion, is dispersed into the peculiarities it would repress.

Uncannily, the poet knows all this, understands the threat, and yet realizes that nothing can be done. Once beyond the reach of a mastering voice, the text disappears into its own itinerary and just as inexplicably returns. So the poet must preserve at all costs the ruse of dramatic time, the reality of a speech that both yields and discards itself at each moment, leaving behind no remnant. After the failure of wheel and night, the poet offers a flurry of substitute tropes: "a last feast," "they flock," "a rite of disbelief," "all their stars." From a disciplinary standpoint, the imagery is capably handled in that its shift from a normative (i.e., Christian) to an illicit variety of religion (the ancient darkness of astrology) implies a parodic dismissal. Yet the parody has its cost. It implies the existence of a valid religion, an authentic totality capable of containing the deleted body. Accordingly, the poet is required by his own tactics to supply a restorative wholeness, the pastoral "without" that promises escape from the treacherous riddle of signs. No sooner does the pastoral enter the text, however, than it degenerates into a profligate scene, seedy, profuse, where the rivers enticingly depart for unknown destinations, lovers commence their tempestuous relations, and even the symbol of lyrical completeness, the birds' song, is separated from "their work," a host of other tasks. Surprisingly, the poet admits the pastoral's inscribed resistance: "the labyrinth is safe but endless, and broken / is Ariadne's thread." Yet even the slight hyperbole, "broken," betrays a further intrusion of the text. What is at risk is not a filament that can be severed or snapped, but an entire architecture of restraint.

Given so relentless and irrepressible a force as the text, its containment is a matter of illusion. Having failed to devise an image that might simulate the remnant body yet not admit its disruptions, the poet turns against the text itself: "as deeper in these hands is grooved their fortune." Since taking revenge suggests not only a just grievance but a long-awaited restoration, both of which are in this instance false, the poet's tactic is essentially a bluff. Unable to control an unruly anatomy, the poet becomes retributive to the hand itself, incising its surface by using the writer's stylus as a weapon, a means of sadistic mastery that scars the recalcitrant body with an inevitable destiny: what Fortune decrees. But the same violence also fashions a parable of the text. For it is the act of writing that proscribes dismemberment by preventing the image from being isolated into a theme. The attempted violence, then, once more rediscovers the body within its deleting synecdoche and even acknowledges its creative promise as "this generation," not simply a succession of biological stages but an irrepressible event.

The poet's ideal is a text that is immediate, instantly comprehensible, and yet *illegible:* unreadable because its production recedes into its truth. In theory, by adjusting combinations of disciplines, the poet should be able to design artifacts that exceed the reach of critical inquiry. So powerful is the semantic entrancement of such poems that their voiced meaning saturates the text, leaving a reader with nothing to do. One of the most reliable markers of these works is that they are usually consigned to the dutiful annotations and paraphrases of literary history. A year after "Casino," Auden wrote "Spain 1937," which offers an invaluable introduction to this group of virtuoso, that is, virtually illegible, texts.

In retrospect, it is odd that "Spain" did not become one of Auden's most acclaimed poems, as the proof of his radical social commitment. If so modest a topic as gamblers can permit a naturalizing sway, the power to entice words from the lexicon and conjure them into phantasms of reality, then that power is incomparably greater with headline events and world affairs. One need only mention the civil war in Spain to achieve a formidable reality-effect. Its name invokes a reserve of further references, most of which have adequately disposed of their textual aspect (newspapers, official documents, secret agreements, memoirs). Furthermore, in the case of Auden's "Spain" (the possessive seems natural, inevitable), the reality-effect is enhanced by the apparent capitulation of the scriptor, who surrenders the text to the biographical author and the speaking poet. As is well known, Auden actually went to Spain, wrote a prose description of its urban life, and donated the proceeds of the first edition to the Red Cross (though the story about driving an ambulance is false).[5] Because of this compelling bond between a biographical hypostasis and a voiced persona, "Spain" offers a good opportunity for a poet with political ambitions.

Yet the poem is a notable unsuccess. Even more puzzling, the causes

---

5. "Impressions of Valencia," *New Statesman and Nation* 13 (January 30, 1937): 159.

of its failure require a considerable amount of additional effort. As noted earlier, the poet is well advised to ignore the audience, because the implicit threat of relegating them to the public tends to encourage their grateful identification with the speaking voice. The poet of "Spain," however, uneasily seeks the approval of the audience, which leads to miscalculations in tone that make the poem ineffective. Its poet is both patronizing and envious, for example, when he remarks that the revolutionaries "came to present their lives" (EA, 212), presumably as their social betters present their university degrees. Phrases such as "they clung like burrs" (EA, 212) and "they floated over the ocean" (EA, 212) suggest the ambivalence, a mix of derision and sentimentality, of someone who feels resentment at being excluded from a group he considers inferior. As Orwell later pointed out, the poet speaks with the bravado of an outsider who has no experience of what he is talking about: "Today the inevitable increase in the chances of death; / The conscious acceptance of guilt in the fact of murder" (EA, 212).[6] What is perplexing about these missteps is that they are entirely unnecessary. "Spain" does not succeed because it devotes considerable effort to fashioning a dimension of the discourse that had been better left out.

The puzzle, however, arises from certain assumptions about what is good and bad in poetry. From the standpoint of the poet, a good poem is illegible, a pure voice that escapes the tumult of the text to achieve an indubitable truth. But from the standpoint of the scriptor, a good poem must break that trance of meaning and provoke inscriptive responses. So the critical conversation about "Spain" might be reoriented, and the poem's obvious deficiencies taken as a deliberate precaution, akin to a handicap. The logic of this reorientation would go as follows: since the reality-effect of "Spain" exerts such a powerful force, as a result of the advantages conferred by both its well-recorded topic and its fortuitous confluence of biographical author and voiced poet (it could have been that Auden never went to Spain or that he composed the poem at Brighton), the scriptor evens the odds by marring its illegibility.

6. Orwell's "Inside the Whale" described this passage as irresponsible radicalism: "Mr. Auden's brand of amoralism is only possible if you are the kind of person who is always somewhere else when the trigger is pulled. So much of left-wing thought is a kind of playing with fire by people who don't even know that fire is hot." See George Orwell, *A Collection of Essays* (New York: Doubleday, 1954), p. 243.

This is accomplished by misaligning the disciplines so that the poem does not succeed. In that case, criticism has been accurate enough in its unfavorable judgment of "Spain" but incomplete in its subsequent reading.

If the opening left by its purposeful misalignment of disciplines is pursued, what emerges from "Spain" is an adept yet traceable repression of the text. The poem is divided into three sections according to the temporal sequence of Yesterday, Today, and Tomorrow. The Today section includes an array of social voices, though except for "the life," they are parodically stylized. The lyricist, for example, sounds idiotically enraptured ("O my vision"); the scientist pompous ("I inquire, I inquire"); the poor abject ("O show us / History the operator, the Organizer"); and the nations emptily bombastic ("Did you not found once the city state of the sponge, / Raise the vast military empires of the shark"; EA, 211). Through this ridicule of any kind of archaism, the parody confirms the repressive tactic of the framing Yesterday and Tomorrow sections. Each of the stylized voices is dated and thereby marked as an obsolescent discourse. The intransigent adversary of the poet is the inscribed memory, actually the discursive unconscious of a text. Because of its record of defiant accents, this unvoiced yet accompanying memory makes it impossible for any speaker, even a poetically accomplished one, to exercise more than a brief and illusory control. To counter this textual resistance, the poet uses an inflationary ellipsis in the Yesterday and Tomorrow sections. The technique involves a form of depreciation, expending and at the same time cheapening language, so that it retains only a directly voiced sense.

> Yesterday all the past. The language of size
> Spreading to China along the trade-routes; the diffusion
>   Of the counting-frame and the cromlech;
> Yesterday the shadow-reckoning in the sunny climates.
>
> Yesterday the assessment of insurance by cards,
> The divination of water; yesterday the invention
>   Of cart-wheels and clocks, the taming of
> Horses; yesterday the bustling world of the navigators.
>
> Yesterday the abolition of fairies and giants;

The fortress like a motionless eagle eyeing the valley,
    The chapel built in the forest;
Yesterday the carving of angels and of frightening gargoyles;

The trial of heretics among the columns of stone;
Yesterday the theological feuds in taverns
    And the miraculous cure at the fountain;
Yesterday the Sabbath of Witches. But to-day the struggle.

                                                    (EA, 210)

The diction is discrete and vivid, in an orthodoxly poetic way. But the suppression of any action, with predicates either absorbed into participial modifiers or omitted altogether, reduces the words to an empty show. Unable to muster the strength for an assertion, and barred from contact with other phrases, each successive utterance defines a depleted space, a discursive refuse pile in which bits and pieces of dead languages lie about in heaps, colorful perhaps but worthless. When taken together, the parodic archaism of the Today section and the inflationary ellipsis of the Yesterday and Tomorrow sections suppress the trace of any divergent discourse. The poet's voice presides over a scene whose details are tamely picturesque: entertaining but severed from illicit exchanges, flattened to a contemporary obviousness.

Yet the ellipsis that is so brilliant a discipline bears another aspect, as a textual gesture. It suggests a condition of amnesia, the forgetting of some nameless trauma. As if having discovered that the act of remembering might itself become a means of deflection, each phrase decrees a near escape from some unspecified hence dangerous event. What shift in social obligations decreed the imprisonment of time within space through the invention of the clock or made the heretic's dissent an intolerable threat? Rather than responding outright, the voiceless yet gesticulating text can only exert a mounting pressure. With each repetition of amnesia, a return of the repressed becomes more imminent until even the poem's most authoritative voice, its personifying of "the life," becomes subject to disruption.

What's your proposal. To build the Just City? I will.
I agree. Or is it the suicide pact, the romantic
    Death? Very well, I accept, for
I am your choice, your decision: yes, I am Spain.

                                                    (EA, 211)

This would seem to confront the trauma by speaking the unspeakable: what is repressed is a *Liebestod*, the agreement of exalted spirits to reject a flawed world for the perfect consummation of death.[7] But the ellipsis also suggests a more subtle anxiety. Just as the city must be built, so the suicide pact must be written. Yet at precisely the instant of conceding this, the poetic voice falls silent. It cannot enunciate the formation of that text. So its silence attempts to gloss over the contract between a nameless other, some cipher of the public, and the active production of that contract, which by two stanzas later has become an entire scene: "that arid square," "that fragment nipped off from hot / Africa," "that tableland scored by rivers" (EA, 212). As a voiced performance, then, "Spain" readily offers a consummating union with visionary truth. But it can also offer an unvoiced text whose production provides a chance for inscriptive responses. Perhaps the trauma carefully deleted from the remnants of past discourses is their gamelike quality, as intimated by that imaginary square: the exchanges across an open grid whose tactical nuances can exceed the subtleties of a chessboard. Or it might be the discovery that even a natural designation, Spain, entails a contrivance that both sunders and joins. Or it may even involve the possibility that a solid reality, a table of inventoried elements, contains a field of discursive structures that are orchestrated, incised, berated by diverging currents.

There is no rule, though, that requires the poet to be put at a handicap. In other works by Auden, the powers of the poet are given fuller reign. "September 1, 1939" provides an instance of a more successfully dominated, which is to say, illegible, text. Its occasion is not merely a historical situation, a civil war, but a specific event, the German invasion of Poland. Very little can surpass the reality-effect of a number or, even better, a date. The magical ciphers fasten a discourse to an actual occurrence, something that really happened. This bond pervades the rest

7. On the romantic death, cf. Auden's later remarks on Wagnerian desire in "Balaam and His Ass": "But the infinite romantic passion of Tristan and Isolde which has no past and no future outside itself cannot be generated by a finite quality; it can only be generated by finiteness-in-itself against which it protests with an infinite passion of rejection. . . . They do not yield because their passion is not for each other but for something they hope to obtain by means of each other, Nirvana, the primordial unity that made the mistake of begetting multiplicity, 'der Finsternis die sich das Licht gebar' " (DH, 121–22).

of the work, gradually congealing it into simple fact. Thus the poet's shrewd choice of a topic almost effaces the worrisome difficulty that there are incongruous discourses implicated in the hard fact itself, as well as highly contentious rivals competing for its interpretation.

To enhance the poet's powers even further, "September 1, 1939" is the beneficiary of a historical accident. At the time it was written, the Second World War was only a vague prospect. For more than a year it was to remain "the phony war."[8] But apart from a few specialists, not many people would place the poem against its actual backdrop of the uncertainties of late 1939. What if war had been averted through diplomatic means; or the French had heroically thrown back the aggressors so it became a Gallic triumph; or the Germans had won, so that the objective academics of today naturally viewed the invasion as an inevitable expression of the universal will? As matters turned out, however, "September 1, 1939" happened to precede the war that was to become the last credible apocalypse (at least for a while), a struggle between absolute good and supreme evil. Subsequent conflicts (Korea, Vietnam, Cambodia, Lebanon, Nicaragua) have been far too beset with ambiguity to be assimilated within this archetype. So the illegibility of "September 1, 1939" arises not only from the poet's shrewd choice of an occasion but from a historical accident.

Rhetorically, the poet seizes an opportunity to intensify the usual strategy of indifference by shifting to one of its variants, resentment. Whereas indifference takes little notice of its recipients, resentment adopts a more active part. It still relegates the audience to the anonymous oblivion of a public. But it fosters a stronger identification with the poet's voice by condoning a deep contempt for that public. "September 1, 1939" marks a day of revealed betrayal. The invasion showed that, under the pretext of official diplomacy (comity, forbearance), the Nazis were in fact taking a course of aggression. So in addition to breaking a treaty, the invasion offered a mortal insult: it ridiculed its unwary victims as dupes. It exposed them as being obtuse, cowardly, and unwilling to notice what was happening (the retributive laws, the domestic terror)

8. Samuel Hynes, *The Auden Generation: Literature and Politics in England in the 1930s* (New York: Viking, 1972), p. 381: "The fall and winter of 1939 were the time of the 'phony war,' when England and Germany were officially at war, but were not doing any fighting."

lest they be obligated in some way. In "September 1, 1939," however, the poet manages this insult by transferring its blame. He intimates that those willing to adopt his voice must have known all along about the treachery. Involved as it always is in a shift of blame, the resentment implies that the despised many, the anonymous public, were the ones who failed in vigilance. So in this admirable disciplinary economy, a member of that public, by simply accepting the poet's voice, can redirect a grievous affront, transcend the contemptible herd, and enjoy a considerably improved stature.

Because its choice of an occasion and use of resentment are such efficient disciplines and require little effort to operate, the poet of "September 1, 1939" can devote full attention to the management of his unruly text. He adopts the pose of a median drunk: past the early glow of euphoria but not yet at the point of incoherence. This moment is accorded an almost sacred privilege. The lucid drunk is one of the popular archetypes of authenticity (*in vino veritas*), an individual who is unfettered, intently focused, enraged against hypocrisy and injustice. There is nothing idealistic or sentimental about this privilege. The drunk serves as a safe repository of community mores. With both critical and perceptual sensibilities blunted, the drunk's discourse declines to the level of everyday wisdom. The resulting *veritas* is a compendium of unquestioned and thus coercive dictates.[9] The drunk does not have a language, only the stale leavings of one, all that goes without saying.

> I and the public know
> What all schoolchildren learn,
> Those to whom evil is done
> Do evil in return.

> The strength of Collective Man.

> Not universal love
> But to be loved alone.

9. Cf. "Balaam and His Ass": "A proverb has nothing to do with history for it states, or claims to state, a truth which is valid at all times. . . . Proverbs belong to the natural world where the Model and imitation of the Model are valid concepts. A proverb tells one exactly what one should do or avoid doing whenever the situation comes up to which it applies" (DH, 138).

> Hunger allows no choice
> To the citizen or the police
> (EA, 245–46)

Certainly this pose has its rhetorically persuasive aspect. But its more important function is to permit the poet a specific license with language. Under ordinary circumstances, such a parade of truisms would be differently encoded: as the mark of a bore or sanctimonious hypocrite. Yet as the words of an archetypal authenticity, the clichés become semantic residues, precious deposits of a generally approved authority. Through the adept selection of a persona, then, the poet takes advantage of a good disciplinary opportunity. He secures the right to a concrete discourse, one whose aphoristic basis is so solid and massive (immediately apparent, universally evident) that it may provide a secure foundation for the truth.

Yet it is this very stability that incites the textual symptoms. As foundation, the aphorisms furnish an incorporative limit: something that entirely contains what it bears. Should a sufficient discursive mass fall outside the aphorism's perimeter, the structure would be off-center and in danger of collapse. As a rule, the poet of "September 1, 1939" exercises complete control, even to the point of sometimes faltering as part of his chosen persona. It is not that a phrase is slurred, but that it is incorrectly gauged, a shade excessive for its task. As if aware of fading powers, the drunk carefully compensates through a minor overperformance, preferring the technical to the ordinary, the elegant to the commonplace. Yet these planned miscues also have a further effect, which is to destabilize the solid aphorisms by admitting the possibility of a variety of accents. Hence the poetic justice of "September 1, 1939": to maintain a persona whose pose of drunken earnestness enables him to repress textual instability, the poet must allow a series of miscues that, in effect, resubmit that instability.

The ensuing textual dialogue unfolds as an unequally voiced struggle between aphorism and miscue. Ordinary usage would not have "the clever hopes *expire*" (EA, 245) but have them disappear, pass away or die. In expiring, they depart, after the fashion of defunct official documents, for some nameless bureau of dead letters. Yet that expiration leaves behind an inconvenient body. Because it might play host to an array of dissident forces, this inconvenient body requires an aphoristic interment: "The unmentionable odor of death / Offends the September night" (EA, 245). The subsequent burial takes the form of an adequate explanation, a credible myth of origins whose "accurate scholarship can / Unearth the whole offense" (EA, 245). Yet this myth of origins provides too little restriction, for its scene of beginnings is one in which figures beget figures: "What huge imago made / A psychopathic god" (EA, 245). Shifting to another myth, that of the intending author, the poet invokes "exiled Thucydides" to entomb the unregenerate body within a cenotaph, confining it "all in his book" (EA, 245). At this moment of near containment, though, the miscues force the poem to a crisis by admitting a medley of hybrid inscriptions: "the enlightenment driven away" (pretentious intellectual history crossed with sentimentality); "the habit-forming pain" (a trope from the rhetoric of a magazine advertisement); "mismanagement and grief" (diplomatic euphemism grafted onto genteel trivialization). These miscues interfere with any efforts to master the textual body, since they readmit the diversity through which it eludes even a classical analysis, "all that a speech can say" (EA, 245).

What gives "September 1, 1939" its uncanny aspect is the sense that the poet recognizes this textual strife and is thoroughly conversant with it, as if its disruptions were a familiar adversary. No ordinary foe but the text is what engages the poet's attentions, even though the evidence of this struggle has been scrupulously erased. Realizing the necessity of a more moderate discipline, the poet retreats from the global to the specific: the scene at the bar itself. Citing such fixtures as the obligatory mirror (to make a small, narrow room appear more spacious), the conventional music and furnishings, even his own angry tones, "the windiest militant trash" (EA, 246), he fashions these details into semblances of the text. Thus, even though he concedes a disruptive diversity ("Each language pours its vain / Competitive excuse"; EA, 245), the poet manages to stifle its clamor within an atmosphere of meaning, "this neutral air," whose banality can support only what is already known ("faces along the bar," "the normal heart"). The brilliance of this maneuver is that its uses metaphorical vestiges of the body to restrict the unruly text. For a while at least, anarchic metonymy is encompassed within more conservative metaphor. Nonetheless, the miscues still pursue their disruptive play. When "all the conventions conspire" (EA, 246), their mingled breathing intimates another body, a giant form briefly gathered into an aggregate yet assembled from varied points. And because the traces of this assemblage remain implacably evident, even the most elemental and static aspects of that body suffer "the error bred in the bone" (EA, 246), a wandering both inherent and irrepressible.

Because each discipline provokes a responsive inscription, the poet's control of the text becomes a matter of magic or enchantment. Through a suitable violence, a restoration of the one true voice lost in the textual din, meaning must be preserved, in other words, destroyed (as further response). Growing cagey, the poet tries a medley of tactics: a parodic paraphrase of the "dense commuters" and their vow; a plea for the social messiah ("Who can release them now, / Who can reach the deaf, / Who can speak for the dumb?"; EA, 246); a splendid defiance of over-whelming odds ("All I have is a voice"); and as a result of such courage, an autogenesis that gives birth to a new Adam, fearless and entire:

> May I, composed like them
> Of Eros and of dust,
> Beleaguered by the same
> Negation and despair,
> Show an affirming flame.
> (EA, 247)

The question may be asked, as the poet assumes it will, What is wrong with hope in a dark time? At the level of sentiment and action, nothing. Abominations arise, and they must be brought to an end. But that is not what is at issue in "September 1, 1939." Its stirring convictions could easily be found in a range of contemporary protests. Rather, the covert project of this work is to reintroduce at the level of discursive discipline the same elements it finds so reprehensible at the level of historical events: subterfuge and violence in support of a repressive totality.

The poet's concluding medley of tactics, a virtuoso effect, is designed to limit the damage of his persona's miscues. The rapid sequence of gestures shifts the emphasis to his aphorisms, which provide interludes of immediate and reassuring sense. Nonetheless, the miscues still manage to serve their disruptive function. Prior to his final petition to some vague god of order, the poet attempts to contain the offensive body within a last, summary metaphor.

> Defenceless under the night
> Our world in stupor lies;
> Yet, dotted everywhere,
> Ironic points of light
> Flash out wherever the Just
> Exchange their messages.
>
> (EA, 247)

This passage withdraws what it concedes, first recognizing the body as an ineradicable landscape, the scene within which meaning must be pursued, and then reducing it to a condition even more manageable than death, a coma. If an adversary can neither be beaten nor be dismissed, a conditional acceptance is best. Yet the miscue of "stupor" is awkward enough to become responsive. A scion from the same stem as "stupid," it makes an accusation, in fact one similar to the insult of the invasion: that what should have been an attentiveness to a scene of diversity has allowed itself to be duped by a cunning reassurance. The insult is disguised only because "stupor" shifts from the sentient to the physiological and hence from a culpable condition to an involuntary one. But as a result of this shift, the metaphor impels the poem not forward to the finale but back into a neglected genealogy; what induced the stupor? Through so casual a misstep, the troublesome text that the poet had almost escaped is reopened. The world in stupor is "dotted everywhere," diacritically marked, its varied items starred with tiny points that, since they lack either legend or accompanying gloss, are limited only by the discourses imaginable at the moment. Brief, existing only in passage, these flashes do not convey a meaning or obey a voice. Instead they permit an exchange, points of convergence among the Just (missed, dumb, or whatever), a group for which poet and text have considerably differing accents.

The struggle between the text and a presiding voice can evolve but never halt. As Auden illustrates in "The Maker," which translates the Greek word for poet, this figure is more accurately thought of not as a lyricist ("songs / Encourage laboring demes, amuse the idle") or an orator ("sophists / Don't do metallurgy" (CP, 555), but as an artisan. A descendent of Haephaestos, the poet is the obscure, faintly despised cripple who forges "the Perfect Object," an ultimate prosthesis whose beautiful fatality avenges the body's treacherous limp.[10] The poet's task is to make these capable contrivances available so that the unscrupulous may have power and the inattentive certainty. Regrettably, though, poets have not supplied their inventions with the necessary warning:

> beware, then, maladroit
> Thumb-sucking children of all ages,
> Lest on your mangled bodies the court verdict
> Be Death by Misadventure.
>
> (CP, 555)

The poet's perennial work, which is distinct and even antithetical to the arranging scriptor's project, is to improve on the last device, to make its violence even more natural and its disciplines inevitable.

•

An occasional poem, based on an actual event, can certainly achieve an impressive reality-effect. But it also takes considerable risks. Because it is obliged to maintain a credible kinship with a record of references, its themes are limited, as well as subject to contradiction: that things were different. Yet these problems can be diminished by moving from a specific occasion to its more human (psychological, spiritual) consequences. What are the advantages of this shift? For one thing, it eliminates the lively competition that occurs at the level of supposedly objective fact. The shift to the more abstract leads into a mythic realm of universal truths. Here dissent would be in poor taste. Moreover, the shift itself is easily concealed: by adapting a pose as the natural *consequence* of another event, which is itself an indisputable given, the discourse of mythic verities gains an associative advantage. Parasitic upon the lan-

---

10. There is also a connection with Blake's Los, another smithy who uses hammer and anvil, but with the difference that Auden's artisan works in a medium that is even more elemental hence more diverse than Blake's mythemes, the cultural sediments of discourse itself. *Blake, Complete Writings* . . . , ed. Geoffrey Keynes (Oxford: Oxford University Press, 1971), p. 259.

guage of external fact, it become factual itself, acquiring the solid realism of the events from which it is derived. This elimination of competitors and parasitic factuality are worthwhile advantages for a practicing poet, yet there is still another. Having reached a plane of mythic universals, what began as a discourse of humble consequences may then, because of its greater spiritual authority (the eternal verities of the soul), come to encompass, explain, determine the prior language of fact. In other words, a purely mythic discourse, even while enjoying the borrowed solidity of its factual beginnings, usurps the place of that factuality and starts to function as an origin unto itself. These complex disciplinary effects are apparent in "Memorial for the City," one of Auden's monuments to the power of the poetic voice.

The poem is set in the ruins of postwar Europe, before the rebuilding under the Marshall plan. Because the war itself is over, "Memorial for the City" is not an occasional poem. Its topic is a mood or atmosphere rather than an event. It assumes the question of the weary survivor: not, Why did this have to happen? but, How is it possible to continue after it did? Thus the poem locates its concern within a suitably abstract realm, the spiritual despair of the West. Even so, it manages to leave the impression of a tough, unillusioned survey, though its inquiry is entirely mythic. A few well-placed details (a crematorium chimney, a tanker sunk by a U-boat, a bombed hotel) impart an objective quality, especially since the poem does not claim to challenge or even to be concerned with such familiar givens, but only to elaborate their human implications. Yet this elaboration is shrewdly expansive, even imperialistic. Because it operates on the remote plane of humanist universals, the poetic discourse of "Memorial" pursues hope by way of revelation. It claims to explore the collective unconscious, discover what went awry, and then divulge a true Image, an authentic essence which if only heeded is capable of preventing such disasters in the future. Through a modest aggression, then, the discourse that only moments before had embraced the humble role of an examiner of consequences, now becomes the source and determinant of what had previously been its objective foundation. If nothing else, the disciplines of "Memorial for the City" illustrate the power of a patient indirectness.

Although its disciplines are so adept as to be almost imperceptible, the poet of "Memorial" is quite aware of the fantastic nature of his realism. Like other cosmographers, he begins with violence, proceeds to catastrophe, and ends with vengeance. Yet to do so intrudes on the domain of religion, which has always known that reality might not survive without its mythic props. So to be on the safe side, the poet invokes a vague Christianity, lest his mythic machinations become too noticeable and thus ineffective. The artistry here is to maintain a light touch. Religion must be invoked as the guarantee of a certain form of explanation, yet not relied on: summoned as a matter of propriety, not necessity. Christianity is well suited to this purpose because its symbols are readily recognized. So its authority can be implicated with a minimum of effort. An epigraph from a medieval mystic, a few biblical allusions (to Adam, the Cross, the Last Judgment) will suffice. These references also add another degree of protection. Should the poet's virtuoso reality-effect be challenged as a quite fantastic fabrication, he is still safely wrapped in the mantle of an impenetrable, if self-conferred, priesthood.

Does it follow that "Memorial for the City" implies an active antagonism, between the scriptor who arranges discursive differences and the biographical Auden who maintains certain intellectual ties? Although the accounts of Auden's religious conversion are probably overstated, there is evidence to support the idea that he found Christianity a useful ally in his struggle against authoritarianism. Is it therefore incredible to suggest that the presiding poet of an Auden text would use religion as simply another disciplinary technique? This is putting it plainly. Yet the question needs to be reversed: who else, other than a believer, would be either inclined or able to illustrate such disciplinary opportunism? In the "Postscript: Christianity and Art," Auden suggests that any overt liaisons between the two must be warily approached. "I sometimes wonder if there is not something a bit questionable, from a Christian point of view, about all works of art which make overt Christian references. They seem to assert that there is such a thing as a Christian culture, which there cannot be" (DH, 458). This seems an odd parting of the ways, between a religion and its symbols. But it is necessitated by the unusual status of Christianity, which is both a specific discourse itself and a commitment to historical development through an exchange among discourses. Even though Christianity has its own recognizable symbols, its historical task would argue against setting them up as imperial or definitive emblems. As Auden insists, "there can no more be a 'Christian' art than there can be a Christian science or a Christian diet" (DH, 458). Thus it is probable that unlike "Spain," in which there is a clear divergence between its scriptor and the biographical figure, "Memorial" presents an even more startling congruence between the two. That is, it is *because* Auden was a believing Christian that he would not have hesitated, as a scriptor who compiles disciplines and traces their inscriptive responses, to fashion a poet who makes ingenious use of a repressive piety.

But is there any basis for thinking that Auden believed in the particular kind of Christianity this presupposes, a historical religion which, unlike its gnostic rivals, did not reject the body and its journey through time? This question, which calls for the elaborate apparatus of traditional source criticism, would lead far afield from "Memorial," except that it attends the poem as its epigraph. "In the self-same point that our soul is made sensual, in the self-same point is the City of God ordained to him from without beginning." The passage from Juliana of Norwich is sufficiently orthodox in its main themes, the spirituality of human existence, the City of God. But it arranges those elements in an unusual way. It asserts that the embodiment of the soul, the temporal dimension of an otherwise inconceivable existence, ordains the City of God, establishes and founds it, not as a distant promise but as a present event. The interest of the passage lies in its seeming to be about the corporeal while actually concerning a modification of the spiritual. Because of the soul's historical body, its journey through an arena of conflicting discursive forms, the City of God is indeterminate, "*without beginning*," irreducible to any one explanation or final truth. That is why the City of God is not promised as some distant reward, a spiritual condition apart from human experience, but ordained, embarked upon at the instant of embodiment as a present recognition of the risk and delight of that experience.

On the strength of its epigraph, a text within a text that incites a dialogue, the title's issue is decided before the poem is begun. "Memorial for the City" is less a pious monument to the dead than a recollection of the inscribed. It designates the arena whose rivalries are continuously active even if neglected or suppressed.

Nevertheless, the presiding poet can still rely on some effective disciplines to sustain the illusion of mastery over the text. The individual sections of "Memorial for the City" make capable use of a parodic succession. Each section deals with a different historical epoch, and each epoch is allotted an imitative style. But there is an interesting shift in the way the styles are used. At first, they are implemented efficiently, unobtrusively. Yet in the course of each section its designated style becomes more exaggerated, awkward, as if flustered at something it can no longer repress. What begins as a just representation, a faithful mimesis, ends as a parodic exaggeration of itself. In this way, each style is effectively discarded as the poem advances to the next phase and eventually achieves its revelatory destination. What are the disciplinary advantages of this parodic succession? It permits the public a double gratification: the thrill of momentarily identifying with an alien discourse and the even greater satisfaction of witnessing its demise. A voice is adopted, even indulged for a while, but then parodically relegated to the wreckage of the past. The power of this discipline extends well beyond its obvious hermeneutic allure, the assurance that since error is continually being discarded, the poet must be approaching the one thing beyond parody, the voice of plain truth. For the parodic succession also offers a seductive semblance of dialogism. Certainly its constant movement acknowledges a range of historical differences. But rather than configuring and contrasting those differences, the parody discards them in seriatim fashion. In place of a continuing exchange, it offers the satisfaction of a triumphant progress.

To enlist a prejudice so entrenched as to be imperceptible, the poet begins his pathology of Western discourse with the Greeks. This is not a definitive origin but a possessed one: the Greeks are ours. The section is cast in the manner of a psychotic intensity, suggestive of a fated world in which nothing, not even pure destruction, can be averted. The one respite from despair is to make events aesthetically beautiful.

> The crow on the crematorium chimney
> And the camera roving the battle
> Record a space where time has no place.
> On the right a village is burning, in a market-town to the left
> The captives are led away, while far in the distance
> A tanker sinks into a dedolant sea.

> This is the way things happen; for ever and ever
> Plum-blossom falls on the dead, the roar of the waterfall covers
> The cries of the whipped and the sighs of the lovers
> And the hard bright light composes
> A meaningless moment into an eternal fact
> Which a whistling messenger disappears with into a defile.
>
> (CP, 450)

The description bears a deliberate similarity to the newsreels shown between features during the war. The camera locks its subjects in an eternal present where nothing can die because it is never quite alive. Atrocities are recorded with an impassive, even lilting equanimity. Any impulse of concern or responsibility, the basis of civilization, recedes into the ecstasy of voyeurism. So it comes as a relief when this intolerable fatalism deteriorates into a sing-song that mimics itself: "One enjoys glory, one endures shame; / He may, she must. There is no one to blame" (CP, 450). The self-parody prepares for a shift to another voice, one that departs from an acknowledged mistake, "our grief is not Greek" (CP, 451). But it also discloses a syntactic body. Far from being implacable or intransigent, the "abiding / Mother of gods and men" (CP, 450), this textual body is awkward, almost dislocated in its movements, as if it were a mechanical apparatus. Thus the textual gestures respond to the aesthetic fatalism not with a corrective but a difference. The inevitable rounds of pastoral and epic are contrived systems, a human artifice; more than merely debris within a "chaos of graves" (CP, 450), they offer a variable structure.

Yet the poet is unperturbed by the text's response. If dislocations can be used to illustrate the contrived hence alterable quality of a discourse, they can also be used as a disciplinary tactic. The second section of "Memorial for the City" might be called its baroque phase, even though it spans the period from Pope Gregory to a fin-de-siècle decadence. It is baroque in its use of a kaleidoscopic montage as a descriptive mode. Historical peculiarities are rushed by at high speed so they seem both comic and disjointed, as in the pantomimes of a silent film.

> The facts, the acts of the City bore a double meaning:
> Limbs became hymns; embraces expressed in jest

A more permanent tie; infidel faces replaced
   The family foe in the choleric's nightmare;
The children of water parodied in their postures
   The infinite patience of heaven;
Those born under Saturn felt the gloom of the day of doom.
                         (CP, 451)

The comic effect is part of the poet's reductive program. Each discourse is confined to an unalterable grammar: a few colorful elements held in an arrangement at once haphazard and rigid. No peripheral details or unsanctioned relations are admitted. Consequently, the intricate maze of historical development is reduced to a series of snapshots, connected only by the accident of temporal sequence.

Yet this repression is hardly tolerated by the accompanying syntax, which constantly strays into unassimilable novelties. The poet's repetition, "the facts, the acts," is designed as an intensifier: a move from the static to the dynamic, that is, from the stated truth to its underlying reality. But in the pairings that follow, this intensifying reduction is at once disrupted and articulated so that its implied synecdoche, reinforced by the poet's distracting half-rhymes, induces a series of discursive contrasts. The pious hymns cannot quite exhaust the performing capacities of active limbs. A culture may wish it could attain permanent ties, but human bonds are as transient as the embraces and faces through which they are symbolized. The day of doom overshadows all, yet it is as much a private nightmare as an astral revelation. Thus in response to the poet's discontinuous monoliths, his collection of six representative cities (New, Sane, Sinful, Rational, Glittering, Conscious, the seventh being the unnameable), the textual body intimates that hard facts do indeed lead into revelatory acts. They become movements in an ebullient drama whose scenes admit a range of distinctive rituals, mercantile, familial, political, scientific.

Although the control wielded by a poet's reassuring voice is finally an illusion, it can be sustained through the expedient of a sequel that reasserts vocal authority. The poet of "Memorial for the City" reacts to the textual dissidence by reducing its potential articulation to an ironic absurdity. If connectedness is what the text counters, that is what it shall get. The third, or postwar, section of "Memorial for the City" adopts the style of a surrealist dream sequence. Time is slowed from its frenetic pace in the baroque segment. Objects becomes weightless, as if floating in a void. Rather than a series of comic collisions, action occurs as an insidious metastasis.

> Across the square,
> Between the burnt-out Law Courts and Police Headquarters,
> Past the Cathedral far too damaged to repair,
> Around the Grand Hotel patched up to hold reporters,
> Near huts of some Emergency Committee,
> The barbed wire runs through the abolished City.
>
> (CP, 452)

In a world where any discourse is on equal footing with every other, where prepositions are the recurrent grammatical element because any-thing can be connected to anything else, objects lack the solidity of either truth or value. The only rules are arbitrary division and brutal restraint, the barbed wire. Thus the poet parodies the baroque section's threat of connectedness with the leveling relativism of this postwar nightmare. Yet in a fascinating reversal, the usually disruptive syntactic body responds to this anarchic threat with a rhythmic equanimity. The diversity of the city's arena does not mean that pattern is abolished, only challenged, to make way for more complex cadences. As a form of intimidation, relativ-ism proposes an all-or-nothing alternative of order or chaos: "a place, a path, a railroad ends, / The humor, the cuisine, the rites, the taste, / The pattern of the City, are erased" (CP, 452). But the syntactic equa-nimity of the text indicates a considerable middle ground. The erasure does not quite leave a void, only a blankness, a field of difference in which the distinctions between an enclosed scene ("a place"), a topogra-phy with an exit ("a path"), and a terminus that leads into a network of further lines ("a railroad") are both important and insistent.

Throughout the poet's endeavor, the textual body proves a stubborn nemesis, engaging each ingenious discipline with a countergesture. Al-ways the poetic ambition is to find a way to stifle this resistance by attaining a final mastery over words. Sometimes subtlety must yield to harsher tactics. If unvoiced inscriptions are the problem, why not simply assign the resistant text a voice and thereby control it by means of an imputed response. In this way, the unruly text might be restricted to a harmless eloquence and the violence then concealed as the modesty of a poet who withdraws before a greater power (shrewdly devised in advance). Thus in a moment of revelatory bravura, the poet goes "behind the mirror" (CP, 452), the devious surface of signs, to attain a modern icon, "our Image." This revealed source has some remarkable qualities. It underlies all the varied states of consciousness, "the same / Awake or dreaming." It is perfectly coincident with a true identity, "it has no image to admire." It is free from the conflicts of the body, "no age, no sex." It is cut off from any repertoire of signs, "no memory." It is detached from its limiting cultural moment, "no creed." In short, it is beyond the grasp of the language it speaks, and in speaking masters, as a being with "no name." Having discovered this carefully wrought icon of the body, the poet need only play the part of liturgist at some awful rite who steps aside in deference to the ultimate: "*Let Our Weakness speak*" (CP, 453). This is the voice that shall at last dominate the text.

The ensuing performance must measure up to such an impressive prologue. Adopting the role of a star witness, the police informant, the poet gives his image of the text an absolutely authentic voice: that of a much abused victim, sworn to truth, implacably dedicated to revenge. "At the place of my passion her [the city's] photographers are gathered together; / but I shall rise again to hear her judged" (CP, 453). Through this pose of apocalyptic retribution, the Image manages to recover the last word, quite effectively finishing the text, forcing it into submission through a voice that eludes its inscriptions to become immediate sense. Everything in this last section is utterly direct. Each statement is absolute in its candor.

Yet such directness is itself the means of syntactic betrayal. The frontal quality of the Image's discourse is striking. It conceals nothing, in fact takes an exhibitionist's delight in displaying what is most shameful. Yet this aggressive directness is oddly defensive. Although it claims a full and complete exposure, it must continuously reexpose itself, attaining each revelation only to be compelled to assert a further nakedness, as if to make up for something withheld in the previous one.

Without me Adam would have fallen irrevocably with Lucifer; he would never have been able to cry *O felix culpa*.

189

It was I who suggested his theft to Prometheus; my frailty cost Adonis his
    life.
I heard Orpheus sing; I was not quite as moved as they say.
I was not taken in by the sheep's-eyes of Narcissus; I was angry with Psyche
    when she struck a light.
I was in Hector's confidence; so far as it went.

(CP, 453)

Through a too persistent directness, then, the syntactic body begins to
suggest a more surreptitious concealment, a candor that is proffered as
a substitute. But since the poet's Image claims to be a final revelation,
an absolute priority, there can be no dark antecedents for the discourse to
withhold. This impossibility is corroborated by the apocalyptic scheme of
the Image's testimony, which follows a familiar itinerary of Fall, pre-
Christian error, crucifixion, the uncertain Pentecosts of the romance
world, and Last Judgment. Such a strongly marked Christian myth, the
whole plan of salvation, bears the conservative connotations of a discourse that is neutral, inclusive, definitive.

Nonetheless, the at once insistent and compensatory directness of the
syntactic body entails a further aspect, something even more deeply
repressed than the various abuses and humiliations that are so gladly
displayed. This shameful disclosure is the remnant of a priority that
antedates the aboriginal Image. Supposedly it has been waiting behind
all written texts, behind even history itself, for its chance to speak. But
the compensatory quality of its candor suggests that this is not the case.
The utter frankness conceals a further text, the point of a derivation,
from the bard Taliesin's challenge in *The Mabinogion:*

> I was with my Lord in the highest sphere,
> On the fall of Lucifer into the depth of hell . . .

> I have been with my Lord in the manger of the ass;
> I strengthened Moses through the water of Jordan;
> I have been in the firmament with Mary Magdalene . . .

> I have been teacher to all intelligences,
> I am able to instruct the whole universe.

I shall be until the day of doom on the face of the earth;
And it is not known whether my body is flesh or fish.[11]

The potential responses of this origin are incalculable. It revises the aboriginal into the contested, indeed a game of one-upsmanship. It frames the Christian as the alien, a relatively late import into a world of older cults. And from the poet's vantage, the reappearance of a repressed precursor, whatever its provenance, marks the impossibility of achieving an ultimate voice. There can be no possession of the last word, no end to the resistances and inscriptions of the text. For language has its own indomitable memory, and no voice can achieve any more than the passing illusion of a priority to the text.

11. *The Mabinogion,* trans. Charlotte Guest (London, 1877; reprinted Cardiff: John Jones, 1977), pp. 482–483.

CHAPTER SEVEN

The Returns of Caliban

There's a flying trickster in that wood,
And we shan't be there to help with our love.
— "Have a Good Time"

In a stage production, Caliban should be as monstrously conspicuous as possible, and, indeed, suggest, as far as decency permits, the phallic.
— "Balaam and His Ass"

Can a voice undo its native violence? Rather than attempting to ignore, repress, or ingeniously outwit its accompanying text, might it pursue another task? Could it not deliberately play the inscriptions: provoking dissonances, actually inciting responses? To develop this question, it is necessary to consider a most unusual voice, one that would otherwise be left in silence (as illicit or obscene) because it undermines its own propriety and sense. Such an utterance gaily, recklessly, subverts the very apparatus that safeguards its preeminence over the text.

It is curious that Auden has Caliban give the afterword to *The Sea and the Mirror*. Ariel would be the more sensible choice. A magician's familiar, Ariel represents "the invisible spirit of imagination," an essence devoid of any distracting material taint, a pure or in other words "a disembodied voice" (DH, 132). Through his entirely natural and compelling discourse, Ariel could soothe any flutters of doubt by listing the sources, themes, truths of the play. A perfect critic, he might fulfill an effigy's discreet if somewhat sadistic fantasy: a complete account which, by stating the plain truth about a work of literature, manages to banish forever the troubling opacities of its text. Yet these fond hopes are dashed when instead Caliban appears. The shocking emergence of this monster restates the perennial question of Auden's poetics. What remains after the magician's entourage, the mythical powers of voice, have left the stage? Caliban stands for the rights of the otherwise silenced text. Grotesque, he is pieced together from sundry creatures, a protean sea-monster who recognizes no unifying ideal. Guttural, his rasping tones spoil even the simplest utterance, afflicting it with an obnoxious noise. Phallic, he admits what must at all costs be covered up, a revolting excess bent upon sordid liaisons, comic displays.

Sometimes destiny can be coaxed from a name. Caliban may be a corruption of Caribbean: "r" and "l" tend to be interchangeable in American languages. So Caliban would suggest a shorter version of "calibbean." He is born not so much from language as from its decay, a monster bereft of any existence outside a prior word. His rightful paternity is masked by the transformative magic of an unnatural intervention, the witch Sycorax. And so Caliban embarks on his imaginative wanderings. Permanently cast in the role of an epilogue, a word upon a word, Caliban is unthinkable without a former text, *The Tempest*, a region dense with exotic names and dissident voices. Within the site of this derivation, Caliban offers a chance for reading. Nothing more than a corrupted name, he is less a character than an interpretive gambit, an invitation to sound texts in a distinct yet far from determined way. For in Caliban there is an unusual convergence between the word as derivative from a field of inscriptions, and its performance as a violence to those inscriptions. Caliban is an actor playing an actor, a character who enacts readings rather than deeds.[1] Such sophistication might seem at odds with his crude, elemental nature, but if anything it makes him more outrageously apt. Caliban is of course also adapted, as a possible anagram, from cannibal (calibann). A savage, he refuses the violence of even necessary restrictions and responds with a complex counterviolence: at once holding such limits up for ridicule and reshuffling their values to release, as in his own case, uncouth, alien accents.

Having usurped the Ariel/critic's rightful place, Caliban enjoys some enviable advantages. He has the undivided attention of the audience.

---

1. Cf. Auden's remark on a similar character, Falstaff: "In Falstaff's world, every moment is one of infinite possibility where anything can be wished" (DH, 193).

There are no other characters with whom he must share the stage, nor any threats of future contradiction. As the bearer of an actual character's name, he has a solid claim to authenticity, based on a presumed access to the author's intention. And as a conspicuous gap in the text, the one element omitted from the play's comic synthesis, he offers an ideal standpoint for a profound insight. Yet Auden's Caliban says nothing about Shakespeare's *Tempest*. He is like Lazarus, back from the dead. There are myriad questions Caliban might answer concerning a realm no living person has ever seen. But they never arise. It is as if an abyss intervenes between character and work, voice and text, so that Caliban may not speak of the play from which he has emerged. Instead he contends with the obvious disappointment of his audience at meeting him and not a more impressive (respectable, credible) character. For this disappointment gives Caliban access to his chosen topic, which is the unconscious expectations the audience brings to the performance. "And now at last it is you, assorted, consorted specimens of the general popular type, the major flock who have trotted trustingly hither but found, you reproachfully baah, no grazing, that I turn to and address on behalf of Ariel and myself" (CP, 334). Caliban's concern is not the original play but its likely readings, which he obstreperously proceeds to enact.

How is a reading shaped? What factors enter into its seemingly spontaneous judgments of value, truth? Caliban approaches that question by traversing a symbolic landscape, not of desire but of its formation. What interests him about human experience is not its extended periods of habit but its rare moments of dislocation, in which a shift occurs from one dominant discourse to another.

> The Journey of Life—the down-at-heels disillusioned figure can still put its characterization across—is infinitely long and its possible destinations infinitely distant from one another, but the time spent in actual travel is infinitesimally small. The hours the traveler measures are those in which he is at rest between the three or four decisive instants of transportation, which are all he needs and all he gets to carry him the whole of his way. (CP, 335)

In effect Caliban confronts his disgruntled audience with the scenes of their discursive instruction. These begin with the "singular transparent globes of enchantment" (CP, 334), a prelapsarian world that imagines itself in direct contact with a maternal, nurturing reality. This "childish spell" can be discovered only in retrospect, for it does not appear until it has been lost. Like any discourse, it remains absorbing, entrancing, until intruded upon by another. In fact its idyllic "globes" are places not of harmony but of neglect, where unity presides only because difference is ignored. Even so, such idylls continue to act as standards of completeness long after they have collapsed. They furnish the criteria against whose impossible perfection all subsequently met discourses are to be measured. Unsurprisingly, from this enchantment onward everything is downhill, in obedience to the demands of its retrospectively fashioned metaphor, the Fall.

After the trance of childhood, Caliban's next scene of instruction is "the Grandly Average Place." Drawn from one of Auden's favorite locales, the train depot, it offers an image of the discursive exchange, where past, present, and future converge. The opportunities are exciting, for love sometimes begins here, in "those promiscuous places of random association" (CP, 335). Yet because this scene is cast against the totality of an Eden forever lost, it seems squalid and threatening, a point of treacherous departure leading "the nearer Nowhere, that still smashed terminus at which he will, in due course, be deposited, seedy and by himself" (CP, 335). Although the act of reading through which ciphers are conjured into sense begins in mystification, it soon becomes a flight, into the "certainties of failure or success" (CP, 335), the safety of a career's rigid perspective. Unfortunately, this flight leads to an intolerable fate, the narrowness of professional interests.[2]

So it is at this moment that the magic of art is summoned to offer its replicas of the child's enchanting globes of enchantment. Here Caliban distinguishes between two different kinds of escapism, which might be dubbed *incestuous rapture* and *phallic ecstasy*. To the unambitious, art's magical representations must restore an authenticity whose truth is immediate, sufficient, nurturing. In these mollifying scenes, reading requires a continuous amusement, guaranteed by a benignly unquestionable if somewhat incoherent authority, "Master," "Captain," "Uncle," "O

2. Cf. the "Empiric Economic Man" of *New Year Letter:* "Or drive himself about creation / In the closed cab of Occupation" (CP, 184).

Cupid, Cupid" (CP, 336). But for the refined minority, "exhausted lions of the season, local authorities with their tense tired faces, elderly hermits of both sexes living gloomily in the delta of a great fortune" (CP, 337), the scenes of reading through which truth is devised must venerate paternal authority rather than maternal solace. Here what is valued is the power that permits a vengeful son's deliverance from the stifling mother, thus severance from the "terrible mess" of "this particularized life," and admission to "that Heaven of the Really General Case where, tortured no longer by three dimensions and immune from temporal vertigo, Life turns into Light, absorbed for Good into the permanently stationary, completely self-sufficient, absolutely reasonable One" (CP, 337).

As portrayed in Caliban's ludicrous figuration, reading does more than restore intentions, as if it were moving from natural marks or sounds to living truths. It entails complex scenes of instruction, an entire landscape of formative expectations, and it is these generative procedures themselves, not their semantic results, that Caliban reveals to his audience. Utterly modest, he has no illusion of winning them over. His only ambition is to offer an anatomy of their displeasure by showing how it is produced. Yet in a perverse way, even so modest a project is recuperative. True to Auden's title, Caliban holds up the mirror to life's sea of diversity, to reflect its sites of origin. Yet in the act of doing so, Caliban does not demystify and thereby restore his audience. He merely replaces one dogmatic stance with another. In the best mimetic tradition, he offers an alluring representation—complete, solid, authoritative—even if it is a representation of reading itself. A casualty of his own eloquence, Caliban cannot elude the violence of his own voice any more than he can avert the fate imposed on every character in a literary work: to be interesting.[3] With each phrase he achieves an illusory yet effective victory

---

3. This problem fascinated Auden. How is it possible for a character to both hold an audience's attention, thus confine interest within its thematic volume, as well as direct that attention into the varied resistances of its text? One solution is to establish a tension through a derangement in the character: this does not lend a voice to the text, but it does open a space in which inscriptions may be heard. For example, the madness of Don Quixote furnishes an opportunity for the text to interject a mundane practicality into the exalted world of chivalric romance. "Don Quixote's madness, on the other hand, might be called holy madness, for *amour-propre* has nothing to do with his delusions. If

over the text so that it becomes docile, a faithful means to a communicative end, thus a further extension of the tyrannical scenes he wishes to debunk. On its own terms, then, the trap is inescapable. In the course of anatomizing the scenes of instruction that produce a complacent totality, Caliban must use a voice whose Jamesian eloquence restores the foundations of that totality.

But if Caliban's dilemma is insoluble at a representational level, that is not the case with his syntactic gestures. True to Auden's later stage directions, Caliban displays an exuberant unrestraint. His relation to the text is not that of suppliant or seducer but of a lover delighting in the quirks of the beloved. This syntactic pose permits both ebullient inclusion and indiscriminate intermingling, as in Caliban's rendition of a nostalgic idyll:

> O take us home with you, strong and swelling One, home to your promiscuous pastures where the minotaur of authority is just a roly-poly ruminant and nothing is at stake, those purring sites and amusing vistas where the fluctuating arabesques of sound, the continuous eruption of colors and scents, the whole rich incoherence of a nature made up of gaps and asymmetrical events plead beautifully and bravely for our undistress. (CP, 336)

While it might be argued that such high spirits strengthen the powers of voice, they also have a provocative effect. As with Caliban's earlier portrayal of the Muse, "so marvelously at home with all her cosy swarm about her" (CP, 326), the overwrought exuberance welcomes such a medley of discursive elements that, when they begin to interact, it can only step back and enjoy the fray. For example, the mytheme "home" is put under the supervision of "strong and swelling One," a suitably phallic image of Caliban's own voice. Yet the swelling of the One, which hints at virile confidence, also introduces an accompanying tremolo of

---

his madness were of Lear's kind, then, in addition to believing that he must imitate the knight-errants of old, he would have endowed himself in their imagination with their gifts, e.g., with the youth and strength of Amadis of Gaul: but he does nothing of the kind; he knows that he is past fifty and penniless, nevertheless, he believes he is called to be a knight-errant" (DH, 136).

sound: the swelling as an ebb and flow that complicate the accents at play within its utterance. The ensuing disengagement of power from sound might afflict anything, even the presiding Minotaur. The name of this fellow monster brazenly links the offspring to the legal father. Yet the obviousness of that lie serves to underscore the extravagant lusts of an origin that all too eagerly yields to less orthodox paternities. As if perplexed by such sonorous play, the strong and swelling One becomes "ruminant," immobilized by different possibilities, its confident utterance held in an uncertain state, a generative throat, and yet at liberty within a field where "nothing is at stake." So it comes as no surprise that the home of this bewildered beast becomes potentially predatory in its "purring sites," for its soothing idyll admits a body and its minute choreography, "the fluctuating arabesques of sound," whose movement is at once an indecipherable complexity and a dancer's sinuous gestures.

Where, though, does Caliban stand in all this? Does he premeditate specific responses? Or more outrageous still, does he merely incite them, permitting his exuberance to release an incalculable resistance? The question can never be resolved. It is certain only that, perverse to the last, Caliban disrupts what he cannot elude, the dominance of his own voice. Through a syntactic exuberance that incites a host of disruptive inscriptions, Caliban matches the violence of his own impressive eloquence.

•

Must there be a permission to play? Auden's ludic voices, like those of his poets, are distinguished by their careful attention to the unruliness of the text, though with different aims. Whereas the poet wants to repress the inscriptions, Auden's players try to provoke them. It would seem logical that because a ludic voice is primarily engaged with the text, then as in the case of the poet, any concern for the audience would be a minor issue. Yet logic is often an unhelpful guide to the exchange between a discipline and its resistances. Caliban, for example, can count on rejection. He knows in advance that his audience will dismiss him because what he proposes is too threatening, indeed obscene: from the practice of augury, a disclosure of revolting entrails. But as a result of this highly probable rejection, Caliban enjoys a double privilege: he can more pointedly anatomize his audience's expectations and more wantonly indulge in syntactic exuberance. Unfettered, he illustrates an important aspect of artistic license, namely, that rejection opens a vista of ludic possibilities.

The converse of this raises an interesting question. If an anticipated rejection frees the ludic voice, by enabling its play to become all the more energetic and even outrageous, does it follow that an anticipated acceptance has a restraining effect, actually muting or inhibiting the play? It seems that when permission is given, the ludic voice is granted a deceptive indulgence, in that this permission implies certain restraints. That is, a provocation is allowed *as long as* it does not admit any inadmissible accents or *provided that* it preserves the mandatory decencies. In such instances of restraint by way of consent, a ludic performance is still possible, but it would not take Caliban as a model, at least not in any direct way. For a voice so licensed would have to be more patient in its portrayals of discursive production by shifting from mimicry to a subtler impersonation. Further, its syntactic gestures would need to be more understated, even reticent. This paradoxical reversal casts the issue of a writer's social concern in an unusual light. Under what circumstances is permission to play likely to be granted? Since a culture jealously safeguards its disciplinary resources, it is likely that permission will be given when the writer takes up a discourse that is either outmoded or little practiced (thus with no immediate value); and denied when the discourse is either current or widely accepted. To the extent that this paradox holds, it follows that Auden's engagements with the most tyrannical contemporary disciplines are apt to occur in works that are the most exorbitantly ludicrous (that is, permission is refused because the disciplines at stake are still operative, hence the play can be more vital). And to continue the paradox, it is Auden's more reserved and subdued performances that are likely to engage discourses with considerably less coercive power (so permission to play is granted because the disciplines thereby put at risk are not that important anyway). If this is the case, then Auden's schoolboy sketches and high-camp farces, precisely the passages that are most embarrassing to his serious commentators (How could a genius of such stature be so puerile, so immature?), would stage his engagement with the era's most dangerous discourses.

Fortunately, however, matters are not so simple. Although the paradox of permission raises issues that may seem sufficiently novel, even avant-garde, it only begins to explore a range of disciplinary structures that are both deeply entrenched and highly resourceful. Whenever there is an opportunity to complicate or defer the subversion of disciplines, the odds are its techniques have long since been perfected. If a permission to play has a repressive effect, it is certainly possible that in a given situation—for example, with a more sophisticated audience—permission might be granted in a preemptive fashion, as a way of maintaining control, by ensuring that matters do not get out of hand. So it would be inaccurate to fashion the paradox of permission as a straightforward reversal. It is too simple to maintain, for example, that play is permitted within a discourse that no longer matters, and forbidden within a discourse that still counts. In certain instances, most likely in times of high passion and moment when force is likely to rule anyway, a culture may indeed make the foolish mistake of putting its most efficient disciplines at risk by refusing to let them be the subject of a ludic voice. At other times, however, the restraint may occur in a subtler manner, so that permission to play would be granted as a means of preemption.

The paradox of permission may itself be apparent enough, but the evidence of Auden's poetry suggests that its discovery was no easy matter. An early work, "1929," indicates that only through a process of trial and error did Auden chance upon the release afforded by an anticipated refusal. Written during his *Wandersjahr* in Berlin, the poem is mainly concerned with the romantic quest for a new and vital language, which in practice means deliverance from one that is moribund.[4] The speaker of the poem senses the presence of natural and spontaneous rhythms: "It was Easter . . ." with its complex overtones of seasonal, liturgical, and mythic renewal. But these regenerative rhythms are outside the boundaries of respectable yet defunct discourses: "as I walked in the public gardens" (EA, 37). So it is necessary to set out for a new country, a place untouched by the memories and inhibitions of the past. The project of the poem is to proceed from what is human yet lifeless to a restoration of what is natural and vital. This distinctly *poetic* hope is expressed in the third section's epic simile, itself a marker of the longing for a return to natural rhythms.

---

4. Auden links this quest for renewal by way of rejection to the romantic dislike of the city, which provides a summary image for worn-out and discredited discourses (EF, 28–38).

Moving along the track which is himself
He loves what he hopes will last, which gone,
Begins the difficult work of mourning,
And as foreign settlers to strange country come,
By mispronunciation of native words
And by intermarriage create a new race
And a new language, so may the soul
Be weaned at last to independent delight.

(EA, 39)

That ambition, however, runs athwart a stubborn impossibility. What is natural, at least in the realms of discourse, is not at all the bright and beckoning future but the familiar languages of the past. These cultural productions only seem to be transparent, imperceptible, spontaneous because they have yet to be recognized as elaborate and highly contrived structures. So the poem's quest for the natural leads not to the sought-after renewal, only back to the morbidity it flees.

What makes "1929" so fascinating is that its speaker understands the impossibility, wants to reveal it, and yet finds it extremely difficult to do so because of a tacitly accorded permission. The poem follows a design that is so innocent, the discovery of a natural discourse, "an altering speech for altering things" (EA, 37), that it must anticipate acceptance of its project. Yet this anticipated permission curbs the ludic strategies of the poem. Bound within a web of implied expectations (that he will find a pure, inward language; that he will have nothing to do with the corrupt and teeming life of the city), the speaker must proceed with restraint. Rather than directly portraying his audience's practices, he must take them upon himself. The voice of "1929" neither allegorizes nor tropes but actually performs the discourses it wishes to disrupt. And for that disruption to occur, the syntactic mime must shift from the promiscuous exuberance of Caliban to a different stance, the vulnerability of being awkwardly direct, of adopting a bluntness akin to stupidity. Enacting sundry rituals of candor, the speaker treats the text as a simple device, a mastered instrument, one that offers little resistance and requires no great skill to operate. In this way, his various disciplines, unguarded against a resistance that stems from within their own text, release inscribed responses.

The initial pose, that of a genial conversationalist, suggests an effortless grace in which huge yet compliant forms are swept along in a harmonious synthesis: "Watching traffic of magnificent cloud / Moving without anxiety on open sky" (EA, 37). True to its self-imposed candor, such a voice is forbidden to hold anything back and thus finds itself obliged to record the next perception:

> But thinking so I came at once
> Where solitary man sat weeping on a bench,
> Hanging his head down, with his mouth distorted
> Helpless and ugly as an embryo chicken.
>
> (EA, 37)

For human beings at least, discursive forms are quite unmanageable, and their future direction (the mouth as a site of the voice's production) is an uncertain matter. Similar responses await the unguarded voices of the next two sections. A Yeatsian sublimity ("Or upright paddle on flickering stream, / Casually fishing at a passing straw"; EA, 37–38) leads to a compulsive automatism ("Yet sometimes man look and say good / At strict beauty of locomotive"; EA, 38). A Frostian pithiness ("home, a place / Where no tax is levied for being there"; EA, 39) stumbles on a less reverent ebullience of sound ("Startled by the violent laugh of a jay / I went from wood, from crunch underfoot"; EA, 39). Thus the successive voices of "1929," even though constrained by a permission to play, manage to incite inscriptive disruptions. Ostensibly, they search for a new language, one that will stir the soul and fix the truth. But their quest is reversed in that its sacred object, an authentic voice, is posited at the outset rather than achieved at the end. As a result, each attempt at a purely natural voice, instead of being guarded by demonic powers, is possessed by them, in the guise of its responsive inscriptions.

Like many of Auden's poems, particularly the earlier ones, "1929" is an experiment whose stages have been left in place. However troublesome to anyone demanding an expressive or thematic totality, this varied format is well suited to the shifts in ludic technique Auden wished to explore. In the poem's fourth section, permission to play is abruptly withdrawn. This occurs because the speaker no longer pursues an acceptable (harmless) poetic quest, the search for a personally valid voice, but instead strays into the public part of the discursive arena. The concern is no longer to find a language of personal authenticity, but to anatomize the components of a politically effective and current discourse, that of apocalyptic retribution. In its final section, then, the ludic voice of "1929" engages a popular mode of political radicalism. For this reason, its previously assumed permission to play is withdrawn. Apocalyptic discourse is too valuable, too spell-binding in its demagogic effectiveness, to be subject even to a poetic play.[5]

Of all four sections of "1929," the last one seems the most distinctly Audenesque and also the most successful, because of its sense of uninhibited fun. But this impression needs to be refined. It is not that the earlier sections are less characteristic of Auden, only less energetic in their use of ludic tactics. With permission to play withdrawn, the final section can more directly engage the practices it wishes to expose, as well as experiment with more overt forms of provocation. "It is time for the destruction of error," its speaker portentously warns.

> The falling leaves know it, the children,
> At play on the fuming alkali-tip
> Or by the flooded football ground, know it—
> This is the dragon's day, the devourer's:
> Orders are given to the enemy for a time
> With underground proliferation of mould,
> With constant whisper and the casual question,
> To haunt the poisoned in his shunned house,
> To destroy the efflorescence of the flesh,
> The intricate play of the mind, to enforce
> Conformity with the orthodox bone,
> With organized fear, the articulated skeleton.
>
> (EA, 40)

This explicitly figures the desire of the politically self-righteous: to exclude any kind of dissidence so as to impose a tyrannical regime. Yet

5. Auden's recurrent fascination with apocalyptic discourse as a mode of demented yet effective power probably sprang from two sources. One is the mock-apocalypses of D. H. Lawrence, which Auden considers in "The Good Life" (EA, 345–48). The other is the increasingly common use of apocalyptic disciplines and motifs within contemporary political rhetoric.

there is no attempt to find an alternative to the apocalyptic discourse, whether through the restored dogmatism of a romantic genuineness, or the devious complicity of a tolerant liberalism. Instead the ludic voice indulges in a camp display, a syntactic posturing that puts the apocalyptic language in motion, as if it were ostentatiously parading across a stage. So at the same time the discourse is explicitly figured, its accompanying inscriptions are given an entry. The orders issued to a dominant my-theme, the devourer, in turn summon an infectious expansion, an un-avoidable sibilance, and an eerie haunting by the incalculably other. In this way, the language of intolerance releases within itself a response whose dissidence interrogates its too emphatic claims. Exactly where such challenges might lead remains a pure conjecture. The stranger who emerges ("You whom I gladly walk with, touch, / Or wait for as one certain of good"; EA, 40), in contrast to the "solitary man" of the earlier Easter, is spectral. This "you" is neither person nor image but a textual movement: a variable point of entry, the stirring within an eddy of sounds, "deep in clear lake / The lolling bridegroom, beautiful, there" (EA, 40).

Auden's later poetry often lacks the sense of daring characteristic of his earlier work, but the analysis it pursues is subtler. " 'The Truest Poetry Is the Most Feigning,' " for example, returns to the paradox of permission that is so important in "1929." Its speaker is a professional hack, a poetaster offering studio advice to would-be hacks on how to write a love poem. "By all means sing of love, but if you do, / Please make a rare old proper hullabaloo" (CP, 470). Because of the over-whelmingly probable acceptance of such an effort (what could be more poetic, more inconsequential), its ludic voice is bedeviled by an unavoid-able permission. Thus the speaker would be expected to show consider-able restraint—and does. But as events turn out, there is a political coup, and the speaker finds the permission to play abruptly rescinded. In its general outline, then, "The Truest Poetry" follows the itinerary of "1929." The restraint imposed by permission is followed by the license of an anticipated rejection. But the later work pursues its ludic tasks with greater skill. Its unpropitious political development poses the ques-tion, Why would a government, even a dictatorship, object to anything so harmless as a love lyric? The implication, supported by poems such as "A Bride in the Thirties" and "In Sickness and in Health," is that not the love poetry itself but its disciplines bear too close a resemblance to certain features of political discourse: the crowd as capricious cruel fair; the rhetor as passionate wooer; a pact of flattery and deception between them.

The ludic voice of the poem, though, is delighted at this withdrawal of permission because it presents an opportunity for more robust play. Unrestrained, it can freely survey an entire range of illiteracy. This begins with the "new pot-bellied Generalissimo" (CP, 471) who understands power well enough to fear the threat of textuality. But its scope also includes the official censor who searches for simple markers of party allegiance; the politically uncompromised who greet the speaker's disingenuous resexing of pronouns with cries of "*Shame!* . . . Toady! Hypocrite!"; and most confused of all, the "true hearts, clear heads" who peg the eventually printed work to a forever absent source, the original inspiration. Interestingly, the most perceptive person in the group is the loutish dictator who, like Plato, appreciates the danger of the text enough to outlaw it. The others believe they have found the key to its final truth.

Yet a ludic voice must achieve comedy without distance, the impossibility of what would otherwise be irony except that it refuses to claim a superior vantage. To escape likely execution, the poetaster reshapes his love lyric into a paean to the new leader:

> Some epithets, of course, like *lily-breasted*
> Need modifying to, say, *lion-chested,*
> A title *Goddess of wry-necks and wrens*
> To *Great Reticulator of the fens,*
> But in an hour your poem qualifies
> For a State pension or His annual prize,
> And you will die in bed (which he will not:
> That public nuisance will be hanged or shot).
>
> (CP, 471)

The italics not only assert an authentic language (the existence of a prior discourse) but supply its proof, a spontaneous immediacy (the pretense of typeface posing as fluent, handwritten script). But the phrases so venerated are fugitives from some Book of Clichés. This return to banality joins with the syntactic overemphasis, which holds up the mannered

205

and trite as if they were prize specimens, to block an ironic exemption. Instead of intimating an obscurely superior discourse, the ludic voice supplies only a list of absurd names. Thus authoritarian modes of reading are made ridiculous, yet this occurs without the intimation of a superior language. The only discursive alternatives that the ludic voice offers emerge from the inscriptions admitted by its syntactic posturing. For example, the shifts within the initial epithets, from vegetative (lily) to animal (lion), and feminine (breasted) to masculine (chested), are predictable enough, given the change in topics. But in the second pair a further transposition occurs so that the discarded feminine, now specified as a local divinity, takes over the active animal kingdom, while the dominant masculine, elevated to a formal function, is set to preside over the great morass, the sprawling fens. In the course of a renaming, then, the victorious leader is transformed from a serious power into an "epithet," a tentative identity uneasily riding on the diverse energies of a place. And that identity is itself only a "title," a possible entry into the uncharted labyrinth of the fens.

•

The paradoxes of permission clearly furnish a useful guide to the tactics of a ludic voice. The more likely the rejection, the more ebullient the play. But this division between refusal and acceptance is only a beginning. Because of the diversity of any audience, anticipating its reaction involves a degree of guesswork, hence uncertainty. So the paradox does not always work like a toggle switch, either on or off. It can at times maintain an unnerving poise, which happens in "As I walked out one evening." Should the ludic voice of this ballad anticipate acceptance or a less favorable reception? In favor of acceptance is the reassuringly restrictive enframement of the literary ballad itself. Although it uses powerful disciplines, the literary ballad sets its performance apart, carefully removing itself from ready appropriation. A deliberate and self-confessed hoax, it passes as the voice of an earlier time, an expression of some primordial but long forgotten collective will.

> As I walked out one evening,
> Walking down Bristol Street,

> The crowds upon the pavement
> Were fields of harvest wheat.
>   (EA, 227)

An anonymous "I," the witnessing balladeer, is not a person but a communal archetype, an avatar rather than a historical individual. Ballad time is not unspecified but unspecifiable, "one evening," any time at all, for its moment is eternal. The reference to "Bristol Street" provides only a perfunctory concession to historical particularity. It is merely pasted onto a scene that has no capacity for change or surprise. Surrounding the balladeer are crowds, metaphorically reduced to "fields of harvest wheat," so that the speaking voice is situated within a vast docility (the fields cannot talk back) of which it is the sole expression. Because this performance offers a gratifying rhetorical fantasy, yet not a readily transferred set of disciplines, its ludic impulses are likely to be accepted. Paradoxically, this requires its play to be muted and discreet.

But weighing against that acceptance is the considerable value of what this particular ballad undercuts. The poem is fashioned as a debate, with the ardent vow of a lover's passion contradicted by the cynicism of the town's more unromantic clocks. "I heard a lover sing / Under an arch of the railway:

> 'Love has no ending.
>
> 'I'll love you, dear, I'll love you
>   Till China and Africa meet
> And the river jumps over the mountain
> And the salmon sing in the street.
>
> 'I'll love you till the ocean
>   Is folded and hung up to dry
> And the seven stars go squawking
>   Like geese about the sky.
>
> 'The years shall run like rabbits
>   For in my arms I hold
> The Flower of the Ages
>   And the first love of the world.'

> But all the clocks in the city
> Began to whirr and chime.
> (EA, 227–28)

It is expected that a literary ballad will restore community mores by correcting or removing an unconventional discourse; but this discipline is typically displaced to a natural event, an earthquake, storm, flood, and so on. But in Auden's ballad the corrected discourse is neither deviant nor pathetic (an unacceptable production or one that no longer works in a more complex world), but current and necessary. The lover's passion preserves the right of the vow. His promises assert the possibility of both permanent identities (as mastering he and submissive she) and fixed relations, a love detached from all historical contingency. Such permanence and constancy are the basis of power and truth. So the lover cannot be lightly dismissed, for his fervent vow is all that stands between a solidly rooted reality and the tumult of the text. Should the clocks have their way and unleash the play of time within the permanencies of identity and truth, the lover's embracing arms might degenerate from obedient limbs into a treacherous text: the arms as a heraldry, a tabloid of images in which China and Africa meet in the folds of a map, or the years run by even faster than rabbits with the turning of a page.

Given such an even balance between the probability of acceptance and rejection, what course is a ludic voice to take? To adjust to this uncertainty, the voice of the ballad must subdue the exuberance of the syntactic provocations. Unsure about the chances of permission, the voice assumes a wry ingenuousness and recedes into an almost incidental narrative framework. In this way, the strife of the text can continue without interference. Aside from supplying an introduction, minor transition, and summary, which are interjected almost as formalities, the balladeer withdraws from the poem. This withdrawal implies a pose of uninhibited approval, so that by the end of the poem, presumably, everything has been shown: "The clocks had ceased their chiming / And the deep river ran on" (EA, 228). In this sense, the ludic voice repeats the gesture of the impassioned lover, enclosing the other within an embrace. But while the lover earnestly believes in the docility of the body he embraces, the ludic voice of "As I walked out one evening" calculates its resistance. The ballad proceeds from the initial quiet of the harvest wheat and brimming river to the lover's vow. But no sooner does the lover speak than he is accompanied by the cacophony of a salmon chorus, squawking stars, and whirring and chiming clocks, as well as coughing Time, knocking glacier, raffling beggars, and a roaring Lily-white Boy. By the poem's end, the river has become deep rather than brimming: not a bounded surface but a fluent medium. Having nowhere definite to go, its varied sounds can only resonate among themselves. In this way the devious reticence of the ballad's speaker restores to the object of the lover's vow, the silent beloved, what would otherwise be missing, the capacity for a dissenting response.

•

In practice it is often a guess whether a voice will be granted or denied permission to play. If readers are always auditors as well as effigies, any conjecture concerning their behavior must admit to a degree of arbitrariness. Dogmatists and reactionaries will of course continue to invoke the myth of the general reader: usually, a prig with a grudge. But myths aside, for each person, at any instant, and for whatever discourse, the permission to play might be granted, refused, or any unlikely combination of each. Consequently, the paradox of permission must be traced through a series of contrasts: similar roles occurring within paired texts which serve as explicit contrasts to one another, the one conceding and the other denying permission to play. Since any persona might indulge in ludic mayhem, the choice of the roles themselves is partly a matter of individual preference. For whatever reasons, then, the specific roles that struck Auden as opportune sites for elaborating this contrast are the liturgist, the lover, and the pastoralist. For each, he composed paired texts, contrasting poems linked by the difference that one anticipates rejection, the other acceptance of its play.

Auden's fondness for poking fun at ecclesiastical pomposity is well known.[6] But this burlesque of official piety implicates not only offertories and doxologies but also some less apparent rituals from the romantic repertoire. For example, Auden's sonnet "Petition" relies on an estab-

---

6. M. K. Spears, "Late Auden: The Satirist as Lunatic Clergyman," *Sewanee Review* (Winter 1951): 50–74.

lished formula for prayer: a request to a divinity, by an appointed media-
tor, for assistance and guidance. But like the poem on which it is partly
modeled, Gerard M. Hopkins's "Thou art indeed just, Lord, if I contend," Auden's "Petition" also poses an important challenge to romantic
practice. It does not approach an obscurely displaced deity and then
either acclaim that displacement's pantheistically diffused splendor or
mourn its inexplicably maturing loss. Instead Auden's more impertinent
address assumes a well-defined divinity and then situates this figure
within a web of contractual obligations: a petition implies certain duties,
so that even the ultimate is expected to do its part. When cast against
the setting of romantic tradition, then, a petitionary poem is quite barbaric, well beyond the pale of the accepted. It boisterously presupposes
an adequate definition of something that romanticism came into being
in order to mystify or defer.[7]

It is a good guess that such a performance would be met with rejection, not from devout religionists (who seldom read poetry anyway) but
from piqued authoritarians (who have need of an absolute that is vague
and thus compliant). So granted the likelihood of its rejection, the sonnet's voice is free to play.

> Sir, no man's enemy, forgiving all
> But will his negative inversion, be prodigal:
> Send to us power and light, a sovereign touch
> Curing the intolerable neural itch,
> The exhaustion of weaning, the liar's quinsy,
> And the distortions of ingrown virginity.
> Prohibit sharply the rehearsed response
> And gradually correct the coward's stance;
> Cover in time with beams those in retreat
> That, spotted, they turn though the reverse were great;

---

7. Romanticism does not necessarily deal with its versions of the ultimate in a
consistent manner. Auden devotes the second lecture of *The Enchafèd Flood* to the way
in which romanticism attains a specious comprehensiveness, a totality within manageable
limits, by setting up mutually exclusive versions of its postreligious absolutes: "On the
one hand, the poets long to immerse in the sea of Nature, to enjoy its endless mystery
and novelty, on the other, they long to come to port in some transcendent eternal and
unchanging reality from which the unexpected is excluded" (EF, 82).

Publish each healer that in city lives
Or country houses at the end of drives;
Harrow the house of the dead; looking shining at
New styles of architecture, a change of heart.

(EA, 36)

The ludic focus of the address is not the Sir or his power but the devious opportunism that constructs both. Unconstrained by the genteel tyrannies of permission, the voice can put a mode of understanding on display. What is it that an effigy demands, either when searching for or when believing itself already in possession of an absolute? Naturally it turns to an invincible force, a presiding Sir, to provide deliverance from treacherous psychosomatic symptoms: the neural excitation that deflects meaning into a maze of divergent synapses; the fatigue that follows severance from a primordial intention; the rasp in the throat, an inhuman noise, that accompanies even the most accomplished utterance; the alarming growths that beset all attempts to exclude other discourses. Rather than impersonating this violence, by adopting it as an at least momentarily convincing performance, the ludic voice of "Petition" fashions it into a theme, an imaged array of standard disciplines and their textual disciplines.

Yet the tone of the sonnet is light, without being either censorious or knowing. Although the ludic voice puts an opportunistic absolutism on display, it avoids any form of ridicule. Instead the invoked Sir suffers a more intricate fate, as its curtly interrupted sibilant calls into doubt any prospect of an untroubled elaboration. The patriarch is demoted to the status of an offspring, "be prodigal," and then sent on its deviant way through the sonnet. The burlesque quality of the syntax, the way it uses false emphasis and teasing ambiguity to set off its pseudoliturgical phrases, continuously converts that departure into a return: the "negative inversion," "ingrown virginity," "rehearsed response," and "turn though the reverse were great." Moreover, these persistent returns, detours from a normal and healthy excursion into reality, are oddly responsive. The dominant Sir, specter of all authority, is also a "sovereign touch," presiding over a realm of varied contacts, perpetual tangents, hence an easy touch, combining regal generosity with royal gullibility. Its act of curing involves a contest, between restoration to normality and

211

preservation of eccentricity, much as its covering in time admits both an exposure and a concealment of the spotted aberrants. Similarly, its harrowing the house of the dead concedes both an obliterating sameness, the smoothing out of interesting irregularities, as well as a ribald plundering, which seizes the remnants of unholy discourses and leads them back in triumph. Of what possible use are such extravagant returns? In this rite of burlesque, they enable the fashioning of altered codes of production, "new styles of architecture," or perhaps playful conversions, a "change of heart" which in turn invite a dialogue among differing structures.[8]

If the ludic voice of Auden's "Petition" is denied permission to play, under what circumstances would the liturgist be granted that right? Clearly, certain conditions must be met. Because liturgy is inherently disruptive, a forcing of not only the latent into the manifest but the mythic into the performed, the stakes must be lowered: it is unwise to commit an important matter to liturgy unless access is limited to the faithful, a precaution impossible with published texts (unless secret or dead languages are used). So it follows that permission to play might be granted the liturgist only if the topic of concern is a minor authority, an incidental prop that is expendable. An apt candidate for this topic is the authority of the poet, as an artificer of future disciplines. In all probability, a ludic voice might count on receiving permission to play if the subject is another poet. Accordingly, the voice would have to heed the limits imposed by specific expectations: to impersonate rather than portray the readings it occupied; and to confine its syntactic excess within a well-mannered moderation. Were these limits given as instructions to

8. Auden omitted "Petition" from what was once the major anthology of his work, the *Collected Shorter Poems*, giving this explanation in his foreword: "I once expressed a desire for 'New styles of architecture'; but I have never liked modern architecture. I prefer *old* styles, and one must be honest even about one's prejudices" (CP, 15). How is this to be read? Some possibilities: (1) the older poet, after the fashion of Saturn/ Wordsworth, destroys his too threatening offspring, the texts that have survived an author's loss of imaginative powers; (2) as a deliberate ruse, designed to reveal the fatality of approaching this, or any other line of poetry, as a communicative instrument that must be pegged to a presiding intention; hence (3) as a test, to discern whether a reader has the necessary independence of mind, or even the courage required to step outside the carefully supervised boundaries of an anthology and explore the distant marches of a writer's uncanonical, unredeemed efforts.

an imaginary writing machine, they might well produce a text such as Auden's elegy, "In Memory of W. B. Yeats."

No doubt an unrestrained play would have been more enjoyable, for example, a poetic version of the mock-trial Auden staged in *The Partisan Review*.[9] But because of the tacit permission it has been given, Auden's elegy must proceed with greater care. An Irish poet, provincial, esoteric, elitist, nostalgic, has died. A younger aspirant, English (actually Icelandic), urbane, commonplace, at ease with modern thought, populist (the shorts, the cabaret songs, the verse letters), writes an elegy. As a ritual to exorcise death, this act of mourning proceeds from loss to restoration. The old must be carried out and laid to rest, so of course a playing within its domain is permitted. But its poetic essence, the source of disciplinary power that really matters to a culture, must be transferred: conveniently enough, to the officiating voice of the elegy itself, which in the process of lamenting the death of a precursor ensures its own immortality.

This required transference, a restraint imposed by the permission to play, is capably achieved. The ludic voice takes up various styles of the mature Yeats: polemical sarcasm, disarming intimacy, prophetic rage. But this mimicry is accompanied by a subversion of the poet's main themes. In this way, Yeats's writings, as a thematic residue, are effectively discarded. Yet their rhetorical tactics as disciplines are retained for further use. The elegy accomplishes this feat of transference within dismissal by creating a gap with nothing to fill it, apart from the elegist's quite prominent skill.

While all this is going on, however, the stylistic impersonations pursue a further itinerary, a separate trajectory through the poem. Through their accompanying gestures, which like any mimicry betray themselves, they act as provocations of the text that summon it to a response. It is this complex trajectory, of a deftly repressive transference and, within it, an incited return, that makes the elegy such a fascinating work.

"In Memory of W. B. Yeats" actually begins as an antielegy. It accepts the conventions of mourning but adapts them to the kind of polemical conflict at which Yeats excelled, except that here the target

9. W. H. Auden, "The Public Versus the Late Mr. William Butler Yeats," *Partisan Review* (Spring 1939): 46–51 (reprinted EA, 389–93).

becomes the oddities of Yeats's own myth. The conventions of the classic elegy require that nature lament the deceased. But this becomes "he disappeared in the dead of winter" (CP, 197), a more banal cycle than the phases of the moon. Instead of a chorus of sorrowful spirits, there is the gaiety of a drinking song, "O all the instruments agree / The day of his death was a dark cold day," so that modern technology replaces the wheels and gyres of Yeats's system. The luminaries who traditionally receive the departed into eternity become "an afternoon of nurses and rumors," as a satiric version of Yeats's singing masters. The achievement of immortality becomes a more pragmatic passage through the vagaries of reading, "The words of a dead man / Are modified in the guts of the living," a historical plurality that thwarts the desire to achieve a perfect, changeless form. And the undying praise of the ages dwindles to the smaller audience of a neglected genre, "A few thousand will think of this day / As one thinks of a day when one did something slightly unusual," which debunks Yeats's dream of a heroic Ireland restored to its ancient mission. To heighten the contrast, these subversions of poetic extravagance are performed in a sarcastic understatement, which connotes the speaker's own reasonableness and common sense: "fairly accustomed," "almost convinced," "a few thousand," "something slightly unusual."

Yet this calculated violence not only destroys but provokes. The syntax of the first section suggests a stance of tough directness, the confidence of a powerful poet wielding a compliant instrument. Every movement is honed to maximum efficiency, so there is little chance of any excess, which is forbidden by the law of hard work. The matter-of-fact sentences exert a minimum of effort.

> He disappeared in the dead of winter:
> The brooks were frozen, the airports almost deserted,
> And snow disfigured the public statues;
> The mercury sank in the mouth of the dying day.
> What instruments we have agree
> The day of his death was a dark cold day.
>
> (CP, 197)

But there is a curious vulnerability to this gesture, a bluntness which because of its absorption in a task misses the dissonant nuances of the surrounding scene. With easy assurance, the elegist illustrates the accuracy of his phrase "dead of winter." This claim is *proven* by appropriate evidence, such as climatic changes, demographic movements, reliable indexes. Yet this earnest proof of the thoroughly obvious neglects the one issue that threatens it, which is also the main concern of the elegy: "the dead." What are the features of that other place, the realm of the dead? And if an elegy marks a shift, from life to death, does it not therefore imply the prospect of a reverse movement, a return? In its intent instrumentality, its oblivious busyness, the syntactic body remains heedless to such issues.

The accompanying text, however, as if provoked by such obtuseness, generously responds. What is disfigured is split apart, dispersed into the *figura* or transient shapes from which it emerged into form. When this violence is transferred to the deceased ("Now he is scattered among a hundred cities / And wholly given over to unfamiliar affections"), it releases a countermythic *sparagmos* in which the text becomes an array of differing versions, rival figurines. And though the conflict among these versions can be slighted, as the mere "noise of tomorrow" akin to the brokers "roaring like beasts on the floor of the Bourse," it nonetheless interjects the rules of the exchange. So whereas the image of an author can be managed through a sarcastic use of his own polemical techniques, the text is another matter. Provoked, it returns as an array of fluent forms, drawn into a bourse that is at once a bundle of ill-sorted contents and the folds of their fluctuating value.

The skill of the elegy's ludic voice is remarkable. Restrained by a permission it cannot escape, it is obliged to impersonate what it subverts in order to keep specific disciplines intact. Yet within the restraints of this permission, the ludic voice affects a syntactic pose, a bluntness that provokes inscriptive returns. Such skill, however, cannot allow itself to fall into a pattern. In the second section the character of the impersonation shifts, from sarcasm to the heartfelt intimacy of a direct address. "You were silly like us: your gift survived it all" (CP, 197). This is calculated to sound like a retraction, the deference of an understudy to the acknowledged master. But its carefully fashioned impression (of concerned intimacy, utter humanity) is quite misleading. If anything, the intimacy presses the attack at closer quarters. Its lowered voice and solicitous manner barely conceal the jibes at Yeats's narrow political allegiance ("the parish of rich women"), selfish preoccupation with aging ("physical decay"), and successive rejections by first mother then daughter Gonne ("yourself"). Such virulent intimacy requires a distinctive gesture, one of complete and relentless possession, not of its victim but of the resistant entity that must be subdued in order to seize that victim, namely, the aggressor's own text. The syntactic pose is that of a stare, in which a complex and varied anatomy intently, obsessively focuses on a discrete point of concern, the authoritative essence of the poet Yeats. Yet this exaggerated concentration provides the text with a point of return. Under its relentless pressure, even a truism can admit differing accents. "For poetry makes nothing happen" transforms emptiness into an event and thereby calls a response out of silence. That response is vital, "it survives," but in an ambiguous way, twice born, as a surreptitious production that promises deliverance to some higher, inaccessible realm yet is only an accompaniment. This maddening double is little more than a gesture, "a way of happening, a mouth," which runs beside the static word. And yet, like the continuously reshaping lips, it divulges its mirth through the subtlest nuance, even as it painstakingly shapes its sounds into compelling truth.

The development of the Yeats elegy is guided by an attentiveness to its restraining permission; in each of the sections, the ludic voice becomes more compliant with that permission, hence less conspicuous in its play (more difficult to read). After the intimacy of the second section, the elegy shifts to the prophetic fervor of its conclusion. Yeats is interred, effectively removed from the scene, by being relegated to a masque. At the court of Earth an impromptu knighthood is conferred, as Time lays a wreath at the feet of the poet. In the background the nations of Europe bay like dogs, while, in an even more distant scene, a solitary fountain springs up in the desert. The both contrived and awkward nature of the composition suggests an allegorical painting, perhaps from Yeats's beloved Municipal Gallery. With their rhythm of mantic inevitability, its heavily accented trochees might almost be chanted rather than spoken. The slow, solemn movement indicates both a funeral procession and a mystical state, the purity of a mind whose incidental thoughts have receded into nothingness so that it may behold the eternal forms. In its syntactic gesture, then, the passage proposes a movement from mourning into ecstasy, a burning away of the worldly and historical in the singing masters' holy fire. The words of the chant are stressed with hard, definitive accents, as befits lapsed particulars that have served their purpose so that now, with a mixture of bitterness and elation, they may be forged into an elemental truth.

Yet as the ludic voice understands well enough, the text is hardly submissive to these provocations. Whatever is discarded, even the empty husk of words, persistently returns. "Let the Irish vessel lie / Emptied of its poetry." But that abandonment can never be more than neglect, for time "worships language," attending upon it long after the departure of a dominant voice. Momentarily, the inscriptions may remain within the unreflective and familiar patterns of usage, "And the seas of pity lie / Locked and frozen in each eye" (CP, 198). But eventually the inert becomes active, the static fluent, not as an inundating chaos but as a region of inscriptions. Even the curse may harbor a lyric, or the tyrannically obvious propose a disruptive freedom.

> Follow, poet, follow right
> To the bottom of the night,
> With your unconstraining voice
> Still persuade us to rejoice;
>
> With the farming of a verse
> Make a vineyard of the curse,
> Sing of human unsuccess
> In a rapture of distress;
>
> In the deserts of the heart
> Let the healing fountain start,
> In the prison of his days
> Teach the free man how to praise.
> (EA, 243)

Perhaps the most remarkable aspect of the elegy's ludic voice is its poise. With complete equanimity, it is equally willing either to let the poem fulfill a repressive design, of providing a new disciplinarian to fill the place left empty by Yeats; or to assemble a collection of mimes whose subtle audacity provokes unvoiced yet telling responses.

•

The permission to play, and by implication the desire to contain that performance within acceptable limits, hinges on disciplinary necessity, not thematic preference. As a result, that permission's devious censorship works at a discursive, not a conceptual, level. Even if the subject matter is alarming, at least to some, a work might anticipate acceptance provided that it preserves a sufficiently vital discipline. This is readily demonstrated by some of Auden's love poems. Although they acknowledge homosexual desire, these poems are in several instances defined against a backdrop of cultural acceptance. Why such surprising tolerance? Certainly Auden was under no illusion about a predominantly middle-class culture suddenly abandoning its official puritanism or, even more unlikely, setting aside its cherished resentment of the uncommon. Rather, Auden's love poetry illustrates some of the curious bylaws of discursive politics. The lesser must be sacrificed to the greater, that is, thematic propriety to disciplinary need. Even though it endorses an unapproved love, this poetry protects the highly useful discipline of a maternal aggression. Unlike the paternal varieties, which overtly bully, maternal disciplines gently envelop and stifle. They do not mete out punishment but make it unnecessary. They beckon the errant child to return to the ultimate source, an absorption within what is always the same since the mother, unlike the legal and thus merely stipulated father, remains implacably original.

Because maternal modes of aggression are useful and readily appropriated (particularly by large, impassive institutions: the corporation, the state), a playing within their bounds is likely to be permitted as a precautionary measure. For that permission entails an effective check to discursive freedom, even if it risks an affront to respectable sensibilities. In "The Letter," for example, a would-be lover has made a frankly sexual invitation, but only to be rebuffed with an ambiguous reply, "Your letter comes, speaking as you, / Speaking of much but not to come" (EA, 25). Irked and more than a little spiteful, the jilted speaker casts himself in the role of Aggrieved Soul, deceived by a cunning schemer. Thus the poem's dramatic setting poses an anomaly: How can such self-indulgence be so confident of its acceptance? The answer is implied within the poem's prehistory, in the initial invitation of the would-be lover. For this offer has been made in all sincerity, perhaps even uttered *in person*. It consequently establishes a contrast between the authentic word and a dissembling text, the body's innocent desire as opposed to an unnatural denial. Because the lover assumes the voice of an undefended and altogether natural affection, he suggests a maternal force, selfless, sacrificial, in mourning as the result of a child's thoughtless offense. And it is as the expression of this natural force, not as the votary of a specific observance, that the poem's ludic voice must calculate a restrictive permission.

Even though it is the event that prompts the poem, the offending letter does not appear. Nonetheless, it is continuously supposed, as a dissonance that upsets the pastoral harmony. The lover portrays himself as a romantic wanderer, at home in the elements and intimate with their mysterious powers. But the gestures accompanying this portrayal are vexed. In accordance with the demands of his persona, the lover tries to be modest and understated; any form of ostentation would seem decadent, unhealthily self-conscious, and thus run counter to the desired impression. Yet it is difficult for him not to indulge in a certain exuberance, if only because he enjoys so great a tactical advantage: whereas the lover can claim a speaking voice, his adversary is banished to an excluded text. The resultant tension within the lover's discourse, between plain dealing and a more exuberant display, provides the basis for an intriguing complexity. Not only is there a contrast between a thematic concern and its accompanying syntactic gestures, after the fashion of an actor whose movements modify or subvert stated meanings; "The Letter" also entertains a further tension within the gestures themselves. Its syntactic mimes are torn between a modest self-effacement and a more self-congratulatory elation.

> today
> I, crouching behind a sheep-pen, heard
> Travel across a sudden bird,
> Cry out against the storm, and found
> The year's arc a completed round
> And love's worn circuit re-begun,
> Endless with no dissenting turn.
> Shall see, shall pass, as we have seen

> The swallow on the tile, Spring's green
> Preliminary shiver.
>
> (EA, 25)

Aware of the unseemly tension, the lover is obliged to offer an explanation. His discourse, because fashioned as a sequel to the offending letter, suffers from a debilitating contagion. The serenity of the pastoral has been lost, having come in contact with the fatal knowledge of a deceitful refusal. Insidiously, through a prior act of reading, the body of the text has become vexed, furrowed with concern: the letter's arrival serves "to interrupt the homely brow" (EA, 25). Thus the lover's tainted innocence begins to emulate, helplessly, the offense of which it is now twice the victim. The natural rhythms of the pastoral grow more erratic, its inspired particularity dissipates into abstraction; and, worst of all, its plain and decent directness succumbs to such coy innuendos as "sudden bird," "worn circuit," and "swallow on the tile."

This pose of helplessness, a maternal vulnerability, has a complex function. Certainly it invites pity for the lover and, conversely, disdain for the offending letter. Yet it also performs a calculated ludic gesture in that it requires still another ruse, a withdrawal into a serenity whose mystical bliss will annul, or at least balance, the telltale glee of the earlier passage.

> Nor speech is close nor fingers numb,
> If love not seldom has received,
> An unjust answer, was deceived.
>
> (EA, 25)

The loss of sensation connotes a retreat into some sheltering inwardness, no doubt the point of contact with a primordial nature. Yet this retreat, a form of contraction, provides the waiting inscriptions with an opportune moment of return. Its gesture withdraws into a realm at once confined and overfull, "nor speech is close," because it is laden with a nearness that cannot be seized. In recoiling from the offensive letter, then, the passage takes refuge in a closeness that proves to be a scene of conflict. What is the primordial source that sustains the maternal body? It may be an impenetrable oblivion, as in the echo from Hopkins's "Spring and Fall"; or it may implicate an indecipherable creativity, as in the even fainter resonance from Isaiah.[10] Nor is there anything either to adjudicate between the two or to exclude still further possibilities. All the inscriptions offer by way of a conclusion is "the stone smile of this country god" (EA, 25), an archaic ambiguity, the infinite patience of an approaching response.

Sometimes, however, even a maternal aggression can go too far, as if testing the limits. This is what happens in "Dame Kind," a late revision of "The Letter" which transposes the earlier poem's anticipated permission into an emphatic rejection. An aged and overweight libertine gazes at his quite unappealing figure in a full-length mirror. His remarks are intended to overcome the reluctance of a hired partner, though they are likelier to intensify that sentiment. Since this dramatic context suggests a refusal of permission, hence the freedom to pursue an unrestrained excess, "Dame Kind" engages in a particularly energetic play. The maternal aggressor is displaced into a sneering debauchee, wily, shameless. And the hireling who yields to such offers is put under a contract of prostitution, though as a purely normal state of affairs, the routine barter of sensibility for expedience.

Such disclosures could be called excessive, except that as usual with Auden's ludic voices, the libertine of "Dame Kind" is bereft of irony. The good-natured quality of the humor recalls Caliban's remarks on "Our Native Muse," who "can skate full tilt toward the forbidden incoherence and then, in the last split second, on the shuddering edge of the bohemian standardless abyss, effect her breathtaking triumphant turn" (CP, 326). Caliban offers an image of troping, figuration itself, as an impulse to meaning that is deflected and then obliquely returned. But this activity requires the properties of a special surface, one that suspends the ordinary laws of space and gravity. In "Dame Kind," this surface is provided by the implied mirror, which quietly intervenes between an utterance and its refracted body. While the voice attempts to achieve an ultimate power, mastery at a distance as well as possession without consent, the accompanying body quietly recedes into the planes and angles of its mirrored image. So even as the voice attempts to impose a

10. "Nor mouth had, no nor mind, expressed / What heart heard of, ghost guessed" ("Spring and Fall"). "For my thoughts are not your thoughts, / neither are your ways my ways, / says the Lord" (Isaiah, 55:08).

dominant force, the refracted body dispels that power into a depthless multiplicity, the varied facets of the mirror text. Irony requires an exemption, the privilege of an unquestioned because normal discourse. But the ebullient accompaniment of "Dame Kind" resists any such unchallenged normality.

The poem's ludic voice relies on this resistance, which it deliberately incites. Set free by a refusal of permission, the syntactic gestures are high camp. With its precious, mannered quality, the ludic voice does not use language but rather idolizes it. The words are not spoken but placed, as if the speaker were using little silver tongs to arrange confections on an ornate salver, lightly but exactingly, so as not to mar their delicate designs. Yet this deliberate preciousness had a ludic consequence. Its fondly held items are put on display, thrown into prominence, so that they may be assayed for their safety, tested for poison, as in an origin of the term *salva:* a professional pretasting to guard against assassination. Any term, given the fact of inscription, must concede similarly improvident histories. The epithet, for example, conducts the primal poetic act, a bestowal of the name that shall forever be. But in "Dame Kind" this endeavor is subject to an impertinence that baits its inscriptions. How does the mirrored body appear? "Steatopygous, sow-dugged and owl-headed" (CP, 503). Each epithet draws on a different discourse (technical, vulgar, mythic), so that the assembled names instigate a rivalry. "Steatopygous" may be justified on the basis of its anatomical precision, yet that is too weak an alibi to silence its inscriptions. For that name also recalls Georg Groddeck's IT, a numinous power adopted from romantic animism, whose perverse and unpredictable energies manifest themselves in the forms of the body. These anarchic accents, however, provoke the curt response of a less grandiose epithet, "sow-dugged." The body in question exhibits the fecundity, or intransigence, or perhaps the cannibalistic frenzy, of a sow. Yet surely this goes too far and so requires in turn the more dignified stance of a possibly classical allusion, the wisdom or foolishness of Minerva's sophomoric owl. Through its deliberate affectation, then, the ludic voice renames the mirrored body so as to ensure its return.

As for Dame Kind, the featured animus of the text, this dubious divinity recedes into the various ceremonies performed in her homage. Each is a distinct liturgy that in turn incites the response of a successor.

"The Primal Scene," the parents in bed, proposes an engendering by way of difference. But this excessive vitality must be overcome through a more sanctified naming, the *"Chi-Rho,"* an early Christian emblem from the first two letters of Christ's Koine name. But that sacred commonness, drawn from *koinos* or the vulgar tongue, only proposes a more vexatious coupling, a writing of the Phoenician *resh*, or head, over the Greek *chi*, chiasmus or figure of exchange. Thereafter stability and order might be reclaimed through a suitable myth, "of unpunishable gods and all the girls / they interfered with" (CP, 503). Yet such divine impunity misses the obvious, which is that even a pantheon must continuously renew itself through mundane (sordid, unsanctioned) liaisons. Of course a retreat into an isolated and self-sufficient inwardness is always possible, "the clear rock basin that stultified / frigid Narcissus" (CP, 504). Yet even here the hallowed ground is subject to the chattering of the nymphs, the returns of a spurned Echo through which the body betrays the confidently spoken word, "where tongues stammer on a First name." So the ludic voice, as maternal aggressor, attempts to gather its recipient within a stifling embrace. But its mannered gestures serve to agitate the inscriptions of the mirror/text.

•

Are there instances in which the voice is obliged to play, where permission, along with its restrictive provisos, is not given but insisted upon, because the stakes are so high? A group of Auden's poems suggest this is the case with the pastoralist. Since descriptive verse has little apparent connection with the disciplinary requirements of more current discourses, this dictated permission may seem strange. What does its insistence protect? To answer that question, it is necessary only to recall that any scene might be infinitely described. The pastoral sets a limit to this intractable possibility. It draws a border, a horizon of governance around its topics, and then encloses their development within a recurrent cycle. It is thanks to such delimitations of an otherwise prolific nature that power can forge its way to truth. Thus the pastoral's innocent (simple, clear) description, if accepted, is a monumental achievement. It enables the tumult of nature to be mastered, by prior agreement, through readily applied conventions. Yet these conventions, even though their effect is to provide a secure backdrop, are neither reductive or exclusive.

223

On the contrary, they promise a corroborative richness, a teeming abundance of tangible detail which, though always waiting out of sight for the present (a moment that in the realm of pastoral becomes eternal), is safely held in reserve should its support ever be required in the future. At one stroke, then, the pastoral supplies convention and novelty, discipline and a well-managed adventure.

Since the pastoral is far too important a form to be relegated to an unchecked play, permission for its ludic voice is virtually ensured. It follows that Auden's pastoralists must be discreet, playing the textual inscriptions but in a circumspect manner. For they move in the presence of an indubitable reality, the Book of Nature, and are expected to assent to its rituals of reverence. In fact, these rituals compose the Book of Nature, which is otherwise without content. Its only substance is a mandatory drama which, if capably enacted, dissembles the reality it can never deliver. As a votary before some ineffable god, Nature itself, the pastoralist can bear witness to what is immediate and real only through strict adherence to a highly artificial protocol.

The successive stages of the pastoral's ritual are readily apparent, for example, in a work such as the title poem to Auden's 1936 collection, "On This Island."

> Look, stranger, on this island now
> The leaping light for your delight discovers,
> Stand stable here
> And silent be,
> That through the channels of the ear
> May wander like a river
> The swaying sound of the sea.
>
> Here at the small field's ending pause
> Where the chalk wall falls to the foam, and its tall ledges
> Oppose the pluck
> And knock of the tide,
> And the shingle scrambles after the suck-
> ing surf, and the gull lodges
> A moment on its sheer side.
>
> Far off like floating seeds the ships
> Diverge on urgent voluntary errands;

And the full view
Indeed may enter
And move in memory as now these clouds do,
That pass the harbor mirror
And all the summer through the water saunter.

(CP, 112–13)

Reality, as an effect of reading, begins as an imperative, "Look," which promises revelation, though only as an excuse for demanding docility. To be worthy, the audience must take the scene as offered, "stand stable here," and also repress any active response, "and silent be." This state of fixed docility induces a quite justifiable terror, the threat of being inundated by a chaos of impressions. So the pastoral deftly anticipates this terror, skirting its rim "at the small field's ending." After a carefully measured instant of vertigo, the poise of a bird hovering over the abyss, deliverance arrives through a rapturous hiatus, a metaphoric revision of the imperiled subject into a weightless particle, "like floating seeds," indifferent to the force of gravity. In this way, a comprehensive reality is at last achieved, "the full view," not as a product of experience but as the result of conformity to a certain ritual.

The enactment of this reading is efficient enough, but it hardly qualifies as inspired. At best it is competently performed, well enough to serve as an exhibition, but without the kind of tactical brilliance that Auden's personae demonstrate elsewhere. A likely reason for this slackness is that the poem's ludic voice, though adept in the necessary protocols, has a most unpastoral project, not the containment but the release of inscriptions. So rather than an inspired intensity, "On this Island" suggests a pose of blissful surrender. Its syntactic gesture is related to the ecstasy ridiculed by Caliban. The phrasal movements convey a sense of trustful reliance, as of a body sustained by an encompassing and benevolent power. There is nothing to fear because even though this buoyant movement continuously hints at a distant horizon, there is no intervening resistance. The floating body does not drift but expand, bearing within itself a realm of pure sameness. As if yielding to a summer breeze, a stream of random associations, the syntactic movements accept the peculiarities of the unruly text, without striving to manage them after the fact, which is to say, limit them in advance. This serenity suggests the confident faith of being sustained by a mysterious yet kindly force.

Yet such serenity is a pretext, a pose calculated to release inscriptive contrasts, and thus offer a means to play. For no sooner does the soothing voice begin to fade than its intently beheld island, archetype of order (protection in the midst of chaos) divulges a curious tale.[11] Drawn from *eyland*, it properly admits no "s": that sinister intruder enters from elsewhere, perhaps through a medieval scribe who, whether because impatient for a faster cursive route or awed by the prospect of a Latinate universality, decided to assimilate *eyland* to *insula*. But this scriptural commingling dissipates much that the secure island would attempt to preserve. The intruding sibilant brings the hissing of the edge, the alarming fact of being *in salo*, awash in the salt sea, into the midst of a solid ground. Of course the "s" of island is unvoiced. Yet the remainder of the poem's final stanza, secure in its blissful ease, gives that sibilance a free reign so that its agitated, corrosive flux, the passing of a limit, finds an entry into the text. In this way, the pastoral's tyrannical "now," though it remains a moment that cannot be escaped, *need* not be, for it proceeds to embrace a treacherous shore, not at the edge but at the center of each word.

The commotion of that shore is curiously measured. Rather than a deafening or monotonous din it is a "pluck" and "knock," a fastidious selection of certain elements and patient attendance upon their inscriptions. What ensues is a "swaying" that bears within itself the sequel of a blissful surrender, both as an irresistible determinant and the eddies of a clamorous memory. Within that swaying's liminal space, where the outlines of a solid truth mingle with the surges of an inscribed legacy, the Book of Nature undergoes some noteworthy revisions. Its barriers become the "tall ledges" whose imposing stature is somehow incredible, a preposterous tale of evolutionary improbabilities. The battered remnants of those ledges stage a desperate pursuit, "the shingle scrambles," in which the fragments are sorted and tossed into a finer array, though never forced into a unity. This border between a term and its unencompassed memory is a realm of nonessence, where each supposedly irreducible element keeps receding into varied facets. Here nature remains

11. For Auden's gloss on the iconology of the island, see *The Enchafèd Flood*, pp. 20–25. "The primary idea with which the garden-island image is associated is, therefore, neither justice nor chastity but innocence; it is the earthly paradise where there is no conflict between natural desire and moral duty" (EF, 20).

poised like the gull on its "sheer side," as a momentary plane of coherence that is both absolute and precipitous, whose semitransparency admits intimations of a further embodiment, perhaps of the "leaping light" or sauntering clouds, whose movements trace an abandoned descent.

If nature is to serve as a firm backdrop, an epistemic web into whose restraining filaments a topic might be dropped with impunity, then different subjects or circumstances call for a radical (in the mathematical sense, of a root represented by a sign) as opposed to an ecstatic approach. The distinction is that whereas the ecstatic abandons itself to an enveloping otherness, which it prudently contrives in advance to be the same, the radical withdraws into a protective recess. Thus its version of nature does not drift toward a distant horizon but recedes into a precious inwardness. Although equally maternal in its disciplinary mode, the radical's incapacitating idyll is situated in time rather than space. Typically, it occupies a nostalgic past, an idealized future, or as with "In Praise of Limestone," a combination of both. Since the discipline of such a restorative inwardness is so invaluable, it must anticipate a permission that cannot be refused.

Restricted by this imposed acceptance, the ludic voice complies. At the poem's center is a scene of perfect fulfillment, the limestone origin.

> If it form the one landscape that we the inconstant ones
>   Are consistently homesick for, this is chiefly
> Because it dissolves in water.
> (CP, 414)

Around this scene is a series of arcs, which describe futile efforts to improve on the limestone's idyllic completion.

> From weathered outcrop
>   To hill-top temple, from appearing waters to
> Conspicuous fountains, from a wild to a formal vineyard,
>   Are ingenious but short steps that a child's wish
> To receive more attention than his brothers, whether
>   By pleasing or teasing, can easily take.
> (CP, 414)

Each of these arcs is triadic in form, in that it explores fields of religious, secular, and aesthetic endeavor. Further, the arcs are chronologically arranged, for example, from early mythic man ("unable / To conceive a god whose temper-tantrums are moral"; CP, 414) to the present speaker ("I, too, am reproached, for what / And how much you know"; CP, 415). So the poem's meditative form is beautifully wrought, with a petallike design that ventures into the perilous domains of history, but only to retreat to the protective center. Like most organic structures, this reassuring form connotes a return to the deep-rooted and innocent (since it is found, not made, thus untouched by human interests).

But though a return may be guaranteed, its contents are not. As with all of Auden's most effective voices, it is tempting to take "In Praise of Limestone" as the expression of the poet, especially when the voice is so accomplished, at the height of its powers. Yet in the case of a ludic voice, its distinctive task is to hold the text within bounds only long enough so that its assembled inscriptions may begin their response. Even magisterial ease can practice forms of play. The syntactic movements of the poem, in contrast to those of "On this Island," suggest Caliban's other nostalgic form, an incestuous rapture. Rather than drifting toward a serene horizon, the syntactic body more wondrously sinks upon itself, but without achieving a final collapse. On the contrary, its decline becomes a successive event, a continuous infolding that approaches the deepest center, a neglected origin that is always there, as the source of whatever is indestructible and sustaining. This trustful reliance accepts a Mediterranean indulgence in which usual proscriptions are lifted.

> What could be more like Mother or a fitter background
>   For her son, for the nude young male who lounges
> Against a rock displaying his dildo, never doubting
>   That for all his faults he is loved, whose works are but
> Extensions of his power to charm?
>
> (SP, 185)[12]

12. The *Collected Poems* offers another version of this passage: "What could be more like Mother or a fitter background / For her son, the flirtatious male who lounges / Against a rock in the sunlight, never doubting / That for all his faults he is loved" (CP, 414). As Edward Mendelson explains in his preface, Auden's earlier versions generally offer "greater immediate impact" (SP, xviii).

The image is startling mainly because it turns the licentious into the commonplace: so capably is the Book of Nature invoked that anything appearing within its bounds is encoded as natural, pure, and thus utterly acceptable. In this rapturous interlude, the usual scruples, as well as their even more tyrannical aesthetic surrogates, are momentarily suspended.

The lascivious vignette repeats the basic meditative design of supportive mother, errant son, and futile works, but in a deliberately disruptive fashion. Each is renamed so that it becomes both an archetype and a caricature: mother as impervious rock (foundation, origin, center); son as indolent nude (shameless, irresponsible); civilized achievement as ludicrous dildo (admission, prop). In this wanton manner, the ludic voice happily endorses what is awkward, inadmissible, unspeakable. Yet its wantonness is also a deliberate pose, a means of playing the text. For the poem's meditative pattern to work, the errant offspring must shuttle between the extremes of an authentic origin and a tempting array of destructive substitutes.

> "Come!" cried the granite wastes,
> "How evasive is your humor, how accidental
> Your kindest kiss, how permanent is death." (Saints-to-be
> Slipped away sighing.) "Come!" purred the clays and gravels,
> "On our plains there is room for armies to drill; rivers
> Wait to be tamed and slaves to construct you a tomb
> In the grand manner: soft as the earth is mankind and both
> Need to be altered." (Intendant Caesars rose and
> Left, slamming the door.) But the really reckless were fetched
> By an older colder voice, the oceanic whisper:
> "I am the solitude that asks and promises nothing:
> That is how I shall set you free. There is no love;
> There are only the various envies, all of them sad."
>
> (CP, 415)

The son may use the rock, or even its absence, to fashion a deviant prosthesis, the works of a culture. But the results must have no bearing on their origin. It is this separation, however, that the licentious namings put at risk. The dildo is the ultimate substitute: the comic prop in which the actual concedes its frailty long enough to summon the makeshift, sterile but useful, as a reminder not only of a lack but of the capacity

229

to lighten it through mimicry. Yet the range of that mimicry is too extensive. The sterile prosthesis can dissemble a plenipotent dick, remnant of the dictionary, a maze of illicit, tricky, and occasionally necessary substitutions. Perhaps such deceit might be tolerated were its outrageous metonymies confined within the regions of their own play. But the energies of the prosthesis are enough to reverse the irreversible, so that they invade even the impervious mass of the precious origin, the center as rock, *petre*, the solid ground on which to put that which shall withstand the ages. The rock is also the punned Peter, a further emblem of evasive motility, of what is alternately irascible, treacherous, intransigent, sanctified. Blissfully unsupervised, licentiously named, the nude young male wields the substitute whose returns come back to haunt even the inviolable rock.

Yet the torment becomes generative as it meets a tacit with an outright violence. Power, as the preservation of an assured meaning, emanates from a virgin birth: an origin presumed to be pure. But that purity is what the ludic voice refuses to allow. It upsets the clear dichotomy of imagination and reality, univocal origins set against historical contingency, if only because the origins always prove to be riddled with dissent.

> The poet
> Admired for his earnest habit of calling
> The sun the sun, his mind Puzzle, is made uneasy
> By these marble statues which so obviously doubt
> His antimythological myth.
>
> (CP, 415)

In contrast to that "earnest habit," the text's inscriptions propose another scene of origins, licentious, ungovernable, obscene. The drive to find the ultimate source seeks an irreducible genesis, that before which nothing further might occur, and from which nothing different might evolve, "the historical calm of a site / Where something was settled once and for all" (CP, 415). But the search can never go back far enough. It can attain only "a backward / And dilapidated province, connected / To the big busy world by a tunnel, with a certain / Seedy appeal" (CP, 415). The authoritative forms are already in ruins, mere shadows of a power whose previous grandeur is strangely unwitnessed. And the scene itself is neither pure nor complete, and bears the scattered traces of possibility, the remnants of a departed impulse. Yet it is this disreputable passageway that offers the only attainable origin, the farthest point that may be reached, which as always turns out to be a point of further departure.

What ensues from the Book of Nature's nonvirgin birth? The textual reply, "a stone that responds" (CP, 414), is the otherwise silent resistance that accompanies any voice.

> Dear, I know nothing of
> Either, but when I try to imagine a faultless love
> Or the life to come, what I hear is the murmur
> Of underground streams, what I see is a limestone landscape.
>
> (CP, 415)

The faultless love of the perfected future is fissured, riddled with devious passages that constantly shift as the limestone dissolves existing solidities and precipitates different ones. To fix or specify this future—the nascent forms waiting within an existing discourse—is out of the question. All that can be known for sure is that the inscriptions of a text, its unvoiced yet discernible memories, will arrange a responsive tumult for them as well, in the surreptitious streams that "spurt," "chuckle," "entertain," and "murmur," with accents that are both a complaint and an invitation, a surprise and a renewal.

•

To take up the initial question, then, a voice can at least arrest its native violence, though this may be the most intricate task it is asked to perform. For this play cannot be approached directly, nor does it attend upon any of the ordinary resources of the speaking voice, whose effect would be to augment a securely conveyed sense. Rather, a ludic voice must pursue its play through a syntactic mime. By means of its performed gestures, it has the capacity not to enunciate (for that can never be done) but to provoke the response of textual inscriptions. These gestures may involve either an instrumental blitheness or a trustful reliance, though these specific provocations in no way serve as a limit. There can be no official grammar of the textual body or its ludic poses, only the different histories of its continuous play.

Index

233

Index

Index

Library of Congress Cataloging-in-Publication Data

Boly, John R. (John Robert), 1948–
   Reading Auden : the returns of Caliban / John R. Boly.
      p.   cm.
   Includes bibliographical references and index.
   ISBN 0-8014-2565-4 (alk. paper)
   1. Auden, W. H. (Wystan Hugh), 1907–1973—Criticism and
interpretation.   I. Title.
PR6001.U4Z6   1991
811'.52—dc20   91-6948